CORINTH

VOLUME XVII

THE GREAT BATH ON THE LECHAION ROAD

CORINTH

RESULTS OF EXCAVATIONS
CONDUCTED BY
THE AMERICAN SCHOOL OF CLASSICAL STUDIES AT ATHENS

VOLUME XVII

THE GREAT BATH ON THE LECHAION ROAD

BY

JANE C. BIERS

THE AMERICAN SCHOOL OF CLASSICAL STUDIES AT ATHENS
PRINCETON, NEW JERSEY

1985

Library of Congress Cataloging in Publication Data

Biers, Jane C.
   The Great Bath on the Lechaion Road

   (Corinth : results of excavations ; v. 17)
   Based on author's thesis (Ph.D.)—University of California, Berkeley, 1975.
   Includes index.
   1. Roman Bath (Corinth, Greece) 2. Corinth (Greece)—Antiquities, Roman. 3. Excavations (Archaeology)—Greece—Corinth. 4. Romans—Greece—Corinth. 5. Greece—Antiquities, Roman. I. Title. II. Series: Corinth ; v. 17.
   DF261.C65A6   vol. 17   938'.7 s   [938'.7]   85-2746
   ISBN 0-87661-171-4

TYPOGRAPHY BY THE AMERICAN SCHOOL OF CLASSICAL STUDIES PUBLICATIONS OFFICE
C/O INSTITUTE FOR ADVANCED STUDY, PRINCETON, NEW JERSEY
PLATES BY THE MERIDEN GRAVURE COMPANY, MERIDEN, CONNECTICUT
PRINTED IN THE UNITED STATES OF AMERICA
BY THE TOWN HOUSE PRESS, SPRING VALLEY, NEW YORK

PREFACE

FINAL publication of a building should wait until the building has been completely excavated or until it has been sufficiently cleared so that its history is fully understood. The Great Bath on the Lechaion Road at Ancient Corinth has not been completely cleared, and many problems still remain to be solved. This publication should, therefore, not be considered the final one. Since, however, further excavation in the near future is unlikely, and the building is rapidly deteriorating, it seemed advisable to publish in this format and in as thorough a manner as possible those parts of the building which had been excavated.

The project was begun under Henry S. Robinson, then Director of the American School of Classical Studies at Athens, and was continued by Charles K. Williams, II, the present Director of Corinth Excavations. The excavators were William R. Biers and myself. The architects for the four excavation seasons were Frank A. J. Clark, W. B. Dinsmoor, Jr., J. W. Shaw, and C. K. Williams, II. The final drawings of the façade are the work of Roger Holzen, except for two bases and the plan of the fallen blocks, which were drawn by John Huffstot. End-of-season photographs were taken by I. Ioannidou and L. Bartzioti.

This publication is based on my Ph.D. dissertation in Classical Archaeology for the University of California at Berkeley. Additional study of the building in Greece and preparation of the manuscript for publication were made possible by a Museum Professional Fellowship grant from the National Endowment for the Arts in the fall of 1975.

I would like to acknowledge here the assistance I have received from many people while working on this project. I owe much to Charles Williams for his advice and encouragement throughout this undertaking, and the chapter on the façade could not have been written without the collaboration of Roger Holzen who, besides preparing the drawings, also guided me in the description of the restoration. My debt both to him and to Charles Williams is a large one. William L. MacDonald kindly agreed to read the chapter on the façade, and I would like to thank him here for his friendly criticism. In the early stages of the project I benefited greatly from the comments of my advisors, J. K. Anderson, R. S. Stroud, and H. S. Robinson.

I am also grateful for the help received over the years from many Corinth Secretaries: Judith Perlzweig Binder, Helen von Raits Geagan, Kathryn Butt, Sharon Herbert, Jean MacIntosh, and Nancy Bookidis. Joan Fisher checked the identification of a great number of the coins for me, and Barbara Johnson and Kathleen Slane advised me on the pottery; the description of the lots in Appendix III is based on work by the latter. Susan Walker gave me invaluable assistance in measuring bricks in the building. I would also like to thank my husband for relinquishing to me the publication of the excavation we undertook together.

JANE C. BIERS

University of Missouri
January 15, 1979

Unforeseen circumstances have delayed publication of this volume. It has been possible to add only a few significant references to publications appearing since the original date of submission of the manuscript.

J. C. B.

July 19, 1984

TABLE OF CONTENTS

Preface	v
List of Illustrations	ix
Abbreviations	xiii
Introduction	
History of the Site	1
Excavation of 1965–1968	2
Building Materials	3
Occupation of the Site	4
I The Western Approach to the Bath	
The Lechaion Road Entrance	7
The Colonnade and Court	8
Chronology	11
Later History	12
II The Marble Façade	
The Façade Walls	14
The Restoration of the Marble Façade	17
The Lower Order	18
Podium Cap	18
Bases	18
Columns	18
Capitals	19
Entablature	19
Cornice	21
The Upper Order	21
Stylobate	21
Bases	22
Columns	22
Capitals	22
Entablature	22
Cornice	23
Crowning Member	24
Unassigned Blocks	24
Chronology	25
The Area at the Base of the Façade	29
The Pool	29
The Foundation Trench	30
Later History of the Area	31

TABLE OF CONTENTS

III The Interior of the Building
Room 1
- Description and Restoration 33
- Chronology 37

Room 2
- Description and Restoration 37
- Chronology 41

Room 3
- Description and Restoration 43
- Chronology 48

Room 4
- Description and Restoration 49
- Chronology 50

Room 5
- Description and Restoration 50
- Chronology 54

Room 6 55

Room 7
- Description and Restoration 55
- Service Areas 56
- Heating Systems 58
- Water Systems 60

IV Conclusions
- Chronology 61
- Identification 63
- Significance of the Excavation 64

V Catalogue
- Architecture **1–102** 65
- Sculpture **103–112** 76
- Terracotta **113–118** 78
- Metal **119, 120** 79
- Pottery **121–137** 79
- Glass **138** 83
- Lamps **139–147** 83
- Inscriptions **148–152** 84

Appendices
- I. Brickwork Specifications 86
  - Table 1: Brickwork 88
  - Table 2: Hypocaust Columns 92
- II. Groups of Finds 94
- III. Groups 19, 25, and 26 103

Concordances
- I. Lot Numbers and Group Numbers 106
- II. Field Inventory Numbers and Catalogue Numbers 107
- III. Inventory and Catalogue Numbers 108

Index 109

Plates

LIST OF ILLUSTRATIONS

Figures in Text
   1 Column Base **1**
   2 Column Base **90**
   3 Column base **98**
   4 Terracotta Heating Tubes **113–115**
   5 Late Roman C Bowl **121**
   6 Storage Amphoras **128** and **129**
   7 Pottery: **130–135**
   8 Glass One-handled Jug **138**

Plates
   1 a. Colonnade and Tiled Court, from the West
      b. Colonnade and Tiled Court, from the East
   2 a. Façade Area, from the South
      b. Façade Area, from the North
   3 a. Foundation Trench in the Façade Area, from the Northwest
      b. Service Area against Central Wall of the Façade, from the West
   4 a. Foundations of the North Wall of the Lechaion Road Entranceway, from the South
      b. Inscription on the Lower Step of the Colonnade
      c. Central Wall of the Façade, Foundations at the Northern End, from the West
      d. Inscription Built into the 6th-century House
      e. Latrine, from the East
   5 a. Room 2, North End, from the North
      b. Service Area North of Room 3 (Corridor 1), from the Northwest
   6 a. South Pool in Room 2, from the North
      b. Room 3 before Excavation of the Central Pool, from the South
   7 a. Central Pool in Room 3 after Removal of Most of the Fill, from the East
      b. Southeast Wall of Room 5, South End, from the Northwest
   8 a. Southeast Wall of Room 5, North End, and Northeast Wall, from the Southwest
      b. Southwest Wall of Room 5, from the Northeast
   9 a. Room 4, West Side, from the Northeast
      b. Room 7, North Corner, from the Southwest
   10 a. East Wall of Room 2, South End, from the North
      b. Northwest Wall of Room 5, from the Southeast
      c. Service Corridor Wall beneath the North Apse of Room 3, from the North
   11 Column Bases **1** and **3**
   12 Column Base **4** and Shafts **7, 8, 11, 12, 15, 17**
   13 Corinthian Capitals **21–26**
   14 Epistyle-Friezes **27, 29, 30**
   15 Epistyle-Frieze **31**. The Captives' Façade, Corinth
   16 Geison Blocks with Dentils **34–37**

17 Stylobates **42** and **43** and Geison Block with Dentils **38**
18 Column Shafts **53** and **55**
19 Corinthian Capitals **59–62**
20 Epistyle-Friezes **63**, **64**, and **66**
21 Epistyle-Frieze **68**
22 Console-Geison Block with Dentils **69–71**
23 Consoles **75** and **76**, Column Shaft with Spiral Fluting **79**, and Corinthian Capitals **80** and **81**
24 Revetment Plaques **82**, **84**, and **85**, Openwork Parapet **86**, and Window Molding **87**
25 Column Base **91**, Geison Block with Dentils **93**, and Epistyle-Frieze **92**
26 Revetment Plaque **94**, Epistyle-Frieze **95**, and Revetment Plaques with Dipinti **96** and **97**
27 Lion's Head Waterspout **99** and Coffered Cornice Blocks **100** and **101**
28 Relief Plaques **103** and **104**
29 a. Fountain Group of Herakles and the Nemean Lion **105**
   b. Head of Pan **106**
   c. Male Portrait **107**
   d. Head **108**
30 a. Head **110**
   b. Seated Figure **111**
   c. Statue Support **112**, front
   d. **112**, back
31 a. Head and Chest of a Ram **109**
   b. Tube from Heating System **113**
   c. Stamped Tile **117**
   d. Tubulus **116**
   e. Stamped Tile **118**
32 a. Spike and Clamp **119**
   b. Plate, African Red Slip Ware **123**
   c. Shaft and Crosspiece **120**
   d. Stamped Base **122**
   e. Bowl, Asia Minor Fabric **124**
33 a. Storage Jar, Dipinto **125**
   b. Storage Amphora **127**
   c. Storage Jar, Dipinto **126**
   d. **126**, detail
   e. Glass Jug **138**
34 a. Storage Amphora **128**
   b. Storage Amphora **129**
   c. Bowl or Dish, African Red Slip Ware **136**
   d. Amphora, Graffito **137**
35 a. Corinthian Lamp **139**
   b. Corinthian Lamp **140**
   c. Attic Lamp **141**
   d. Corinthian Lamp **142**
   e. Attic Lamp **143**
   f. Corinthian Lamp **144**
   g. Attic Lamp **145**
   h. Lamp **146**
   i. Corinthian Lamp **147**

LIST OF ILLUSTRATIONS

36 a. Latin Inscription **148**
   b. Latin or Greek Inscription **149**
   c. Greek Inscription **152**
   d. Latin or Greek Inscription **150**
   e. Greek Inscription **151**
37 a. 1802 Plan
   b. 1910–1911 Plan
38 Plan of the Great Bath on the Lechaion Road
39 Schematic Sections through the Bath
40 Plan of the Façade Area, Actual State (Room 6)
41 Plan of the 6th-century House and Latrine
42 Restored Plan of the Façade
43 Perspective Reconstruction of the Façade
44 Restored North Wing, Elevation
45 Restored Center, Elevation
46 Plan of Fallen Marble Blocks in the Façade Area
47 a. Preserved Blocks in the North Wing of the Façade
   b. Preserved Blocks in the Center of the Façade
48 Reflected Plan of the Soffit of the Façade Cornice, Upper Order
49 Fallen Masonry
50 Plan and Elevation, West Wall of Room 1, South End
51 Plan and Elevation, West Wall of Room 1, North End
52 Plan and Elevation, South Wall, West Section of Room 1
53 Plan and Elevation, North Wall, West Section of Room 1
54 a. Plan and Elevation, West Wall, West Section of Room 1
   b. Section of Wall Between Rooms 1 and 2
55 Plan of Room 3
56 Roman Corinth

ABBREVIATIONS

Agora	*The Athenian Agora, Results of Excavations conducted by the American School of Classical Studies at Athens*
	V H. S. Robinson, *Pottery of the Roman Period: Chronology*, Princeton 1959
	VII J. Perlzweig, *Lamps of the Roman Period*, Princeton 1961
	XXI M. L. Lang, *Graffiti and Dipinti*, Princeton 1975
AJA	*American Journal of Archaeology*
Annuario	*Annuario della Scuola archeologico di Atene*
Antioch	*Antioch-on-the-Orontes*
	III *The Excavations 1937–1939*, R. Stillwell, ed., Princeton 1941
	IV, i F. O. Waagé *Ceramics and Islamic Coins*, Princeton 1948
Archaeological Reports	Supplement to *Journal of Hellenic Studies*
ArchAnz	*Archäologischer Anzeiger* [*Jahrb*]
’Αρχ’Εφ	’Αρχαιολογικὴ ’Εφημερίς
AthMitt	*Mitteilungen des deutschen archäologischen Instituts, Athenische Abteilung*
Baalbek	*Baalbek*, I, II, T. Wiegand, ed., Berlin/Leipzig 1921, 1923
BCH	*Bulletin de correspondance hellénique*
BonnJahrb	*Bonner Jahrbücher*
BSA	*Annual of the British School at Athens*
Corinth	*Results of Excavations conducted by the American School of Classical Studies at Athens*
	I, i H. N. Fowler and R. Stillwell, *Introduction. Topography. Architecture*, Cambridge, Mass. 1932
	I, ii R. Stillwell *et al.*, *Architecture*, Cambridge, Mass. 1941
	I, iii R. L. Scranton, *Monuments in the Lower Agora and North of the Archaic Temple*, Princeton 1951
	I, iv O. Broneer, *The South Stoa*, Princeton 1954
	I, v S. S. Weinberg, *The Southeast Building. The Twin Basilicas. The Mosaic House*, Princeton 1960
	I, vi B. H. Hill, *The Springs: Peirene, Sacred Spring, Glauke*, Princeton 1964
	II R. Stillwell, *The Theatre*, Princeton 1952
	IV, ii O. Broneer, *Terracotta Lamps*, Cambridge, Mass. 1934
	VIII, iii J. H. Kent, *The Inscriptions 1926–1950*, Princeton 1966
	IX F. P. Johnson, *The Sculpture 1896–1923*, Cambridge, Mass. 1931
	X O. Broneer, *The Odeum*, Cambridge, Mass. 1932
	XII G. L. Davidson, *The Minor Objects*, Princeton 1952
	XVI R. L. Scranton, *Mediaeval Architecture*, Princeton 1957
Dacia	*Revue d'archéologie et d'histoire ancienne*
Δελτ	’Αρχαιολογικὸν Δελτίον
DOPapers	*Dumbarton Oaks Papers*
Garnett	K. S. Garnett, "Late Roman Corinthian Lamps from the Fountain of the Lamps," *Hesperia* 44, 1975, pp. 173–206
Ginouvès, *Laodicée*	R. Ginouvès, "Architecture," in J. des Gagniers *et al.*, *Laodicée du Lycos. Le nymphée*, Quebec/Paris 1969

LIST OF ABBREVIATIONS

Ginouvès, Théâtron	R. Ginouvès, *Le théâtron à gradins droits at l'odéon d'Argos* [*Études péloponnésiennes* VI, École française d'Athènes], Paris 1972
Hayes	J. W. Hayes, *Late Roman Pottery*, London 1972
Hayes, *SLRP*	J. W. Hayes, *Supplement to Late Roman Pottery* [BSR, Suppl.], London 1980
Hesperia	*Journal of the American School of Classical Studies at Athens*
IstMitt	*Mitteilungen des deutschen archäologischen Instituts, Abteilung Istanbul*
Jahrb	*Jahrbuch des deutschen archäologischen Instituts*
JHS	*Journal of Hellenic Studies*
JRS	*Journal of Roman Studies*
Krencker	D. Krencker *et al.*, *Die Trierer Kaiserthermen*, Augsburg 1929
McDonald	W. L. McDonald, *The Architecture of the Roman Empire*, rev. ed., New Haven 1982
MAAR	*Memoirs of the American Academy in Rome*
MAMA	*Monumenta Asiae Minoris antiqua*
Milet	*Ergebnisse der Ausgrabungen und Untersuchungen seit dem Jahre 1899*, T. Wiegand, ed.
I, v	*Das Nymphaeum*, Berlin 1919
I, vii	*Der Südmarkt und die benachbarten anlagen*, Berlin 1924
I, ix	*Thermen und Palaestren*, Berlin 1928
MonAnt	*Accademia nazionale dei Lincei, Rome. Monumenti Antichi*
PBSR	*Papers of the British School at Rome*
Πρακτικά	Πρακτικὰ τῆς ἐν ’Αθήναις ’Αρχαιολογικῆς ’Εταιρίας
ProcBritAcad	*Proceedings of the British Academy*
RömMitt	*Mitteilungen des deutschen archäologischen Instituts, Römische Abteilung*
Stuart and Revett	J. Stuart and N. Revett, *The Antiquities of Athens* I–III, London 1762–1794
Strong	D. E. Strong, "Late Hadrianic Architectural Ornament in Rome," *PBSR* 21, n.s. 8, 1953, pp. 118–151
Thatcher	E. D. Thatcher, "The Open Rooms of the Terme del Foro at Ostia," *MAAR* XXIV, Rome 1956, pp. 170–261

INTRODUCTION

IN A ROMAN CITY of the size and importance of Corinth one would expect to find numerous small bathing establishments and one or possibly two of the large imperial type. From the literary record it is known that by the 2nd century after Christ there were baths in many parts of the city, including one put up by the emperor Hadrian and a second by the Spartan Eurykles, which is cited as the most famous.[1] Before 1965 three Roman baths had been uncovered in the course of the excavations conducted by the American School of Classical Studies at Athens.[2] Two other buildings, which were assumed to be baths, were always partially visible above ground, one to the north of the Theater, the other east of the Lechaion Road, the principal road between the Forum of Corinth and the harbor of Lechaion on the Corinthian Gulf (Pl. 56). In the early 1960's it was decided that the excavation of the bath east of the Lechaion Road might add significant information to our knowledge of the city of Corinth during the Roman period.

HISTORY OF THE SITE

The site lies north of the village square of modern Ancient Corinth. It is bounded by a village street on the east and on the west by a warehouse purchased by the American School for storage of context pottery. Before the start of the excavation, walls were visible in the eastern part of the site, and there existed a restored plan of the building, drawn by Sebastian Ittar, Lord Elgin's architect, in 1802, when even more standing masonry was preserved above the modern ground level (Pl. 37:a).[3] In 1896 the American School in one of its test trenches (Trench XIV) uncovered the northwest corner of one room and the north boundary wall of the Bath, together with a road running along its north face.[4] The plan of these structures and

---

[1] Pausanias, II.3.5. He mentions only these two by name.

[2] A small bath is located west of the Odeion (unpublished), another was in the South Stoa (*Corinth* I, iv, pp. 145–151), and a third lies north of the Peribolos of Apollo (C. K. Williams, II, "Excavations at Corinth, 1968," *Hesperia* 38, 1969, pp. 62–63; "Excavation at Corinth, 1973," *Hesperia* 43, 1974, pp. 25, 32–33). The latter is probably the one identified by Pausanias as the Baths of Eurykles. (For further discussion of identification, see pp. 63–64 below.) A hypocaust discovered in 1973 by the Greek Archaeological Service near the fountain of Hadji Mustapha at the foot of Acrocorinth undoubtedly indicates the location of another bath (see Corinth Notebook 576, pp. 61–67). Excavations by the University of Texas for the American School in 1969 revealed an underground room with permanent washbasins and a courtyard with a large outdoor swimming pool identified by the excavator as a Greek bath dating to the 4th or 5th century B.C., repaired probably in the 1st century after Christ and used until the 4th century (James Wiseman, "The Fountain of the Lamps," *Archaeology* 23, 1970, pp. 135–136; idem, "The Gymnasium Area at Corinth, 1969–1970," *Hesperia* 41, 1972, pp. 16–26). A Greek bath of the last quarter of the 5th century B.C. (the Centaur Bath) was located southwest of the race track in the southwest corner of the excavation zone of the Roman forum (C. K. Williams, II, "Corinth, 1975: Forum Southwest," *Hesperia* 45, 1976, pp. 109–116; idem, "Corinth, 1976: Forum Southwest," *Hesperia* 46, 1977, pp. 45–52).

[3] See F. Madden, *Catalogue of the Manuscript Maps*, Charts and Plans ... in *the British Museum* III, London 1861, p. 85. For a rough list of all Elgin drawings, see *Antiquities of Athens and other places in Greece, Sicily, etc. Supplementary to the Antiquities of Athens* by James Stuart, F.S.A. and Nicholas Revett. Delineated and illustrated by C. R. Cockerell, A.R.A., F.S.A., W. Kinnard, T. L. Donaldson, W. Jenkins, W. Railton, Architects, London 1830, monuments of the Peloponnese, p. 28, note a. Also F. W. Hasluck, "Some Topographical Drawings in the British Museum," *BSA* 18, 1911/12, pp. 272, 275; A. H. Smith, "Lord Elgin and his Collection," *JHS* 36, 1916, pp. 219, 254.

Early travelers to Greece had also noticed the building and referred to it in their descriptions of Corinth. See G. Wheler, *Journey into Greece* VI, London 1682, p. 440; R. Chandler, *Travels in Greece*, Oxford 1776, p. 240; W. M. Leake, *Travels in the Morea* III, London 1830, p. 244; R. Burgess, *Greece and the Levant* I, London 1835, p. 166; C. G. Addison, *Damascus and Palmyra* I, London 1838, p. 18; C. G. Saunders-Forster, *Beneath Parnassian Clouds*, London 1887, p. 148. Other travelers may be referring to the building, but the identification is not certain. See R. Pococke, *A Description of the East* II, ii, London 1745, p. 174; E. D. Clarke, *Travels in Various Countries* III, London 1814, p. 738; E. Dodwell, *A Classical and Topographical Tour through Greece* II, London 1819, p. 192; W. Drew Stent, *Egypt and the Holy Land* I, London 1843, p. 25; C. E. Beulé, *Études sur le Peloponèse*, Paris 1855, p. 448; W. G. Clark, *Peloponnesus*, London 1858, p. 55. An early 19th-century drawing shows some of the walls with houses built against them: Th. du Moncel, *Excursion par terre d'Athènes à Nauplie*, Paris [1846], pl. 8.

[4] H. F. de Cou, "A Roman Building in Corinth. A Report of the Excavations of 1896: Trench XIV," *AJA*, ser. 2, 1,

the Ittar drawing were incorporated into a restored plan, which was completed by W. B. Dinsmoor in 1910/1911 (Pl. 37:b) and added to the over-all plan of Corinth. No further work was done on the building until the campaign of excavation which was begun in the spring of 1965 and carried on annually for four eight-week seasons until 1968.[5]

EXCAVATION OF 1965–1968

The excavation of 1965–1968 was concentrated in building lots purchased by the School where standing masonry was still visible and in garden land to the west of these walls. As shown on the plan (Pl. 38), the new excavation revealed that the Bath could be approached from the west through an entrance set between shops fronting the Lechaion Road and opening onto a colonnade along the western edge of a large tiled courtyard (see Chapter I). Facing the entrance was a marble façade two storeys high which adorned the west exterior wall of the building and framed a pool, set in the angle formed by its walls (Pl. 43; see Chapter II). The building itself, oriented so that the axis of its main rooms lies approximately north–south, had heated rooms on the west side, but the principal entrance was elsewhere. Plate 38 shows the six rooms[6] which were partially cleared in the course of the excavation (see Chapter III). The *frigidarium* (Room 1) was a large cruciform room from which there was access to the west to a *tepidarium* (Room 2) and a *caldarium* beyond (Room 3). A third heated room (Room 5) projected in a wing to the northwest but could not be entered from Room 3. To the east of Room 5 a fifth room (Room 4), of which only a very small extent has been cleared, was once connected with Room 5 by a doorway, closed in a later alteration. A fourth heated room (Room 7), to the southwest, corresponds in position to Room 5; only a corner of it has been cleared, and where its entrances were is not known. These smaller rooms (Rooms 4, 5, and 7) were probably reached from Room 1 by doors in the north and south walls of the west section of that room. Of the numerous service areas necessary in so large a bath only two were excavated, one to the north of Rooms 2 and 3 and a second much smaller one, which was added to the façade area in a later period.

The excavation began with the clearance of the northwest area of Room 5 and parts of Rooms 1 and 2. In 1966 the excavation of Room 5 was continued to the east, and Room 4 and the service corridor below were cleared to their present state; Room 1 was excavated to floor level, and fill was removed from around the fallen vaulting of Room 3. In 1967, with the acquisition of land to the west, trenches were laid out at the far west, and the tiled court and colonnade were discovered. In Room 3 fallen vaulting was removed, and the northern half of the room was exposed. On the outside of the building, excavation of the façade area and the fallen architectural remains was begun. In the final season more of the court and colonnade and the northeast corner of Room 7 were cleared, and more marble blocks from the façade were recovered. In August of 1970 a small test was carried out for two days in Room 3 and in the façade area.

Several difficulties were encountered during the excavation, the greatest of which was the large amount of fallen vaulting which in Rooms 1, 2, and 3 covered the entire area. Some of these fallen masses were removed after they had been photographed and after those with architectural features had been drawn. Others, however, were too large to break up and had fallen in such a way that excavation would have proved dangerous. This was particularly true of Room 4 where work could not continue to the east because of a large mass of fallen vaulting on the east edge of the cleared area. A second large mass which is resting on the north apse of Room 2 and on the north wall of the west section of Room 1 also prevented excavation to any depth. The weak state of some of the standing masonry was troublesome; supporting fill had to be left against the wall between Rooms 1 and 2. A third problem was caused by village water rights which demanded free access at ground level across the court on the west side of the building. Sufficient land had to be left to support a water

---

1897, pp. 495–506. The trench was filled in, and nothing is visible there today.

[5] For previous brief accounts of the excavation of the building see *Archaeological Reports*, 1965/66, p. 6; 1966/67, p. 7, fig. 10; 1967/68, p. 8, fig. 9; 1968/69, pp. 9–10, fig. 9; *BCH* 90, 1966, *Chroniques*, pp. 753–754, figs. 6–9; 91, 1967, *Chroniques*, pp. 634–635, figs. 4–6; 92, 1968, *Chroniques*, pp. 788–791, figs. 6–10; Δελτ 21, 1966, Χρονικά [1968], pp. 136–138, plan 2, pls. 128, 129:a, b; 22, 1967, Χρονικά [1969], p. 184, pl. 133:e; 23, 1968, Χρονικά [1969], pp. 135–136, pls. 79:d, e, 80, 81:a; *AJA* 71, 1967, p. 297; 72, 1968, p. 268, pl. 90, fig. 12.

[6] For "Room 6" see below, p. 14, footnote 5.

conduit crossing from south to north to irrigate the gardens to the north of the excavation. Consequently a large baulk of earth remains between the tiled court and the building itself. The depth of fill encountered was also a problem. In clearing the tiled court as much as three and a half meters of earth had to be removed before the brick floor was reached, and in Room 2 the fill was almost five meters deep.

Because of these difficulties many areas within the land acquired by the School were not entirely explored. Even with their clearance the excavation of the building could not be completed, since it would extend to the east across the street which borders the excavation on that side. Here, as late as 1910–1911, a small section of standing masonry was visible (Pl. 37:b). The building also extends further to north and south. There are, therefore, many questions that have not been answered. Although an entrance into the courtyard has been found, the main entrance into the building itself has not been discovered, and without the complete plan the function of the various rooms cannot be discussed. Since only a small part of the heating and water systems has been uncovered, these are not fully understood, and although some evidence indicates an earlier building on the site, not enough has been found to enable any reconstruction of its plan and function. The existence of an earlier building may perhaps explain why the orientation of Room 1 is different from that of Rooms 2 and 3 (Pl. 38), but too little of it has been cleared to be certain (see below, p. 63).

Although difficulties were encountered and problems still remain, the excavation did produce a great deal of information of various kinds. Coins and pottery found in a thick layer of fill over the floors of the building provided evidence for the date at which it went out of use, and in certain areas small deposits were found which dated phases of reconstruction. No evidence of a stratigraphic nature, however, was found for the period when the building was constructed. The construction date is based on stylistic evidence from the architecture. The stratigraphic evidence is presented by Groups in Appendices II and III; the numbers of the relevant Groups are given in the discussion of the areas for which they are chronologically significant.

BUILDING MATERIALS

The construction throughout the building is of brick-faced concrete, except for the vaults which are of concrete poured on a wooden form. Three types of bricks were employed in the main building period, and bricks with different dimensions and horizontal jointing of different thicknesses were used in reconstruction of and repairs to the building. These are all presented in tabular form in Appendix I.

Stone including several kinds of marble was used for most of the decorative architectural elements,[7] and the building was revetted on both interior and exterior. Both white and colored marbles were employed. The latter have been identified as Numidian, Proconnesian, Karystian, *fior di pesco*, and *rosso antico*. Granite and *lapis lacedaemonius*, or green porphyry, were also used.[8] Two of these materials were imported; the rest came from different areas in Greece. From near Chemtou, the ancient city of Simitthu, in Tunisia, came Numidian marble, also known as *giallo antico*. Its basic color is yellow, but different shades occur, ranging from golden yellow through orange to pink.[9] The Numidian marble used in the Bath is mostly pinkish yellow in color. Proconnesian, although classed as a white marble,[10] ranges in color from white to bluish gray. Its quarries have been found on the island of Proconnesos, today called Marmara, which lies in the Sea of Marmara. From Greece itself came Karystian, or *cipollino*, which is a light-green marble with veins of darker green. The quarries were located at Karystos, on the island of Euboia.[11] Other varieties of *cipollino* were quarried by the Romans in Italy but were not apparently used in the Bath at Corinth. *Fior di pesco*,

---

[7] Some of the moldings were in stucco (Group 17 and Corinth inv. nos. A 605–A 607).

[8] The identification of the provenance of Greek marble has been a topic of much discussion in recent years, and it has been amply demonstrated that visual means alone are not sufficient. No attempt has been made, therefore, to distinguish between kinds of white marble, except for identifying some as Proconnesian. For scientific methods of determining provenance, see G. Moschini and B. M. Stievano, "A Contribution to the Identification of Italian, Greek and Anatolian Marbles through a Petrological Study and the Evaluation of Ca/Sr Ratio," *Archaeometry* 22, 1980, pp. 173–182, and bibliography cited there. Studies of the ancient quarries and of objects certainly from them are also producing further advances. See J. B. Ward-Perkins, "Nicomedia and the Marble Trade," *PBSR* 48, 1980, pp. 23–69.

[9] R. Gnoli, *Marmora romana*, Rome 1971, pp. 139–141.

[10] *Ibid.*, p. 227.

[11] *Ibid.*, pp. 154–156.

which is veined in red and gray, was quarried in southern Euboia.[12] *Rosso antico* was used sparingly in the Bath. It is a deep purplish red stone which comes from Cape Tenaro in the southern Peloponnesos.[13] Green porphyry, known as *lapis lacedaemonius*, is dark green in color with specks of light-green rectangular crystals. The quarries have been discovered in the Peloponnesos about 20 kilometers south of Sparta.[14]

OCCUPATION OF THE SITE

Four periods of occupation were revealed by the excavation of 1965–1968: Roman, Byzantine and Frankish, Turkish, and modern.[15] The Great Bath was probably built at the end of the 2nd century after Christ or in the early 3rd century. It underwent a series of modifications in the 3rd century, at the end of the 4th or in the early 5th, and again in the early 6th century. It went out of use in the late 6th century. In the 6th century a house and latrine were built within the colonnade to the west (see pp. 12–13 below). After the Bath was abandoned debris accumulated in the building itself. These levels were covered by fallen vaulting and crumbled masonry from a massive destruction of the building by earthquake, which must have taken place sometime between the late 6th or early 7th century and the 11th century. The vaults of Rooms 1 and 2 and the south apse of Room 3 survived. Evidence for re-use of at least one of these rooms perhaps as early as the 9th century was found in a cache of coins recovered in the fill in Room 2.[16] At the western edge of the site a large deposit of amphoras is evidence for a shop or workshop of the end of the 11th century along the Lechaion Road.[17] Other evidence for this period comes only from the fill which overlay the earthquake destruction level to the west of Room 3 and dates from the late 11th to the mid-12th century.[18] During the 12th and 13th centuries a substantial house was built at the west, over, and partly on, the walls of the 6th-century house.[19] One wall rested on the back wall of the colonnade of the Bath along the west side of the tiled court. A flagstone courtyard lay to the east of the house, which apparently had a lower courtyard with stairway up to the house on the west.[20] Numerous bothroi of this period were found throughout the area,[21] and further west lay a curious vaulted structure dating to the late 12th to 13th centuries,[22] whose use is not understood. East of the house with the flagstone courtyard lay a further complex of Byzantine walls of the late 12th to 13th centuries,[23] and to the north over Rooms 4 and 5 of the Bath more Byzantine house walls were found dating

---

[12] *Ibid.*, pp. 157–159.

[13] *Ibid.*, pp. 160–164; R. H. Higgins, R. Hope Simpson, S. E. Ellis, "The Façade of the Treasury of Atreus at Mycenae," *BSA* 63, 1968, pp. 331–336.

[14] Gnoli, *op. cit.* (footnote 9 above), pp. 115–118; H. Waterhouse and R. Hope Simpson, "Prehistoric Laconia: Part I," *BSA* 55, 1960, pp. 105–107.

[15] See pp. 61–63. Context pottery from Byzantine, Frankish, and Turkish levels is stored in the following lots in Corinth. Turkish: nos. 2263, 2264, 2267, 2268, 2342, 2344, 2345, 3494, 3496, 3498, 3536, 3547, 4694(?); Byzantine and Frankish: nos. 2265, 2266, 2269–2272, 2274, 2275, 2343, 2346–2378, 3493, 3495, 3497, 3499, 3500, 3502, 3533–3535, 3537–3546, 3548–3551, 4642–4656, 4661, 4666, 4671, 4684, 4685, 4687, 4689–4692, 4695(?)–4707, 4710–4713, 4719, 4720, 4723, 4724, 4729, 4732, 4741–4745, 5117, 5118, 5121, 5122, 5124–5131, 5144, 5160–5166, 5174. For Roman pottery see Appendices II and III. Structures uncovered in the upper levels were recorded on working plans, Corinth Drawings nos. 415, 604, 605, 627A, 628, 689, 698.

[16] Six gold coins of Theophilos, A.D. 829–842, Corinth inv. nos. 65-14–65-19 (*BCH* 90, 1966, *Chroniques*, p. 754, fig. 8; Δελτ 21, 1966, Χρονικά [1968], pl. 129:b) were found in a loose fill of stones and tiles in Room 2 *ca.* 2.00 m. above the floor of the room. Eight bronze coins of Romanus I, A.D. 919–921 and later, Corinth inv. nos. 65-37–65-44, were found in similar fill but *ca.* 3.00 m. above the floor.

[17] Four meters of this shop were cleared from north to south with an exposed width of 3.00 m. Several floor levels were found, the two earliest of which dated to the 6th century (Lots 5119, 5120) and were associated with a bench in the northeast corner. The uppermost floor level dates to the end of the 11th century (Lot 5117) and is associated with the amphoras. The shop was re-used, therefore, in the Byzantine period, as was the case with others further to the south on the Lechaion Road (*Corinth* XVI, p. 37).

[18] Lot 4654.

[19] Lots 5130, 5131.

[20] This seems a reasonable explanation for a rectangular foundation which was found against the west wall of the house at a lower level than the interior floor level.

[21] Lots 4648, 4651, 4684–4693, 4719, 4720, 4741–4745, 5160.

[22] Lots 5122, 5129.

[23] Lots 4645–4647, 4649, 4650, 4655, 5162, 5163.

to the same period, one with an oven overlying an earlier built bothros.[24] A beaten earth roadway or village street ran from above the northeast corner of the tiled court across the site to the area above Room 7 of the Bath. The street was bordered by a substantial drain. The two belong to the 13th century[25] and in the area of Room 7 overlay a complex of four walls which must be dated to the 12th century.[26] A grave of the 13th century was found north of the road, and a few others were also found in the area.[27]

The walls of these Byzantine houses were constructed of rough field stones and some re-used material from the Bath and were quite substantial, sometimes with deep foundations which in one case went through the Roman masonry almost to the floor level of the Bath. Floors, where preserved, were of beaten earth with the exception of the flagstone courtyard in the house at the west.

During the Byzantine period the houses were scattered over the whole site, but for the Turkish period no structures were found over the area of the colonnade and the tiled court. Instead, buildings at that time were confined to the space within the standing masonry and to an area over Rooms 4 and 5 of the Bath. Here, a Turkish house was found with walls constructed of stone and mortar.[28] Three sides of the plan, a simple rectangle, were recovered; the west wall lies outside the excavation area. Remains of a paved courtyard were found to the north, and there was an entrance into the house from this court at the northeast corner.

To the east and south of the house, and at the south end of Room 1 of the Bath, were found several shallow, clay-lined pits.[29] Their purpose is not known, but it has been suggested that they were for settling clay. Remains of walls dating to this period were found in Rooms 1 and 2.[30] They corroborate the drawing of the 19th century which shows houses built into the standing masonry of the Bath.[31]

In 1858 a disastrous earthquake destroyed the village of Corinth, and most of the population was moved to the site of New Corinth. When, however, the village of Ancient Corinth began to grow again, the walls of the Bath were once more employed as house walls, until the earthquake of 1962 rendered the houses unsafe. Thus the site of the excavation had a continuous history of occupation through Byzantine and Turkish times and again in the more recent period.

[24] Lots 2348–2350, 2358–2360, 2364, 2365, 3539, 3541, 3543. For a Byzantine plate (Corinth inv. no. C-66-43) from this bothros, see W. R. Biers, "The Horseman and the Angel," *Archaeology* 30, 1977, pp. 333–337.
[25] Lots 4650, 4656, 4703–4705.
[26] Lots 5165, 5166.
[27] Lot 4644.
[28] Lots 2344, 2345, 3536.
[29] Lot 3498.
[30] Lot 3494.
[31] See footnote 3, p. 1 above.

I
THE WESTERN APPROACH TO THE BATH

THE LECHAION ROAD ENTRANCE

THE ENTRANCEWAY, on the east side of the Lechaion Road (Pl. 38), was partially cleared together with a section of colonnade and a large expanse of tiled court. At the west end of the passage there was presumably an opening off the Road, set between shops which lined the street, but this is the area which still lies beneath unexcavated fill. Although a lime pit had been cut into the entranceway at its east end and a house and latrine built within the colonnade in the 6th century (pp. 12–13 below), enough remained to enable some reconstruction of the structures along this western side of the Bath.

The passage is 10.90 m. wide between its north and south walls, which return at the east end in two spur walls on the line of the west wall of the colonnade (Pl. 38). The spur walls rest on a marble stylobate that marks the entrance from the passage into the colonnade through its west wall. The floor of the entranceway has been destroyed by the lime pit, approximately 1.10 m. deep, which was set between the foundations of the north and south walls of the entrance passage and those for the marble stylobate. The clearing of this lime pit and of the vaulted Byzantine construction at the west edge of the excavation[1] revealed the poros blocks of these foundations. Those of the south wall were excavated on their north face to their full depth of approximately 1.52 m. The foundations of the north wall, which are in a much better state of preservation, were exposed for three courses on the south face (Pl. 4:a). The foundations of the marble stylobate as seen on their west face are of the same construction as the two lower foundation courses of the north wall of the entrance; the marble stylobate lies on a level with the top course of the latter (Pl. 4:a). Except at the south and north ends, a heavy incrustation of mortar and brick fragments covers the face.

Although the floor of the entranceway has been destroyed, its level is given by cuttings 0.07 m. deep on the upper west edge of two of the blocks of the marble stylobate (Pl. 1:a). These cuttings are roughly worked and, therefore, not meant to be seen. The floor would thus have been level with the stylobate, slightly overlapping two of the marble blocks.[2] No evidence exists as to the nature of the flooring.

Above the foundations the walls of the entranceway are built of rectangular poros blocks, each the full thickness of the wall (0.70–0.72 m.). Two courses of the south wall are preserved standing to a height of 0.68 m. above the top of the foundations. The north wall is very poorly preserved with only one block remaining at the west end in the scarp. The two spur walls at the east end of the entranceway are preserved to a height of 0.67 m. on the south and 0.515 m. on the north.

The stylobate (Pl. 1:a) is composed of white marble blocks, 0.28–0.30 m. high, which were placed on the foundations apparently without clamps to hold them together. Five of these blocks are preserved with a gap of 1.40 m. south of the northernmost one. The total length of the stylobate, which does not run right up to the face of the walls of the entranceway, measures 10.40 m. The width of the blocks varies from 0.78 to 0.87 m. Although some of the upper surface of the stylobate blocks is still obscured by later construction, enough is exposed to show that in two areas the surface is dressed less smoothly. On the second block from the north an area approximately 0.52 m. wide shows the marks of a claw chisel, and on the fourth block there is a similar area approximately 0.95 m. wide (Pls. 1:a, 38). The distance between the centers of these two areas is about 3.75 m. The presence of the two roughly worked areas indicates that on the stylobate between the entranceway and the colonnade there should be restored two columns at an estimated axial spacing of approximately 3.75 m. with narrower spaces on each side. That on the south side appears to have

---

[1] See p. 4 above.
[2] The North Basilica in Corinth exhibits the same rough working of one face of its stylobate blocks below a certain level (*Corinth* I, i, p. 206, figs. 139, 140). One face of the threshold block in the Southeast Building is cut back cleanly, and the lower level is the same as that of the floor (*Corinth* I, v, p. 17, pl. 11:3).

been approximately 2.80 m., that on the north about 2.65 m., as measured from the axis of the columns to the ends of each spur wall.[3]

Various architectural blocks were found in the excavation of this west section of the Bath, built into later constructions. An unfluted column of Karystian marble,[4] which is still built into the vaulted Byzantine construction, quite possibly comes from the entranceway. One other block which may also belong is the epistyle-frieze block **92**. This was built into a Byzantine wall which rested in turn directly on the west wall of the house built within the colonnade in the 6th century. The length of the block (2.75 m.) is appropriate for the northern span flanking the wider central opening, noted above as approximately 2.65 m., but is insufficient for the intercolumniation restored to the colonnade to the east.[5] If not from the entablature of the entranceway, the block may have come from the façade on the Lechaion Road. Its use at either end of the passage, however, should be considered a re-use, indicated by the clamp cuttings and mason's mark on the front face (see Catalogue and Pl. 25).

COLONNADE AND COURT

The visitor to the Bath, after passing through the entranceway from the Lechaion Road, found himself in a colonnade (Pls. 1, 38) which bounded the west side of the tiled court. The east side of this court was defined by the two-storey marble façade of the Bath itself.

Only a stretch of the colonnade 17 m. north to south was cleared. Its interior width is approximately 3.50 m., excluding the two stylobates and the steps to the east. Its floor is at a lower level than that of the entranceway, and the transition is provided by a step of white marble against the east face of the western stylobate. Four blocks of this step are preserved.

The colonnade floor was in mosaic, which is preserved only in two patches with a maximum width of 0.25 m. and lengths of approximately 2.40 m. for the southern section and 0.47 m. for the northern. These lie against the marble step at 0.295 m. below the stylobate (Pls. 1:b, 38). The pattern consists of two borders, one black and one red, which bound a red wave pattern, all set against a white background. The tesserae are somewhat irregular in shape, but the majority are 0.012–0.015 m. in maximum dimension with a thickness of about 0.02 m. Evidence of a reflooring of the colonnade was found in a thin layer of cement with marble fragments embedded in it, which was preserved over the patches of mosaic. The recovery of this evidence for the floors is fortunate in view of the poor preservation elsewhere in the colonnade. At the southern end the floor had been badly torn up in the area of the latrine, and at the northern end a pit approximately 0.50 m. wide had been cut into the bedding for the mosaic to a depth of 0.39–0.49 m. (Pl. 1:a). When this was cleared of its debris a cement floor was encountered below.[6]

The back (west) wall of the colonnade, which also formed the rear wall of the shop fronting the Lechaion Road,[7] was cleared for a length of 5.00 m., excluding the spur wall. Nothing of the back wall of the colonnade

---

[3] These are the figures obtained by measuring from the central point of the southern, roughly worked area and, for the northern, from an estimated central point to the ends of the spur walls. This spacing differs from that restored to the stylobate of the colonnade to the east (see pp. 9–10 below).

The marble blocks also have various cuttings on their upper surfaces which have no obvious purpose in the construction of the stylobate. They may belong to an earlier use, although some most probably date to the period when the colonnade was being destroyed.

[4] Corinth Notebook 357, no. 139. Architectural pieces inventoried in Notebook 357 are stored on the site.

[5] See pp. 9–10 below.

[6] No further investigation of this cement floor was undertaken. The possibility that it is the top of one of the layers of bedding specified by Vitruvius for construction of mosaic floors (*de architectura* VII.1) does not seem too probable. In the first place this level was not found further to the south in the colonnade, where the bedding has been destroyed to this depth for the insertion of a drain. Secondly, at a depth of 0.39–0.49 m. this level could only be the top of the solid surface below the *statumen*. Vitruvius does not specify that this should be concrete but only that the soil be firm (VII.1.1). Furthermore, we have no evidence that the methods described by Vitruvius were generally followed at Corinth. For discussion of these layers of bedding and the proof of the existence of a layer above the *nucleus*, cf. R. E. M. Moore, "A Newly Observed Stratum in Roman Floor Mosaics," *AJA* 72, 1968, pp. 57–68.

[7] See footnote 17, p. 4 above. Somewhat surprising is the lack of evidence for occupation of the shop earlier than the 6th century after Christ. A bothros which exposed the levels below the earliest Roman floor reveals only fill. One must assume that the earlier floors lay at a higher level than the 6th-century floors. A similar destruction of earlier levels occurred in the shops

to the north of the entranceway was cleared. Both foundations and upper courses are built of rectangular poros blocks in the same style as the walls of the entranceway, the south wall of which bonds with the back wall of the colonnade. The foundations of the colonnade wall were exposed for a length of 4.25 m. by the building of the drain for the later latrine. Made of smaller blocks than the wall itself, the foundations are visible for a depth of 0.87 m. The wall above (Pl. 4:e) is preserved in three courses to the same height as the south wall of the entranceway and is set back 0.08–0.09 m. from the east face of the foundations below. The blocks are of varying lengths, and some are L-shaped, extending down into the course beneath. The wall, which is one block thick, has in its east face several cuttings which belong to the period when the colonnade was converted into a latrine.

The east stylobate of the colonnade, of white marble, is poorly preserved in the area of the latrine, the southern part of the excavated section of the colonnade (Pl. 4:e). Here the foundations are exposed. They are of brick-faced concrete (Appendix I, Table 1:2) with a total width of 0.59 m. The bottom of the foundations has not been reached, but on the west side they are exposed for a depth of approximately 1.60 m. by the drain for the later latrine. On the east side they are bounded by the west wall of a drain which runs the length of the colonnade.

At the southernmost end of this exposed area of the colonnade one block of the east stylobate remains projecting from the scarp for a length of 1.63 m. On the upper surface of the block, which is 0.27 m. in height, are preserved an empolion cutting with a diameter of 0.075 m. and a pour channel with a preserved length of 0.275 m. The surface of the stylobate is less carefully dressed here, but it was not possible to determine whether a round base or a square plinth had rested on it.

The northern part of the east stylobate is well preserved in the area opposite the entranceway (Pl. 1:a). Here the blocks are of two widths. The four southernmost are approximately 0.90 m. wide, whereas those farther north measure only 0.715 m. with the northernmost block cut back to a width of 0.67 m. at its north end (Pl. 38). The height of the blocks, as measured on the southernmost one, is 0.30–0.32 m.; this block has anathyrosis on its south end.

On several of the blocks the upper surface is cut down along the western edge for a depth of about 0.03 m. so that the stylobate would have had a visible width of approximately 0.70 m. (Pls. 1:a, 38). Presumably here the mosaic floor overlapped the marble. The rebate is not of uniform depth nor is it continuous. At two points approximately in line with the estimated positions of the columns of the entranceway the cutting is interrupted. This probably reflects the position of two of the columns of the colonnade which, if they were in position before the stylobate was cut down, must have had bases or plinths large enough to impede the trimming-down of the blocks. A marble block, 0.59 m. square and with a height of 0.32 m., is cemented to the stylobate at the estimated position for the northern column (Pl. 1:a). This block is approximately 0.26 m. narrower than the uncut extent of the stylobate and is not centered in the uncut area but placed at the south side. If the hypothesis is correct that the stylobate here could not be cut down because a column base or plinth was already in position, then the block now *in situ* must belong to a reconstruction or repair, since a plinth of its size would not hinder any cutting down of the stylobate. This argument is supported by a re-used column base on a square plinth (**90**; Fig. 2), which is cemented to the marble block. The east face of the base is unfinished, and it must originally have stood against a wall. That this block and re-used column base are part of the colonnade in a later phase (see below), as a colonnade, and are not just material re-used in the east wall of the 6th-century house is further indicated by the impression left by a square block of the same dimensions in cement on the stylobate to the south (Pl. 1:a). The impression, too, is not centered on the uncut area of the stylobate but is placed at its north side.

Assuming that the cuttings on the stylobate represent the first period of the colonnade, the interaxial spacing of the two columns opposite the entranceway can be roughly calculated by measuring the distance between the central points of the uncut areas. This gives a distance of approximately 3.55 m., about 0.20 m. less than that estimated for the central interaxial spacing of the entranceway columns. The distance between the position estimated for the axis of the southern column of the central pair on the stylobate of the

---

on the east side of the Lechaion Road near the Peribolos of Apollo. C. K. Williams, II, "Excavations at Corinth, 1968," *Hesperia* 38, 1969, p. 63, note 30; idem, "Excavation at Corinth, 1973," *Hesperia* 43, 1974, p. 32.

colonnade and the empolion cutting on the southernmost exposed block of the stylobate is approximately 8.80 m. Since the restoration of the entranceway suggests narrower intercolumniations on either side of a wider one (see p. 7 above), the interaxial spacing between the columns of the colonnade on either side of the center might be approximately 2.90 m. At a later time, the wider central intercolumniation was abandoned. The interaxial spacing between the empolion cutting of the re-used base 90 *in situ* and the estimated position for the axis of the plinth once set in cement to the south is approximately 3.10 m. This is only 0.20 m. more than the interaxial spacing estimated for the remainder of the columns in the original period. Whether this change affected the spacing of the rest of the colonnade is not known, since the stylobate is not well enough preserved here to tell.

For a reconstruction of the elevation of the colonnade there is very little evidence. A few architectural blocks are preserved, built into later structures. A column base on a round plinth (91; Pl. 25) was found in a late wall that had been laid on the stylobate at the south end; the lower diameter of the plinth is suitable for the position of the pour channel on the stylobate.[8] Although 91 is similar to bases restored to the colonnade of the Lechaion Road, its upper diameter is smaller.[9] Two fragments of unfluted Karystian marble columns were found in this part of the excavation;[10] in the absence of other suitable fragments it would seem that the colonnade had columns of Karystian marble. No fragments of Corinthian capitals were found in the area, but two fragments of Ionic ones were recovered.[11] For the entablature, the epistyle-frieze block (92) tentatively restored to the entranceway suggests the style which may also have been employed in the entablature of the colonnade. Three geison blocks with dentils (93) may also belong. All are of slightly varying dimensions, but the height preserved in two of the blocks is the same. They are, however, similar in dimension to blocks restored to the Lechaion Road further south and may be from the colonnade of the road.[12]

When the colonnade was rebuilt, as hypothesized above, the column bases, at least those at the center, were set on plinths with a height of 0.32 m. The column bases had a height of 0.235 m., including their own plinth, and the lower diameter of the columns was 0.38 m. There is no evidence for changes made to the entablature.

The tiled court was reached from the colonnade by two white marble steps. A gutter of cut stone, to the north of the lower step and level with the floor of the court, begins at a point opposite the north wall of the entranceway and drains to the north (Pls. 1:b, 38). A corresponding gutter presumably ran south from a point opposite the south wall but is now missing. The steps down to the court have treads of 0.30 m. and risers of 0.198 m. Five blocks of the upper step are preserved. They rest against the east face of the stylobate, which in the area where the steps are now missing to the south can be seen to be smoothly dressed only for the upper 0.15 m. In the area above and beside the gutter to the north, the stylobate blocks are smoothly dressed on the whole face, but a discoloration suggests that the upper step originally continued to the north. The lower step, however, could not have continued beyond the point where the gutter begins. The projected line of the step overhangs the gutter (Pl. 38), and the cement bedding north of the preserved step blocks has its upper surface at too high a level to accommodate the blocks of a lower step.[13] The lower step is built of blocks of varying lengths, some of which are obviously repairs since the upper step does not rest on them. The central blocks belong to this repair, and on one of these the name Eusambatis is scratched (Pl. 4:b).[14]

At the base of the steps marble slabs were laid level with the floor of the court. These are now badly

---

[8] It is interesting that pour channels were not found on the stylobate to the north. This may indicate two different periods for the stylobate blocks.

[9] Cf. *Corinth* I, i, p. 148, pl. XVII:D.

[10] Corinth Notebook 357, nos. 130, 133.

[11] Corinth Notebook 357, nos. 2, 12.

[12] Cf. *Corinth* I, i, pl. XVII:H, I.

[13] This lack of a lower step, however, is most unusual since normally the steps of a colonnade continued for its full length even where there was a gutter in front. It is possible that both the upper and lower step were interrupted at this point by a basin or cistern which collected water from the roof above.

[14] H. of letters 0.03–0.04 m. Carelessly incised. The letter forms suggest a date in the 3rd or 4th century after Christ. Cf. *Corinth* VIII, iii, no. 517. Unfortunately the date of the inscription does not provide a chronology for the repair to the steps, since the name could have been scratched on either before or after the block was placed in position.

shattered, and only two of the original slabs are preserved. Just south of the gutter three plaques of different dimensions belong to a repair (Pls. 1:b, 38). They close off an original drainage outlet from the court, which is still visible from inside the drain below them.

The courtyard which extends eastward from the colonnade is paved with bricks (Appendix I, Table 1:3) set on edge in a herringbone pattern.[15] The east boundary of the court is marked by a drain (Pl. 38) which, although of later construction, probably delimits the original extent of the brick-paved area. The court thus should be restored with an east–west width of approximately 13.00 m. Its limits to north and south have not been reached, but it has been cleared for a maximum length of 17.00 m. along the length of the colonnade. The paving is well preserved except where two bothroi of Byzantine date have cut through it and along its west edge where, at the north end, it has been broken through into the drain below; at the south end the bricks of the court have been torn up together with the marble slabs over the drain.

Beneath the court lies a drain which runs from the east and empties into the north–south drain along the colonnade at the west side of the court (Pl. 38).

CHRONOLOGY

A comparison of the construction of the foundations and walls of the entranceway with that of the foundations of the stylobate of the colonnade indicates that two different periods are involved. It seems likely that the walls of the entranceway were built in the second half of the 1st century after Christ, the time when shops further south on the east side of the Lechaion Road were constructed.[16] The earlier floor, if it is a floor, found within the colonnade has not been dated, and for the chronology of the tiled court there is little evidence. It seems obvious from the relationship of the court to the steps of the colonnade that the two were built at the same time, but the only ceramic evidence comes from the small amount of pottery which was excavated from beneath the court (Group 1). This provides a *terminus post quem* of the late 1st or perhaps early 2nd century for the laying of the paving, but since the only point at which this test could be made was in the northern Byzantine bothros that cuts through the courtyard floor, the evidence is not very satisfactory. The similarity between the epistyle-frieze block restored to the entranceway (**92**) and the epistyle-frieze blocks of the Captives' Façade[17] makes it likely that they should be dated to the same period. The dating of the Captives' Façade is, however, not certain. It was originally dated to the middle of the 2nd century, but in recent years that date has been questioned, some scholars assigning the façade to the early years of the 3rd century, another to somewhat earlier than the middle of the 2nd century. The most recent arguments propose that some elements of the façade are Augustan and were re-used in the construction of the Captives' Façade.[18] Since, however, the epistyle-frieze block from the entranceway can not be definitely assigned to the

---

[15] The bricks were laid on a bedding of smooth stones and mortar *ca*. 0.16 m. thick, which in turn rests on a second layer of packing of about the same thickness, consisting of small fragments of brick and stone laid flat on mortar and brick packing. Below this lies earth.

Approximately 115 sq. m. of the court were cleared, and the architectural blocks from the façade of the building and from the excavation of the colonnade and the levels above are now displayed there (Pl. 1:a).

[16] C. K. Williams, II, *Hesperia* 43, 1974, p. 29.

[17] Cf. *Corinth* I, ii, pls. III, V, figs. 41, 44–46, 53, 54.

[18] For the Antonine date, see *Corinth* IX, pp. 106–107; *Corinth* I, ii, p. 87. C. K. Williams and C. Vermeule support an early 3rd century date. Study of the Northwest Shops west of the Captives' Façade showed that the former probably should be dated to the early 3rd century and that they are apparently contemporary with the Captives' Façade (*Archaeological Reports*, 1963–64, p. 7). Vermeule compares the reliefs on the bases for the Captives with scenes on the Arch of Septimius Severus in Rome (*Roman Imperial Art in Greece and Asia Minor*, Cambridge, Mass. 1968, p. 83). The wind-blown rosette in one of the coffers and the busts of Sol and Luna decorating two others have also been dated to the Severan period (B. S. Ridgway, "Sculpture from Corinth," *Hesperia* 50, 1981, p. 444). It has been suggested that the Captives' Façade may commemorate the victories of Septimius Severus over the Parthians in A.D. 197–198, as did other monuments, namely the arch in the Roman Forum, built in 202 or 203, and the arch at Lepcis Magna, probably built in 203 (Vermeule, *op. cit.*, p. 87; C. K. Williams, II, "Excavations at Corinth," Δελτ 23, 1968, Χρονικά, [1969], p. 135, note 4). For a date before the middle of the 2nd century, see W.-D. Heilmeyer, *Korinthische Normalkapitelle* [*RömMitt*, Suppl. XVI], Heidelberg 1970, p. 70, note 277. Most recently, Henner von Hesberg has proposed an Augustan date for certain blocks from the Captives' Façade, among them most of the epistyle-frieze blocks ("Zur Datierung der Gafangenenfassade in Korinth," *AthMitt* 98, 1983, pp. 215–238).

entranceway and since it has been re-used, its date has limited usefulness for the chronology of the entranceway. Even if the assignment were sure, it could not be said whether its re-use was part of the original construction of the entranceway or represents a later repair.

There is little other chronological evidence for this area of the Bath. The mosaic floor in the colonnade is not well enough preserved to provide any satisfactory dating evidence of a stylistic nature, although a date in the 2nd century would not be inappropriate for the use of the wave pattern, found elsewhere in Corinth in a floor dating to the 2nd century.[19] From a technical point of view, the tesserae, in their irregularity of shape and their size, are comparable to those used in late 2nd-century structures at Corinth.[20]

Although we have no evidence for the date of the laying of a floor over the mosaic, this may have taken place at the same time as the reconstruction of the columns of the colonnade. The re-used column base (**90**) dates originally to either the Hadrianic or the Severan period.[21] The reconstruction followed, datable, pending further excavation, only as later than the base.

LATER HISTORY

A great deal of evidence for the later history of the entranceway, colonnade, and tiled court does, however, exist. During the 5th and 6th centuries debris accumulated over the court (Group 14), and at the east end a service area for the Bath was constructed in the early 6th century.[22] Probably in the late 5th to early 6th century the lime pit was dug in the entranceway (Group 27) cutting off access to the Bath from the Lechaion Road at this point. In the first half of the 6th century a house was built into the northern half of the colonnade, and a latrine was constructed in the south.

Only two rooms of the house have been cleared (Pl. 41), and its full extent to north and west has not been reached. The walls were built partly of re-used material: large poros blocks probably from the back wall of the colonnade or from the walls of the entranceway. One re-used block bears part of an inscription (Pl. 4:d).[23] The east and west walls of the house were built directly on the marble stylobates of the entranceway and colonnade, and both rooms were entered from the west through a doorway whose threshold block is still *in situ*. In the northwest corner of the north room was found a hearth; in the southeast corner of the south room there were remains of a stairway to an upper storey. A tall, white marble basin was found in this room.[24]

The chronology of the house is established by the numerous coins and pottery found in fill which had accumulated along its north wall (Group 28). The latest coin, dating to A.D. 565–578, gives a *terminus post quem* for the hearth and associated floor level found above this fill in the north part of the house. The pottery found above this fill, presumably belonging to the last occupancy of the house, dates from the late 6th to early 7th century (Group 29). The pit dug in the mosaic bedding of the colonnade contained early 6th-century pottery (Group 30). The pit thus is evidence for the destruction of the colonnade at that time.

[19] Cf. the Peribolos of Apollo (*Corinth* I, ii, pp. 52–54, fig. 37).

[20] Cf. the ceiling of the north hall of the Odeion (*Corinth* X, p. 41) and the northern and middle mosaics of the Mosaic House (*Corinth* I, v, pp. 114–115). For reservations, however, about the usefulness of tesserae size as a criterion for date, see L. Foucher in *Actes du colloque international sur la mosaïque gréco-romaine*, Paris 1965, p. 216.

[21] The base **90** is a mixture of the Greek and Roman forms of the Ionic base, the double scotia found on the Roman imperial base combined with the Attic type where the top of the scotia is in line with the torus above. These bases have been discussed by L. S. Meritt in her article, "The Geographical Distribution of Greek and Roman Ionic Bases," *Hesperia* 38, 1969, pp. 198, note 49, 199, 203, note 65. The references are taken from her article. The earliest examples of this mixture of the two types are found at Nîmes and on one base at Hadrian's Villa at Tivoli. For Nîmes, the Maison Carrée, see J. C. Balty, *Études sur la Maison Carrée de Nîmes*, Brussels 1960, pls. XXII:3; XXIII:1; for the Fountain at Nîmes, see R. Naumann, *Der Quellbezirk von Nîmes*, Berlin 1937, pl. 19:1; for Hadrian's Villa, see S. Aurigemma, *Villa Adriana*, Rome 1961, fig. 53 and J. Chillman, "The Casino of the Semicircular Colonnades," *MAAR* 4, 1924, pl. LII:3. The type occurs again at a later period in the Severan Basilica at Lepcis Magna (R. Bianchi Bandinelli, E. V. Caffarelli, G. Caputo, F. Clerici, *The Buried City, Excavations at Leptis Magna*, New York 1966, figs. 122, 126, 132, 133).

[22] See p. 56 below.

[23] The block was built into the partition wall between the two rooms. H. of block 0.43, W. 0.49, L. 0.59 m.; H. of letters 0.18 m.: C · F P Ç. For a similar open P, cf. *Corinth* VIII, iii, nos. 324:a and 327:j, dated to *ca.* mid-1st century.

[24] H. 0.745, D. interior of mouth 0.50 m.

The lime pit west of the two rooms of the house appears to be earlier: on the basis of the pottery in it (Group 27), it went out of use before the house was constructed. Furthermore, the west end of the south wall of the house seemed to be set on the floor of the pit, and no lime was noticed adhering to its north face. This evidence may, however, be misleading, since no floor level that could be associated with the house was found above the debris that filled the pit.

South of the house the colonnade was further destroyed by the building of a latrine (Pls. 4:e, 41). It is rectangular in plan and extends further south into undug fill. Its west wall was formed by the back wall of the colonnade; on the east it may have been closed by a wall built directly on the stylobate or the foundations of the colonnade. Water to flush the latrine was brought in from the east by a water channel set into the debris that had accumulated over the tiled court (Pl. 41). Re-used blocks closed the north part of the latrine drain. One of these is a marble relief of the same type as one built into the vaulted Byzantine construction (p. 4 above) at the west edge of the excavation (**103, 104**).

Within the rectangle formed by the drains were the remains of the gutter for the latrine. Two blocks were still *in situ*, one parallel to the west wall and the second at right angles at the north (Pls. 4:e, 41). Other fragments of gutter blocks were built into Byzantine walls, including a fragment of a spirally fluted column split in half.[25] All are re-used blocks with a trough cut into the upper surface to serve as a water channel. The one found *in situ* along the west wall bore on its three sides a victors' list from the Isthmian games, dating to A.D. 127.[26]

The latrine was probably in use until near the end of the century as is shown by the pottery, lamps, and coins found in the fill that accumulated over its destroyed floor (Group 24), in its drains, and in the drain along the colonnade (Appendix III, Groups 25, 26). The latest material dates to the early 7th century, by which time one may conclude that the latrine had been abandoned.

[25] Corinth Notebook 357, no. 117.
[26] W. R. Biers and D. J. Geagan, "A New List of Victors in the Caesarea at Isthmia," *Hesperia* 39, 1970, pp. 79–93.

II
THE MARBLE FAÇADE

THE MARBLE FAÇADE stood against the west wall of Room 3, the southwest wall of Room 5, and the northwest wall of Room 7 (Pl. 38). Because Rooms 5 and 7 lie at an angle to Room 3, the façade walls took the plan of a central wall, measuring 11.30 m., with two wings extending to the northwest and southwest.[1] The northern wing was cleared for 7.15 m., the southern for only 3.30 m., but the length of each wing has been estimated as 13.20 m.[2] The façade itself, restored on paper to a total height of 11.04 m.,[3] consists of two orders of freestanding columns grouped in pairs, except for single columns in the two angles of the walls (Pl. 43). The columns of the lower order stand on a podium formed with projecting piers, and a section of the entablature is broken out above each pair and above the single columns. In the recesses between the pairs of columns were windows which lighted the rooms of the Bath behind, and niches set in the wall above the piers were framed by the columns.[4]

At present the walls of the façade and the area at their base, where lay a shallow ornamental pool,[5] are separated from the cleared area of tiled court to the west by the baulk of earth carrying the irrigation channel for the fields to the north. Thus there is no visual conception, when on the site, of the relationship of the façade to the colonnade and entranceway. The ground plan of the building (Pl. 38) indicates, however, that entranceway and façade were designed to complement each other: the angles of the façade are in line with the walls of the entranceway.[6]

THE FAÇADE WALLS

The foundations of the façade walls, which are exposed only at the north end of the central section (Pl. 4:c), are of concrete poured into wooden forms, the marks of which are still to be seen. Vertical indentations from two posts remain, as does the impression of the horizontal boards. The foundations, cleared only for a depth of 1.27 m., project 0.55 m. from the podium of the façade above, and a layer of bricks marks their top.

The walls above foundation level are constructed of concrete, faced with regular courses of bricks (Appendix I, Table 1:1). The podium is approximately 1.20 m. thick, excluding the piers. The two piers of the central wall were fully excavated, but on the northern wing only one complete pier has been revealed so far,

---

[1] The two angles at the junction of the wings with the central wall are unequal. The angle at the north is approximately 133°, the one at the south approximately 125°.

[2] The restoration of wings of this length is based on three epistyle-frieze blocks from the upper order (**63–65**) which were found fallen in front of the northern wing. All these blocks projected out over columns, and a restoration of three pairs of columns on this wall is thus necessitated. An entrance at hypocaust level through the northwest wall of Room 5 (Pl. 10:b) supports this proposed arrangement. The entrance indicates that there was a service area at this wall. If it ran the length of the wall as does the area at the northeast wall of this room (Pl. 38), then the addition of its probable width and the known width of Room 5 results in a length for the northern wing which would indicate that the façade is correctly restored.

[3] This measurement does not include the parapet restored at the top, since there is no evidence for its height.

[4] This type of architecture, essentially decorative in character, is typical of the "baroque" style found in many Roman buildings of the 1st and 2nd centuries in the Near East and elsewhere. In Greece other buildings besides the Bath façade illustrate the baroque style, the Captives' Façade in Corinth itself being a good example. For definition of the term "baroque" as applied to Roman architecture, see Margaret Lyttelton, *Baroque Architecture in Classical Antiquity*, Ithaca 1974, chapter 10 (for monuments of the 2nd century in Greece), pp. 278–281 (for Corinth).

[5] An area (originally numbered 6 as a room) *ca.* 15 m. long from north to south by 8 m. wide was first cleared to just below the top of the façade podium. Except for an area in the northwest corner and at the south, fill was then removed down to the Roman floor level.

[6] The façade area with its three richly decorated walls resembles the Marble Halls of many bath buildings in Asia Minor. This type of room, the "Marmorsaal" or "Kaisersaal", was also usually accessible from a courtyard. In the Corinth Bath, however, the area did not function as a room, being open to the sky and enclosing a pool within its walls.

For remarks on the "Marmorsaal" in bath buildings, see J. B. Ward-Perkins, *Roman Imperial Architecture*, 2nd ed., Harmondsworth 1981, pp. 292–296; Fikret K. Yegül, "A Study in Architectural Iconography: *Kaisersaal* and the Imperial Cult," *Art Bulletin* 64, 1982, pp. 7–31.

and it was not cleared to its full depth on its northwest side. The corner of a second pier, uncovered further to the northwest, was exposed only to a depth of 0.30 m. below the top of the podium. The southern wing could be cleared only to a depth of about 0.40 m. below the top of the podium, and here the northeast end of one pier was revealed. In the angles of the façade the piers were built with a V-shaped indentation (Pls. 2:a, 40) and were constructed of bricks in which a V-shaped notch was cut, used irregularly with ordinary bricks. All the piers project for approximately 0.435–0.52 m. from the face of the wall.

Two vertical channels had been cut in the brick face at the north and south ends of the central wall (Pl. 40). The northern channel measures approximately 0.20 m. in width by 0.28 m. and extends down from the podium cap for 1.18 m. The southern channel, 0.19 m. in width by 0.15 m., appears to be more regular, but it has been exposed for a depth of only 0.17 m. The positions of the two channels have approximately the same relationship to the ends of the wall. They probably belong with a later construction in the area.[7]

The height of the podium below the bases of the lower order of the façade is 1.83 m. as measured on the central wall, but originally its visible height was approximately 1.30 m. This is indicated by the bedding for a molding which is preserved at the base of the northern wing at its southeast end at 1.30 m. below the top of the podium (Pls. 2:a, 40). The imprint in the mortar indicates that the molding had a width at base of 0.15 m., but no fragments of base molding with that width were found in the excavation of the area; a molding with cyma reversa and cavetto has tentatively been restored here (Pls. 44, 45). Although various clamp holes and traces of mortar on the face of the walls indicate that they were once revetted with marble, the type of marble used is not known, since no fragments were found *in situ*. Two clamp holes, one in the northern angle pier, the other in the pier to its northwest, lie at 0.76 m. below the top of the podium, indicating that the revetment probably consisted of two rows of marble panels, but no complete plaques of appropriate dimensions have survived.[8]

The wall above, against which the marble façade was placed, is preserved to a maximum height of approximately 1.30 m. above the podium and is 1.15 m. thick. Clamp holes indicate that this part of the façade wall was also once revetted with marble. Two fragments of the revetment are still *in situ* on the southern wing, one a fragment of *fior di pesco*, the other a small fragment of bluish gray marble, possibly Proconnesian.

Two rectangular niches were uncovered in the central wall, an apsidal one in the southern wing, and both an apsidal one and the southeast side of a rectangular one in the northern wing (Pl. 40). Two apsidal niches flanking a rectangular one have been restored in both northern and southern wings (Pl. 42), with similar niches in the upper storey.

The apsidal niches exposed in the northern and southern wings are 0.45 m. deep and 0.91 m. wide. The floor of the niche in the northern wing begins at approximately 0.22 m. above the top of the podium, but a packing of brick fragments was found inside, preserved to a height of 0.41 m., suggesting that the level of the floor was raised. The apsidal niche in the southern wing is obscured by later rebuilding and cannot provide additional evidence on this point. The floors of these niches were extended outwards by means of brick-built platforms, the best preserved of which is in front of the apsidal niche of the southern wing.[9] Here it has a height of 0.255 m. and extends forward for 0.215 m. (Pl. 40). The platform is partially preserved in the niche of the northern wing, where it can be seen to be part of the original construction, for the bricks in the floor of the niche extend beyond the face of the wall. The original width of this platform was approximately 0.58 m. as indicated by setting lines on the pier cap, and the extension of the platform from the face of the wall may be restored as 0.215 m., the same as that of the apsidal niche of the southern wing.

The two rectangular niches in the central wall are 0.965 m. wide and 0.465 m. deep. The southern niche is obscured by later construction, but the northern one begins at 0.22 m. above the top of the podium. Inside the niche the remains of non-bonding courses of bricks are preserved, suggesting that the floor was raised at some time. Below the niche the wall is damaged but still sufficiently preserved to show that the bricks once

---

[7] See p. 30 below.

[8] Since the podium cap of the angle piers is cut straight across (Pl. 40), the revetment of these piers has been restored as concealing their V-shaped indentation (Pl. 43).

[9] For similar platforms but projecting forward from aediculae, cf. *Baalbek* II, p. 27, fig. 55, pls. 29, 30.

projected beyond the face of the wall, indicating that there was a brick-built platform here as well as in front of the apsidal niches. A setting line parallel to the face of the wall, at a distance of 0.30 m. from it, is scratched on the marble pier cap in front of the niche and indicates the extent of the platform (Pl. 40). These rectangular niches were barrel vaulted, as is shown by a fragment of fallen masonry found in Room 5 (Pl. 49:b). Although the fragment probably belongs with the rectangular niche of the northern wing, the niches of the central wall have been restored with similar barrel vaults.

The height of the niches is not preserved. Their restoration is based on the proportions of height to width (2.57:1) of the apsidal niches in Room 1 (Pls. 52, 53). On this basis the height for the niches in the lower order of the façade should be approximately 2.35 m.

A rich decoration of marble or mosaic covered the walls and ceilings of the niches. A small fragment of *fior di pesco* is preserved *in situ* in the southern niche of the central wall, and from the excavation of the façade area several fragments of revetment were recovered of the same kind of marble and of the same thickness. These have a carved molding on one face (**82-85**). Other fragments, not catalogued, were carved with a larger version of the same molding. The soffit of the vault and the lunette on the back wall were decorated with mosaic. Extensive traces of a mortar setting bed for tesserae are still preserved on the fallen fragment of masonry found in Room 5 (Pl. 49:b). The walls of the apsidal niches of the façade were probably also decorated with mosaic, since a great many glass and stone tesserae (Group 33) were found around a fragment of an apsdal niche that fell into Room 5 (Pl. 49:c). The small brick platforms projecting from the apsidal niches were perhaps revetted with *fior di pesco*, since one small fragment was found *in situ* on the southern wing immediately northeast of the niche. None of the sculpture which once stood in these niches has survived except for a small marble head (**110**), which was found in the area and perhaps comes from the façade.

Nine windows have been restored to the lower section of the façade wall and nine to the upper (Pls. 42, 43). Two were exposed in the northern wing, three in the central wall, and one in the southern (Pl. 40). The brick window sills seem to have lain at 0.20 m. above the podium cap except for the middle window of the central wall, where the sill seems to have lain at 0.28 m. At these levels the window openings begin, as shown by the facing bricks that run through the thickness of the wall, providing the sides of the windows. Subsequently either the window sills were raised, or the windows were bricked up. The central window of the northern wing preserves a brick packing to a height of 0.58 m. above the top of the podium (Appendix I, Table 1:4), and in several other windows one or two courses of bricks still remain. In the southern wing the exposed window is bricked up to a height of approximately 0.67 m. above the podium. This wing showed two periods of reconstruction, the second belonging to the time when the exposed apsidal niche was filled in and the northeast wall of Room 7 of the Bath was widened.[10] The same coarse, white mortar was used, covering up the division through the wall for the southwest side of the window and obscuring the northeast side of the niche, providing evidence for extensive damage to the wall of the façade at this point.

The evidence clearly indicates that there was modification to the windows. It is not clear, however, whether at first the sills were simply raised or whether the windows were totally filled in. Since some evidence has suggested that the floors of the niches were raised (see p. 15 above), it is possible that the sills of the windows were raised at the same time.[11] Subsequently the windows may have been fully bricked up as the evidence of the south wall would indicate.

---

[10] To a height of 0.48 m., the vertical layer of mortar between the packing and the northeast side of the window measures 0.02 m. in thickness and is pink in color. Above that level the vertical thickness is only 0.015 m., and the mortar is coarse and white. Dimensions of bricks in the lower part were not obtainable because of the good preservation of mortar bedding for revetment. For those of the upper part, see Appendix I, Table 1:5. For other reconstruction to this wall, see p. 55 below.

[11] Unfortunately, in most of the windows too little of the brick coursing is preserved to permit comparison of dimensions with those of the walls of the building. The extensively preserved brickwork in the window of the southern wing is coated with mortar, which made measurement of the lower section impossible. Only for the central window of the northern wing is it quite clear that later construction has filled it in. Elsewhere it is perhaps possible that courses of bricks were laid inside the windows in the original period of the façade. If so, the original sill height was more than 0.20 and 0.28 m. (see above). The original height may be preserved in the window of the southern wing, where the first brickwork would indicate a sill height of 0.48 m. above the top of the podium. If this was the original scheme, the packing in the window of the northern wing must be a replacement of the original construction.

The height of the windows of the lower order has been restored as 2.60 m. (Pls. 44, 45). No evidence was preserved to confirm their height, although the level of the window soffit in relationship to the top of a rectangular niche is known from the fallen fragment of masonry found in Room 5 (Pl. 49:b). In addition to the barrel vault of a rectangular niche, the fragment preserves the right side of a window. The brick facing for the side of the window ends at 0.40 m. above the top of the niche, and the socket for a lintel block is preserved above.[12] Since, however, the height of the niches is conjectural, the restoration of the window height must also be uncertain. The windows of the upper storey have been restored as 1.00 m. square. No evidence was preserved for these dimensions.[13]

A molding, set inside the windows, has been restored on the basis of three fragments found in the façade area or in Room 5 (**87–89**); it was carved in one piece with the revetment for the sides of the window. A similar molding has been restored as a frame for each window (Pl. 42).

Quantities of window glass turned up in the excavation of the debris which had accumulated in front of the façade (Groups 10–13, 21, 23). It seems likely, therefore, that the windows were glazed, although no marble or metal framework for glass was found in the excavation.[14]

THE RESTORATION OF THE MARBLE FAÇADE

Since the only blocks found *in situ* were two column bases (**1, 2**), the marble façade has been restored on paper on the basis of fallen blocks from several destruction periods. Most of the recovered architectural blocks have been restored to locations on the northern wing and central section, having fallen from these walls during the earthquake which finally destroyed much of the building. Because no façade blocks, with the exception of angle column **11** (Pl. 12), were found fallen in front of the southern wing within this final destruction layer, although it was widespread over the whole area, the blocks from the southern wing would seem to have fallen in an earlier destruction and most of them to have been removed in antiquity.[15] It has been assumed that blocks found at a very low level in the fill which accumulated in front of the façade before the final destruction period are blocks remaining from an earlier destruction, perhaps the one damaging the southern wing. They have therefore been assigned to that wing. Although many blocks from the other walls are preserved, many are missing, notably the entablatures and cornices of the angles, the bases and most of the columns of the upper order, and almost all the upper-order entablature and cornice of the central wall (Pl. 47). The lack of these blocks, particularly those from the angle entablatures and cornices, has caused problems for the restoration, and although the major scheme of the façade has been established, it must be emphasized that the restoration of the entablature and cornice of both orders at the angles is only tentative. Furthermore, the restoration of some of the blocks to a particular location (Pl. 47) may not be correct, although for others the place where they fell in the final destruction (Pl. 46) has been a strong indication of their original position. No evidence for the type of parapet or crowning pediment was found, and the crowning molding of the podium is also conjectural.

---

[12] Instead of lintel blocks there may have been shallow brick arches over the windows, similar to those over the niches in the west wall of Room 1 (Pl. 54). This would explain the oblique angle of the wall surface (Pl. 49:b, upper left side of masonry). The restoration, however, assumes decorative lintel blocks (Pls. 44, 45).

[13] Smaller windows have been restored by analogy with other restored façades. Cf. the restoration of the Library of Celsus at Ephesus (*Forschungen in Ephesos*, V, i, *Die Bibliothek*, Vienna 1953, pls. I, II).

[14] E. D. Thatcher has shown, however, that in certain circumstances heated rooms could be open and be maintained at a satisfactory temperature (Thatcher, pp. 170–215).

It is interesting to note that Thatcher found that the sills of the windows in the open rooms of the Terme del Foro had been raised by the addition of brick courses. He speculates that this was done because it was found that the lower sill height allowed too much draft (p. 199). Were the sills of the windows in the Corinth Bath raised for this reason, too? A marble window mullion (Corinth Notebook 357, no. 20), which has no holes for the attachment of grill work for glass panes, was found in Room 5 near the south wall of the room. It might belong to a late reconstruction of the windows, since similar window mullions were found in Basilica A at Philippi, dated to the end of the 5th century (P. Lemerle, *Philippes et la Macédoine Orientale à l'époque chrétienne et byzantine* [*Recherches d'histoire et d'archéologie*, Bibl. des écoles françaises d'Athènes et de Rome, CLVIII], Paris 1945, p. 517, pl. XXXI:2–18). The window mullion in Room 5, however, was found with other blocks which were certainly brought in from outside (three footing slabs from a semicircular latrine, Corinth Notebook 357, no. 21 a–c). The window mullion, therefore, may not belong to the façade.

[15] For this reason restored elevations have been drawn only of the northern and central walls (Pls. 44, 45).

The Lower Order

The height of the lower order of the façade has been restored as 5.29 m., excluding the podium cap. The height of column, capital, and base is 4.28 m.; the entablature and cornice measure 1.01 m. (max.): epistyle 0.27 m., frieze 0.34 m., and cornice 0.38–0.40 m. Epistyle and frieze are carved in one block, separately from the cornice.

Podium Cap

The piers at the base of the wall are capped by white marble blocks 0.14–0.155 m. high and 0.655–0.715 m. wide, set into the wall approximately 0.10 m. They are connected by narrow marble slabs of the same height, set into the wall between the piers. A continuous line of marble forming the podium cap thus divided the lower section of the walls from the upper, and from the columns and entablatures of the façade. The podium cap slightly overhangs the face of the wall below, and the connecting course projects approximately 0.10 m. from the face of the wall above. The cap block from the southern angle is carved together with about 0.18 m. of the connecting course for the southern wing to the southwest. The blocks of the connecting course are well preserved, the pier-cap blocks less so (Pl. 2). The sides of the podium cap are roughly worked, and dowel holes, both here and along the upper edge (Pl. 40), indicate that some form of molding must once have been attached.[16] An iron clamp is still *in situ* on the upper face of the southern angle cap block, extending back into the face of the wall at the junction with the block of the connecting course, but no fragments of crowning molding suitable for attachment along the edge were found in the excavation. A plain cyma-reversa molding has tentatively been restored here (Pls. 44, 45), echoing the cyma reversa of the stylobate of the upper order (**42–50**).

On the upper surface of the two pier-cap blocks which are fully exposed, setting lines mark the centers of the blocks (Pl. 40), and on the cap for the northern pier of the central wall there is also the setting line, parallel to the wall, for the brick platform of the niche in the wall behind. The preserved pier-cap for the northern wing, in addition to the setting lines for the platform, also has a rectangular cutting, 0.10 m. deep and 0.26 m. from the face of the wall, which would not have been obscured by the platform projecting from the niche. Along the front edge of this block, at the southeast side, the surface has been dressed down for a width of 0.14 m. The pier-caps have empolion cuttings and pour channels for two column bases, one at each end, and the surface there is dressed down to a slightly lower level than in the center of the blocks.

Bases

The two bases from the lower order still *in situ* were found in the northern angle (**1**) and at the south end of the southern pier-cap of the central wall (**2**; Pl. 46). Other fragments of similar bases (**3–6**) were found during the excavation of the façade area and of Room 5. One (**3**) was resting out of line on the pier cap of the northern wing and has been restored to its present position.

The two bases preserved from the central wall (**1, 2**) are carved with a Lesbian leaf on the cyma recta and guilloche on the half round above, a leaf frieze on the torus below. The decoration differs from that of the base from the northern wing (**3**), which is carved with overlapping leaves on the cyma recta. Only a small fragment (**4**) has supplied evidence for the guilloche that decorated the lower torus of the bases of the northern wing.

Columns

The bases of the lower order supported columns, all of which vary slightly in diameter. Along the wings of the façade stood monolithic, unfluted columns of Karystian marble. One complete shaft was found (**7**) and fragments of three others (**8–11**). They were uncovered just as they fell from the façade (Pl. 46) and have been restored on paper to their exact positions (Pl. 47). **7** and **9** belong to the northern wing, **8** to the northern angle, resting on base **1**, and **11** to the southern angle. The findspot of **10** suggests that it belongs to the same column as **9**, although the two do not join.

---

[16] The row of dowel holes along the upper edge was probably for the attachment of the crowning molding. The lower row, which lies at *ca.* 0.05 m. above the lower edge of the podium cap, is perhaps from the clamps for the marble revetment of the wall. The location of this lower row suggests a height of *ca.* 0.10 m. for the crowning molding.

One fragmentary unfluted column shaft of red marble (**12**) was found near the north wall. On the basis of its diameter it must be restored to the lower order, and its findspot suggests the central pier of the northern wing. The two columns of this pier have thus been restored as columns of this type (Pl. 44).

The four columns on the piers of the central wall were monolithic fluted columns of *giallo antico*. The fluting of one of these columns left an impression in the mortar of a later construction on the southern pier of the central wall, and fragmentary fluted column shafts were all found fallen in front of this wall (**13–20**; Pl. 46). Three of these fragments (**13, 16, 18**) are restored to the same column because their flutes are wider and shallower than those of the others. At least four columns are represented in the preserved fragments, and although none of the columns are complete, their height should equal that of the other lower-order columns, 3.55 m.

Although the unfluted column, **8**, has been restored with confidence to the northern angle of the façade, it must be noted that there is no dowel cutting in the bottom of this shaft to correspond with the empolion cutting in the base still *in situ* in that corner (**1**). Nor are there dowel cuttings in any of the other shafts of Karystian marble. One of the fluted columns of the central wall, on the other hand, did have a dowel cutting (**13**). The surface around the empolion cutting in **1** has been roughly cut away, suggesting that the lead had been removed. Since the base was found in undisturbed destruction fill, the metal must have been removed in antiquity before the destruction; this fact suggests that the bases were not originally made to be used with the Karystian shafts.

Capitals

Corinthian capitals of three sizes were found in the façade area. It is assumed that the largest of these (**21–26**) belong to the lower order of the façade, although two types of capitals of this height were found. Three have a height of 0.51–0.52 m. (**21, 23, 25**), and a fourth (**22**) is the same type as **21** and belongs with it. A fifth capital (**24**) was found in Room 5 rather than in the façade area, but its dimensions and similarity to **25** make its attribution to the façade probable. The size of the upper surface of a fragmentary sixth capital (**26**) suggests that it also belongs with the lower order. Two of the capitals which are of the same type (**21, 22**) were found close to the central wall (Pl. 46). The diameter of their resting surface is approximately 0.39 m., about 0.05 m. smaller than the estimated top diameter of the fluted columns restored to this wall (cf. **15, 16**). The other four capitals (**23–26**), although battered, are stylistically different from the first two. Their findspots suggest the northern wing of the façade for two of them (**23, 24**), and the diameter at base of one of them (**24**) indicates that they are a suitable size for the unfluted columns of the wings. The findspot of the third capital (**25**) suggests the south angle for its restoration. The fragmentary capital (**26**) is perhaps from the southern wing.

The restoration of the capitals to these locations is based on their findspots and on a certain correspondence of size. It must be observed, however, that there is no correspondence between the cuttings in the one shaft top and those in the bottoms of the two capitals assigned to the central wall. The two capitals (**21, 22**) were carved without any, whereas the one fluted shaft fragment which preserves the top (**16**) does have a dowel cutting. This column was apparently fastened to the wall by a hook clamp, and since the area around its empolion cutting was roughly hacked away, presumably for removal of the lead, it must be suggested that this column, at least, was either reset or re-used in its assigned position in the façade. The one Karystian column shaft from the northern wing which preserves its top (**7**) has only a shallow cutting for centering. It thus lacks a dowel cutting to correspond to those in the bottoms of the two capitals assigned to this wall (**23, 24**).

Entablature

The entablature of the lower order is represented by seven blocks (**27–33**). Five (**27, 28, 30–32**) preserve carved ends notched at the back to fit adjacent blocks. They thus belong to the projecting part of the entablature above the piers. One of these blocks (**30**) has been restored to the north pier of the central wall on the basis of its findspot (Pl. 46). Two others (**31, 32**) have been tentatively restored to the southern wing, since both fell before the final destruction of the façade. **32** is still embedded in fill in the south part of the area and does not show on Plate 46; **31**, although found in the northern part of the area, was embedded in 6th-century fill below the level in which the other blocks in the northern sector were found. The remaining two projecting blocks (**27, 28**) have been restored to the southeast and central piers of the northern wing. **28**, which is still embedded in the west scarp and is not shown on Plate 46, fell southwest of the central pier, and has, therefore, been restored to this position. **27** fell southwest of the southeast pier (Pl. 46) in a group of blocks which have all been restored to that pier.

A third block has been restored to the northern wing (**29**). It was originally set back in the wall, and on the basis of its findspot (Pl. 46) has been restored to the area between the angle and the southeast pier, adjoining **27** which is restored above the pier. The adjacent ends have clamp cuttings which appear to correspond. If these two blocks are correctly placed together, the epistyle blocks above the columns projected 0.26–0.31 m. from the face of the adjacent blocks, slightly less than the full extent of the worked ends of the projecting blocks, since, at least in the case of **29**, the end of the block set back in the wall was dressed back from its face for 0.06–0.11 m. The soffit of block **29** was decorated and, therefore, meant to be visible. Since the block was narrow, only approximately 0.08 m. was built into the wall.

The east end of **29** is broken. It thus does not preserve the junction with the entablature over the angle column to the southeast. No entablature blocks have survived which may be assigned to this angle, but, because the angle columns stood on projecting piers (Pls. 40, 42), the entablature in the angles must also have projected from the wall. For lack of evidence the restoration of the entablature and cornice of the angles is based solely on what seems to be logical.[17] Because the central wall of the façade faced those entering the colonnade on the west side of the tiled court, this central wall seemed to be more important than the wings. Furthermore, the preserved angle column base (**1**) has the same decoration as the other base preserved from the central wall (**2**). The epistyle of the lower order in the angles has, therefore, been restored with its west face in line with the projecting entablatures of the central wall and with its south and north faces, respectively, at right angles to that wall (Pl. 42, dashed line). A wide angle is thus made with the northern and southern wings of the façade.

The seventh fragment of entablature (**33**), which is undecorated and preserves only the frieze, is perhaps from a repair to the façade.[18] It has not been assigned to a position in the restoration.

The use of a two-fascia epistyle deserves comment, since the traditional Ionic and Corinthian epistyle has

---

[17] There seem to be no exact parallels from other buildings to help in the restoration of the angles, although the ground plan of the façade with its projecting wings forming oblique angles with the central wall can be paralleled. Cf., for example, the court of the Domus Aurea in Rome (A. Boëthius, *The Golden House of Nero*, Ann Arbor 1960, fig. 51; McDonald, fig. 24). Cf. also the frequently cited wall painting from the house of M. Lucretius Fronto in Pompeii (McDonald, fig. 25), which can be interpreted as having the same type of ground plan. All examples, however, of courts or rooms with wide angles in the corners either have no façade treatment or the decoration is placed only against one wall. Even on buildings with decorated façades where the wings are at right angles to the central wall, the projecting single column and the projecting entablature in the corners usually seem to be avoided. More often the projecting entablatures on side and central walls meet at the angle, as on the Nymphaeum at Miletus (*Milet* I, v, pl. 43) and the Nymphaeum at Side (A. M. Mansel, *Die Ruinen von Side*, Berlin 1936, figs. 36, 37). In the Kaisersaal of the M Building, also at Side, an apse is placed in each angle, thus avoiding the projecting columns (*op. cit.*, fig. 90). The Marble Court at Sardis, however, has single columns in the corners, and the entablature above is broken out over the columns (F. K. Yegül, "The Marble Court of Sardis and Historical Reconstruction," *Journal of Field Archaeology* 3, 1976, p. 171, fig. 2). This is essentially the type of restoration followed for the lower-order entablature of the Bath in the angle, the differences being that the columns of the Marble Court stand on a continuous podium and the walls are at right angles to each other.

The restoration of the lower order of the Bath in the angles differs from that of the upper order, which was dictated by cornice block **70** (Pl. 22). If, however, this block does not belong in its assigned position (Pl. 48), then the restoration of the upper order is incorrect but that of the lower order still possibly correct. Both restorations are shown, since both are possible, given the limited state of the evidence available for the restoration. The restoration of the upper-order cornice block, **70**, to its assigned position is based on its findspot. But the sequence in which the blocks fell in front of the northern wing is peculiar (Pl. 46). Both the console-geison blocks with dentils restored to the upper order of the northern wing (**69, 70**) were lying beneath stylobate blocks of the upper order (**42, 43**). Furthermore, one geison block (**70**) was sandwiched between a lower-order epistyle-frieze block (**29**) and the stylobate block **43**. Joins between several of the blocks (**42 and 43, 27 and 29**), however, suggest that all are correctly restored to the northern wing.

[18] For other blocks which are possibly repairs, see pp. 23–25. Two blocks with ancient repairs (**63, 70**) are also evidence for damage to the façade and subsequent repair. A similar function is conjectured for a partially undecorated epistyle-frieze block from the Captives' Façade at Corinth (*Corinth* I, ii, no. 31, pp. 76–77).

three. This type of epistyle seems to come from Asia Minor, where it is found, although rarely on the main face, as early as the Hellenistic period.[19]

The crowning moldings of the epistyle in Asia Minor from the Hellenistic period onwards are usually cavetto, ovolo, and astragal, although ovolo and astragal, cavetto and cyma reversa, and cyma reversa alone are also known.[20] The astragal and cyma-reversa crowning of the epistyle from the Bath does not follow this tradition but is closer to the normal practice for Roman buildings in Greece: a cyma reversa or a cyma reversa and a cavetto.[21]

Cornice

From the cornice of the lower order eight blocks are preserved but none in complete form (**34–41**). Three blocks (**34–36**) have been restored to the central wall of the façade on the basis of their findspots (Pl. 46). One of the three (**36**) belongs to one of the piers; the other two were set back in the wall (Pl. 47:b). The other five blocks (**37–41**) have been assigned to the southern wing. All fell before the final destruction of the façade, and although **39** was found in the northern part of the area, it is assumed that it belongs with the other blocks brought down in the earlier destruction of the south wing.[22] So much of the upper-order entablature and cornice of the northern wing is preserved that it seems likely that all the lower order of that wall remained standing until the final destruction.

The cornice in the angles has been restored to follow the restoration of the entablature below, forming a wide angle with the wings of the façade.

The Upper Order

The total height of the upper order cannot be restored with certainty because no bases for it were found. Their height may be estimated, however, on the basis of the ratios of the heights of the separate elements of the upper order to those of the lower. These ratios range from approximately 1:1.13 to 1:1.29 which suggests a base height for the upper order of 0.18 m. The combined height of stylobate, shaft, and capital is 3.485 m., and with the addition of the conjectured height of the base, the total may be restored as 3.665 m. The height of the entablature and cornice is 0.79 m.: epistyle 0.25 m., frieze 0.22 m., and cornice 0.32 m. As with the lower order, epistyle and frieze are carved in one block.

Stylobate

Nine blocks or fragments of blocks are preserved from the upper-order stylobate (**42–50**). Most of the preserved fragments are from the projecting parts of the façade. The amount of projection varies from 0.30–0.385 m. On the basis of its findspot (Pl. 46) one complete block (**42**) has been assigned to the southeast pier of the northern wing. Adjacent to this block and set back in the wall between the pier and the northern angle of the façade, a second complete block (**43**) has been restored. A clamp cutting in the northwest end of this block corresponds with one in the southeast end of **42**. A fragmentary third block (**44**) has also been assigned to the northern wing; its height is similar to that of **42**.

Four blocks are assigned to the central wall. Three are fragments of projecting blocks, and on the basis of their positions when found (Pl. 46) one (**46**) has been assigned to the south pier of that wall, the other (**45**) to the north pier. The third fragment (**48**) may also have fallen from the north pier, but from its north corner.

---

[19] Strong, p. 136, note 73.

[20] Strong, p. 136. The preferred Ionic epistyle crown of the Greek period was the ovolo, but there are numerous examples of the use of the cyma reversa (Lucy T. Shoe, *Profiles of Greek Mouldings*, Cambridge, Mass. 1936, p. 171).

[21] Cyma reversa: the epistyle of both orders of the Captives' Façade (*Corinth* I, ii, figs. 44–46, 53, 54); Philopappos Monument at Athens (Stuart and Revett, III, chap. V, pl. VII; *Annuario*, n.s. 3–5, 1941–43, fig. 28, pl. XI; D. E. E. Kleiner, *Archaeologica*, XXX, *The Monument of Philopappos at Athens*, Rome 1983, pls. IV, V). Cyma reversa and cavetto: Odeion in the Agora at Athens (H. A. Thompson, "The Odeion in the Athenian Agora," *Hesperia* 19, 1950, pl. 36:b); the colonnade of the Roman Agora in Athens (A. K. Orlandos, Ἀρχ'Ἐφ, 1964 [1967], p. 18, fig. 22); porch of the Tower of the Winds, Athens (Stuart and Revett, I, chap. III, pls. VII, VIII); Babbius Monument at Corinth (*Corinth* I, iii, p. 27, fig. 15).

[22] See p. 17 above.

The fourth block from the central wall (**47**) was set back in the wall between the piers. It is a complete block and is evidence for the use of small blocks as well as large for the stylobate of the upper order.

Two stylobate blocks (**49, 50**) are assigned to the southern wing. Both fell before the final destruction of the façade, since they were uncovered at a lower level. One (**49**) was found in the northern part of the area. The other (**50**), which is still embedded in the west scarp and does not appear on Plate 46, is an unusual L-shape.

Bases

Although no fragments of column bases have been recovered which may be assigned to the upper order, the upper surfaces of several of the stylobate blocks preserve rectangular setting beds, one (**42**) with setting lines. Empolion cuttings and pour channels are also preserved. There must, therefore, have been bases of some kind for the upper order, and a Greek Ionic base on a small rectangular plinth, a common type of base in Roman Greece, has been restored here (Pls. 43–45).

Columns

A variety of material was employed for the columns of the upper order (**51–58**). White marble, *fior di pesco*, *giallo antico*, and Proconnesian all seem to have been used, as were both fluted and unfluted columns. The height of the columns is preserved in one shaft found in the excavation of the tiled court at the far east end (**51**); it has been restored to the southern wing of the façade. A second unfluted shaft, of which only a fragment is preserved (**52**), probably also fell from this wing, since it, too, was found at a low level.

The fluted columns are represented by a fragmentary shaft in *giallo antico* (**58**) and by one large and four small fragments in Proconnesian marble (**53–57**). The estimated diameter at the bottom of these shafts is approximately 0.03 m. less than the bottom diameter of the fluted columns of the lower order (**13–20**). The fluted columns **53–58** have, therefore, been assigned to the upper order, even though their diameter is approximately 0.038 m. greater than the bottom diameter of the unfluted shaft **51**, already restored to this order. Although the larger fragments (**53, 58**) were found in front of the façade in 6th-century levels below that of the final destruction, they have been restored with the rest of the group to the central wall of the façade (Pl. 47:b), because one small fragment (**57**) was found in the final destruction level in front of this wall. It therefore seems likely that there were fluted columns of this type in the central wall, set above the fluted columns of the lower order. Three shaft fragments (**54–56**) were found in Room 5, north of the façade. One (**56**) may have fallen from the façade before the final destruction and have been re-used within the building, since its preserved end is cut straight across for some later use.

Capitals

Four capitals (**59–62**) have been assigned to the upper order on the basis of their similar height. The find position (Pl. 46) suggests that three of the capitals (**59–61**) fell from the central wall of the façade and the fourth (**62**) from the northern wing. The abaci of all these capitals have been trimmed down so that the upper molding and the central rosette or leaf are completely missing. On **62** a slightly higher band has been left along the front. This cutting down of the capitals indicates that, as carved, all were too tall for the upper order.[23]

The capitals from both lower and upper orders (**21–26, 59–62**) can be divided into three stylistic groups. To one belong **23–26** and **59–61**. Although none of these capitals are well preserved, it can be observed that they are all the same type. A single capital forms the second stylistic group (**62**), and two capitals form the third (**21, 22**). All three are unfinished at the back.

Entablature

The entablature of the upper storey is represented by six blocks (**63–68**). Most of them projected from the wall, since their ends are carved and notched at the back. Because of their findspots (Pl. 46) four have been

[23] For further discussion of the significance of this recutting, see p. 26 below.

restored to the northern wing (**63–66**). The length of **63** is appropriate for the exposed southeast pier on this wall. The second (**64**) fell further west and has been assigned to the central pier. The third (**65**) is still embedded in the scarp and does not appear on Plate 46, but its location even further to the west and within the level associated with the final destruction of the building suggested the existence of a third pier on the northern wing of the façade.[24] The fourth block assigned to this wall (**66**) was set back in the wall and has been restored to a position between **65** and **64** (Pl. 47:a), because its decoration is similar to theirs.

To the southern wing has been assigned a fourth projecting block (**68**), found below the level associated with the final destruction of the façade. It does not appear on Plate 46. It is a re-used block, preserving on its back face an epistyle with figured frieze from another building.

The sixth epistyle-frieze block from the upper order (**67**) may have fallen from the central wall (Pl. 47:b). Its height is the same as that of the other blocks, and since it was found in final destruction debris, it must belong to the façade. It is undecorated and perhaps represents a repair.[25] The restoration of the upper entablature in the angles is unlike that suggested for the lower order but is necessitated by a coffer preserved on cornice block **70** (Pl. 48).[26]

The frieze decoration of the upper order varies from block to block in details of spacing, number of leaves or petals, and arrangement of S-scrolls. On three blocks (**64, 66, 68**) the arrangement of the S-scrolls is not consistent. Other details (half palmettes on **63** and **68**, the undecorated panel on the soffit of **65**) suggest a certain lack of care in the carving of the upper-order entablature. The decoration differs from that of the frieze of the lower order.[27]

With the epistyle-frieze blocks of the upper order there is a return to the traditional Greek form of the three-fascia epistyle divided by plain stepping and crowned by a cyma reversa. Examples of the use of a three-fascia epistyle in one order and a two-fascia in the other are known, but it is unusual for the three-fascia to be used in the upper order, an arrangement clearly indicated here by the relative heights of the two friezes.[28]

The proportions of epistyle and frieze in the upper order differ from those of the lower. The epistyle of the upper order is 0.03 m. taller than the frieze (0.25 m. epistyle, 0.22 m. frieze), whereas the lower order epistyle is 0.07 m. smaller than the frieze (0.27 m. epistyle, 0.34 m. frieze). Such a great difference between the proportions of the two orders is highly unusual.[29]

Cornice

The cornice of the upper order is restored on the evidence of six blocks (**69–74**).[30] The consoles at the ends of the projecting blocks of the central wall of the façade projected diagonally to the outer corners of the cornice. On the wings, the consoles at the ends of the projecting blocks were at right angles to the face of the wall, and consoles projected diagonally from the inner angles of the block (Pl. 48).

Four of the blocks (**69, 71, 72, 74**) are evidence for the projecting cornice above the piers; another (**70**) was set back in the wall. The sixth block (**73**) is too fragmentary to indicate whether it projected or not. The fragmentary block **71**, which preserves a corner console projecting towards the outer corner of the cornice, fell in front of the central wall of the façade and has been assigned to the south corner of the north pier on the basis of its find position (Pl. 46). The projecting block **72** was found at a low level and had been used as a step block into the service area constructed against the façade wall in the early 6th century. It is, therefore,

---

[24] See footnote 2, p. 14 above.
[25] Cf. p. 20 above and footnote 18.
[26] See footnote 17, p. 20 above, and p. 24 below.
[27] Usually the decoration on the frieze of one order resembles that of the other. See, however, the Market Gate at Miletus, where the frieze of the upper order is different from that of the lower (*Milet* I, vii, pl. XVI). The style of the frieze decoration, however, is similar.
[28] For buildings in Asia Minor with three-fascia epistyles in the lower order and two-fascia above, see Ginouvès, *Laodicée*, p. 120 and note 4.
[29] In the Pantheon in Rome there is a very slight difference in proportions between the two orders. See K. de Fine Licht, *The Rotunda in Rome*, Arhus 1966, figs. 114, 130.
[30] In the restored elevations (Pls. 44, 45) the decoration in the coffers does not appear.

assumed to have fallen from the southern wing. Block **69** fell near the northern wing in a group of blocks, all of which have been restored to the southeast pier of that wall. The block set back in the wall (**70**) fell just west of the north angle of the façade together with blocks which all appear to have fallen from a position between that angle and the first pier of the northern wing. **70** has, therefore, also been assigned to that wall. Its northwest end would thus have been adjacent to the southeast end of **69**, but the blocks do not join since they are both broken at these ends. The present condition of the northwest end of **70** suggests, however, that a console projecting diagonally from the northwest angle is correctly restored (Pl. 48). The southeast end of **70** would have been adjacent to the angle cornice block. No cornice blocks have survived from the angles, but the evidence of the adjacent block (**70**) with its coffer cut diagonally must be taken into account and has suggested the restoration shown in the reflected soffit plan, Plate 48.

Several features of the cornice of the upper order are of particular interest. The first is the presence of diagonal consoles. At the outer corners of a cornice these are not uncommon;[31] diagonal consoles from the inner angles seem to occur less frequently.[32] The use of both in the Bath façade is unusual. A further interesting feature is the ovolo molding crowning the consoles. In Greece in the Roman period this is normally a cyma reversa.[33] The ovolo crowning molding is typical of Asia Minor where it is found in the 1st and 2nd centuries.[34] It occurs in Greece on the cornice of the façade of the Library of Hadrian, although there it is undecorated.[35] It does not occur on the Captives' Façade at Corinth, where a simple bed-mold is used (Pl. 15).[36]

Crowning Member

No evidence has survived to enable certain restoration of a crowning pediment or parapet, but the upper surface of the cornice is dressed down, leaving a higher band along the front and side edges. This suggests that some sort of crowning feature must once have existed and that it projected over the piers. Since no marble parapet blocks were found, a brick-built parapet revetted with marble has been restored (Pls. 43–45).

Unassigned Blocks

Several blocks were found which seem to belong to the façade but whose exact position is uncertain. The most interesting of these are two console blocks (**75, 76**) which projected 0.58–0.62 m. from the face of the wall. The carving of the acanthus leaves on the front is very similar to the carving of two of the capitals assigned to the lower order (**21, 22**), which suggests that they belong to the façade. Furthermore, the length of the worked area of the blocks is about equal to the projection of the piers at the base of the wall. These two blocks were found fallen in front of the northern wing of the façade (Pl. 46). One (**76**) was found at a low level, the other (**75**) lay just below the debris from the final destruction of the building. Two rectangular blocks (**77, 78**) of similar height and width to the console blocks were found in the southern part of the area. In neither is the full length preserved, and both seem to be unfinished. The similarity in two dimensions suggests that all four blocks may have had a common function in the façade. What this was, however, can only be conjectured. The traditional uses for consoles are as supports for the lintels of doorways and windows, or for the cornice of an entablature,[37] but the façade of the Bath has no door lintels, and the construction of the windows, at least in the lower order, leaves no room for their use there.

---

[31] Cf. the cornice of the upper order of the Captives' Façade at Corinth (*Corinth* I, ii, fig. 54). For other examples, see Ginouvès, *Laodicée*, p. 113, note 2.
[32] Both occur at Baalbek (*Baalbek* II, pls. 24, 27 below, 28).
[33] Strong, p. 134.
[34] Strong, p. 135; Ginouvès, *Laodicée*, p. 112, note 1.
[35] Stuart and Revett, I, chap. V, pl. VIII.
[36] *Corinth* I, ii, figs. 56, 57.
[37] W. B. Dinsmoor, *The Architecture of Ancient Greece*, London 1950, glossary *s.v.* console. Consoles are also found as part of the frieze of the Trajaneum at Pergamon (H. Stiller, *Altertümer von Pergamon*, V, ii, *Das Traianeum*, Berlin 1895, pls. X, XII) and of the Temple of Bacchus at Baalbek (*Baalbek* II, pl. 7).

Consoles were also used as supports for small columns with entablatures[38] and as statue supports.[39] They were also employed as supports for projecting epistyles[40] and as supports for arches and balconies.[41] The restoration of the façade does not suggest that either arches or balconies were used in it, and although the façade had entablatures projecting out over single columns, there is little room here for both a console and a column capital. Unlike the structures where consoles were used in this way, the façade columns stand close to the wall. The height of the blocks is less than the height of the capitals of both upper and lower order, and, therefore, it is not possible to restore the console blocks to the angles as supports for the epistyle, used alone without capitals, nor is their height such that they can replace any other element of the façade in the angles. It seems more likely that these four blocks should be restored either as statue supports or as supports for small columns with entablatures. The great length of the unfinished areas of **75** and **76** indicates that the function of the blocks was truly supportive and not merely decorative. In the absence, however, of any evidence to indicate which of these two functions they performed, the consoles have not been included in the restored elevation of the façade (Pls. 43–45). The two blocks from the southern part of the area (**77, 78**) may have had a similar function. Their unfinished condition indicates that they probably belong to a repair to the façade.

Two capitals also have no place in the restoration at present. One (**80**) was found in fill over the apsidal niche of the northern wing, the second (**81**) in the center of the area. Both are unfinished and are too small to belong to the scheme as now restored. A fragment of a spirally fluted column (**79**), found in destruction fill near the northern wing, has also not been included in the restoration; its diameter is too small to permit its assignment to the upper order.

CHRONOLOGY

This type of façade, with its projecting and recessed entablatures, is common in many areas of the Roman Empire in the 2nd and 3rd centuries after Christ.[42] A date in either of these two centuries, therefore, seems

---

[38] See, for example, the Basilica Nova in Rome (F. Többelmann, *Römische Gebälke*, Heidelberg 1923, figs. 94, 101, 102); the Porta Aurea at Spalato (B. Schulz, "Die Porta aurea in Spalato," *Jahrb* 24, 1909, figs. 1–3); the city gate at Anazarbus in Cilicia (P. Verzone, "Anazarbus," *Palladio* 7, 1957, figs. 24, 25); the Artemis Propylaea at Gerasa (C. H. Kraeling, *Gerasa*, New Haven 1938, pl. XXV:a).

[39] For columns with consoles as statue supports, see the Camp of Diocletian in Palmyra (K. Michalowski, *Palmyre 1959*, Warsaw 1960, fig. 45); Diokaisareia (*MAMA* III, p. 52, fig. 77); Soli-Pompeiopolis (P. Verzone, "Soli-Pompeiopolis," *Palladio* 7, 1957, fig. 19). A gate at Diokaisareia has consoles restored as statue supports (*MAMA* III, p. 53, fig. 78). See also a gate at Korykos (*MAMA* II, p. 174, fig. 183).

[40] See Hadrian's gate at Attaleia (Antalya) in Pamphylia (K. Lanckoroński, *Städte Pamphyliens und Pisidiens* I, Vienna 1890, p. 20, fig. 8, pl. V); the theater at Sagalassos (*op. cit.*, II, p. 159, fig. 137, pl. XXIX). For the latter, however, there is little evidence in support of such a restoration.

[41] See, for example, consoles supporting the ends of brick-built arches in the shops of Trajan's Market along the Via Biberatica in Rome and others restored to a 2nd-century insula (Boëthius, *op. cit.* [footnote 17, p. 20 above], figs. 74, 73); also in the frigidarium of the Baths at Guelma, Algeria (Krencker, fig. 274). Double and single consoles with sculptured heads on one end were found in the Baths at Aphrodisias. Their suggested function is as supports for the epistyle of the colonnade of the small portico (*MonAnt* 38, 1939, col. 268, figs. 45, 46).

[42] The origin of the pavilioned wall is the subject of much scholarly dispute which it is not within the scope of this work to investigate; the Bath façade is unlikely to throw any light on the problem, and whatever the origin of this style of architecture may be, it will not affect the date of the Bath façade. For the purposes of this publication it seems necessary only to show that the façade fits into the over-all stylistic picture of baroque architecture in the 2nd and 3rd centuries. A closer dating must rest on parallels for the individual elements. For similar pavilioned walls in North Africa, see, therefore, the theater at Sabratha, dating to the last quarter of the 2nd century (G. Caputo, *Il Teatro di Sabratha*, Rome 1959, fig. 53), and the Severan Nymphaeum at Lepcis Magna (M. Lyttelton, *op. cit.* [footnote 4, p. 14 above], pl. 224). In Asia Minor the pavilioned wall was a common feature of many cities. See Ward-Perkins, *op. cit.* (footnote 6, p. 14 above), pp. 297–299.

In the carving of certain details of the façade, namely the two-fascia epistyle of the lower order and the ovolo crowning molding for the consoles of the upper order, influence from Asia Minor has been noticed, and other details will be pointed out in the discussion of the chronology of the façade which follows, but this influence may be indirect since these same details are found on other buildings in Greece. Parallels from Asia Minor, however, as well as parallels from North

probable for the Bath façade, but before a closer dating can be suggested it is important to try to distinguish original blocks from repairs or re-used material. As has been pointed out in the discussion of the restoration of the façade, some elements have dowel cuttings, others do not. This was noted in connection with the lower-order bases, columns, and capitals from the northern wing (**1, 3, 7–10, 23, 24**) and in the discussion of the two lower-order capitals (**21, 22**) and fluted columns (**13–20**) from the central wall.[43]

Other anomalies suggest the presence of re-used material in the façade: Three different types of capitals were employed. The fluted columns of the upper order (**53–58**) are only slightly smaller in diameter than the fluted columns of the lower order (**13–20**) and are larger in diameter than one unfluted column of the upper order (**51**). The frieze decoration of the lower order (**27–32**) differs from that of the upper order (**63–68**) as do the proportions of epistyle to frieze. Furthermore, the epistyle-frieze blocks of the lower order have dowel cuttings in their soffits, whereas the upper-order epistyles have none.

Many of the blocks which show signs of re-use also have dowel cuttings, whereas none of the blocks without dowel cuttings appear to be re-used, with the exception of one epistyle-frieze block (**68**). That block, however, was not re-used in its original state but was recarved for use in the façade. It therefore seems likely that blocks with dowel cuttings are not original. Thus, three of the bases from the lower order (**1–3**) which have empolion cuttings, or at least a pour channel, for use with dowels, may be re-used. This fact would explain the marks around the empolion cutting on base **1**, which could have been caused when lead from the first use of the base was removed, before the base was placed in the façade. The empolion cutting on base **2**, however, is still cleanly cut. One fluted column of the lower order (**13, 16, 18**) also may be re-used, since it has dowel cuttings and also a hook-clamp cutting in its upper surface. This shaft has slightly wider and shallower flutes than the other fluted columns of the lower order, and the latter may, therefore, have been carved at a different time and possibly specifically for the façade. None of these fragments preserves base or top so that it is not known whether these columns had dowel cuttings. The red marble column from the lower order (**12**), since it has an empolion cutting, may be re-used. The fluted columns from the upper order (**53–58**) are possibly re-used, because they do not differ much in diameter from the columns of the lower order and are larger than one unfluted shaft of the upper order (**51**). One fragment of these columns (**55**) preserves a hook clamp, a further indication of re-use or resetting. The Karystian columns from the lower order (**7–11**) were probably carved originally for the façade: besides their lack of dowel cuttings, two of these shafts are unfinished at the back, which makes them unsuitable for use in a freestanding position.

Only two of the capitals preserved seem to be original. These are **21** and **22**, which have no dowel cuttings and also are unfinished at the back. The largest group of capitals, **23–26** and **59–61**, are probably re-used, despite their comparatively large number. First of all, they are finished on all sides, which was unnecessary for use in the façade. Secondly, the lower-order capitals of this group, **23–26**, all have large rectangular cuttings in their upper surfaces, which seem larger than necessary to match the dowel cuttings in the soffits of the lower-order epistyle blocks, **27, 30, 31**. Similar cuttings may once have existed in the capitals from the upper order, **59–61**, but may have been removed when their abaci were cut down. The fact that these capitals had to be cut down for use in the upper order also suggests that they were not carved originally for the façade. In addition, **25** has a hook-clamp cutting as well as a rectangular cutting. On the basis of this evidence, therefore, all these capitals except **21** and **22** should probably be considered re-used material.

Since the decoration and proportions of the epistyle-frieze of the two orders are so different, it seems likely that they are of different periods and that the lower-order blocks are from another building, because they are the ones with dowel cuttings. The mason's mark on one block, **31**, is a further indication of this origin.

The remaining elements of the façade not yet discussed are the cornice blocks of both orders and the stylobate of the upper order. Of these, the upper-order cornice, because of its unusual design, was probably carved for the façade. The cornice of the lower order and the stylobate should probably also be considered original, although stylobate block **43** appears to have been reset, and the cutting in **47** may have had the lead removed in antiquity. Turning to the unassigned blocks, the two console blocks, **75** and **76**, are stylistically

---

Africa and Sicily, will be used to help date the different elements of the façade, although dated parallels from Greece itself are probably more important.

[43] See p. 19 above.

similar to the two capitals considered to have been carved especially for the façade, and they thus are probably also original. The two unfinished capitals, **80** and **81**, may belong to a repair.

The division of the blocks into re-used and original, as presented above, shows that a great deal of the preserved material seems to fall into the first category.[44] The mixture of origins explains the uneven quality of the various elements of the façade, from the clean, sharp carving of the bases **1–3** to the careless work of the upper-order frieze blocks, **63–68**. It must, however, be admitted that the profiles of the various individual moldings do not appear to differ substantially. In addition, one of the lower-order bases, **1**, is well suited by its decoration for the corner where it stands, and, further, all the bases were evidently designed for a façade since they are undecorated at the back. The interpretation presented above is not without its problems, but, given the extent of the evidence, it seems the most likely one that can be offered at this time. On the basis of the separation of the re-used and original blocks the chronology of the façade can now be discussed.

The re-used material is considered first since it presents a *terminus post quem* for the construction. The fluted columns of the upper order (**53–58**) have their closest parallels in the Hadrianic period,[45] but the use of this type of fluting is also attested in the Severan period.[46] The capitals **23–26** and **59–61** belong to the 2nd century, probably to the second half.[47] Unfortunately the figured frieze on the back of one of the epistyle-frieze blocks of the upper order (**68**) is too broken and worn to provide a *terminus post quem* of any certainty.[48]

The bases (**1–6**) have no exact parallels. Two similar bases, one in Rome, the other in Corinth, which combine a less vertical cyma recta together with a lower and upper torus, are not closely dated.[49] A date in

---

[44] This was apparently not uncommon in the Roman period. Cf. re-use of capitals at Piazza Armerina in Sicily (P. Pensabene in A. Carandini, "La Villa del Casale a Piazza Armerina," *Mélanges de l'école française de Rome* 83, 1971, pp. 209–216). Stillwell comments on the practice of re-using material at Antioch (*Antioch* III, p. 150). For Corinth see Von Hesberg, *op. cit.* (footnote 18, p. 11 above), and for recutting and re-use of marble statues at Corinth in the Roman period, see B. S. Ridgway, "Sculpture from Corinth," *Hesperia* 50, 1981, p. 442, note 79, pp. 446–448.

[45] Cf. Hadrian's Villa (E. Hansen, "La 'Piazza d'Oro' et la sua cupola," *Analecta romana Instituti Danici*, Suppl. I, 1960, pp. 15 left, 18 lower left); the Pantheon (Licht, *op. cit.* [footnote 29, p. 23 above], p. 110, figs. 118–120).

For other columns of the same type in Rome, see Licht, *op. cit.*, p. 110, note 26. Two similar columns are lying in the Forum near the Curia. For some fragments of unknown provenance, see F. W. Goethert, *Katalog der Antikensammlung im Schloß zu Klein-Glienicke*, Mainz 1972, nos. 260, 261, pl. 90. A fragment from Corinth has the astragal carved with bead and reel (inv. no. A 368, surface find, not from the area of the Bath).

[46] Cf. H. Stuart Jones, *A Catalogue of the Ancient Sculptures Preserved in the Municipal Collections of Rome. Palazzo dei Conservatori*, Oxford 1926, Galleria 29a, pl. 41. The pilaster belongs with a pilaster capital dated to the Severan period (*ibid.*, Galleria 70, pl. 41; E. von Mercklin, *Antike Figuralkapitelle*, Berlin 1962, no. 389b, fig. 767; G. Pesce, *Il "Palazzo delle Colonne,"* Rome 1950, p. 96).

[47] Two very similar capitals with almost identical measurements have been found at Piazza Armerina (Pensabene, *op. cit.* [footnote 44 above], pp. 209–210, figs. 59, 60; H. Kähler, *Die Villa des Maxentius bei Piazza Armerina* [*Monumenta artis romanae* XII], Berlin 1973, nos. 17, 20, p. 23, pl. 11:c, f). The capitals are considered by Pensabene to be re-used in Piazza Armerina and to date to the 2nd century. This dating is disputed by Kähler who argues that they belong with the remaining capitals from Piazza Armerina and date to *ca.* A.D. 300 when the Villa was built (Kähler, *op. cit.*, note 142). Although Pensabene's division of the other capitals into three different groups is not so easy to defend, the earlier date for the two which are similar to those from the Bath seems likely. As pointed out by Pensabene, similar capitals from Asia Minor and Syria date also to the 2nd century (Pensabene, *op. cit.*, p. 210; *idem, Scavi di Ostia*, VII, *I Capitelli*, Rome 1975, no. 349, p. 98, note 1). The capitals from the Bath, together with those from Piazza Armerina, compare best with those from Miletus and Antioch, dated to the second half of the 2nd century. Miletus, North Market, South Gate: *Milet* I, vii, fig. 131; Wiegand, *Jahrb* 29, 1914, fig. 14 (for better photograph). Antioch: *Antioch* III, no. 51, p. 155, pl. 30 (dated to late 2nd century, perhaps early 3rd). The leaf on the abacus is very similar to the leaf on **26**.

[48] Not only is the frieze in poor condition but the sketchy treatment of the drapery and the small size of the figures also make it difficult to assign a date. The technique, however, suggests that possibly the frieze belongs to the second half of the 2nd century or the early 3rd. The deep drillwork outlining the figures is paralleled on other reliefs of this period. Cf. F. Matz, *Die dionysischen Sarkophage* I, Berlin 1968, nos. 8, 11, 11A, pls. 10–12, 17–21 (Attic sarcophagi); III, Berlin 1969, nos. 181, 222, 225, 237, pls. 205, 238, 239, 246, 258. I am grateful to Mary Sturgeon for her help with this block.

[49] Both bases have a decoration of overlapping leaves on the cyma recta, but the leaves are more ornately carved than on **3** and **4**, and only two rows are used. The base in Rome is not dated; the other, from Corinth, cannot be securely dated, since it has been only tentatively assigned to the Temple of Tyche, itself dated to the first half of the 1st century (*Corinth* I, iii, pp. 60, 66, fig. 40, pl. 24:1. For the base in Rome, see H. Stuart Jones, *op. cit.* (footnote 46 above), Galleria 18, pl. 30; M. Wegner, *Schmuckbasen des antiken Rom*, Münster 1965, pp. 25–26, where he also refers to the Corinth base).

A Greek antecedent for the use of the cyma recta on a column base occurs in the Athenian Portico at Delphi, where it is

the second half of the 2nd century, however, would not be inappropriate for the overlapping leaf decoration of base **3**: it is a common motif in Rome in the later 2nd century at which time it is used on the soffit of the corona.[50]

The re-used fluted column of Numidian marble (**13, 16, 18**) also cannot be dated, but the epistyle-frieze blocks from the lower order (**27–33**) compare closely with the sima of the Captives' Façade at Corinth (Pl. 15)[51], and the acanthus leaves of a capital from the South Basilica at Corinth are also stylistically close. The basilica capital has been dated to the Antonine period, but the sima from the Captive's Façade may be earlier.[52] The twisted-ribbon motif as a division of the fasciae is also used in the Captives' Façade and appears on the theater at Philippi above the third fascia.[53] The leaf frieze as a soffit decoration and the curved ends of the panel are common in Asia Minor in the 2nd century,[54] as is the use of a two-fascia epistyle.[55] In Athens the two-fascia epistyle is found on one building dated to a period before the 2nd century, and it was quite common during the 2nd century.[56] It was also used in the 2nd century at Olympia, Eleusis, and Corinth.[57]

The first of the original elements to be discussed are the two capitals **21** and **22**, best paralleled by capitals from the temples to Commodus at Corinth[58] and by capitals from the Severan Basilica at Lepcis Magna.[59] This would assign the capitals to the late 2nd or early 3rd century. The two console blocks, **75** and **76**, are stylistically close to the capitals in the carving of the acanthus leaves, and the obvious drill work of the leaf frieze suggests a similar date for these pieces.

The other element of the lower order thought to be probably original is the cornice, which can be dated by comparisons with its sima decoration, best preserved on **37**. The sima from the Antonine monopteros in the Athenian Agora is similar in style.[60]

The third element which appears to have been carved for the façade is the epistyle-frieze of the upper order (**63–68**). The decoration on the frieze is similar to that of the Captives' Façade at Corinth[61] and to the

---

used with a small torus below and a large one above, the latter channeled horizontally (P. Amandry, *Fouilles de Delphes*, II, part 1, *La colonne des Naxiens et le portique des Athéniens*, Paris 1953, pls. 21–26). For latest discussion of these bases and full bibliography, see B. Wesenberg, *Kapitelle und Basen* [*BonnJahrb*, Suppl. XXXII], Düsseldorf 1971, pp. 130–141. The cyma recta also occurs in the Colosseum, used with a lower torus (cf. J. Dürm, *Die Baukunst der Römer*, Darmstadt 1885, fig. 213), and bases from the Tuscan order use it with an upper torus above and a plain fillet below (cf. *Corinth* I, iii, fig. 2, pl. 6:2). The combination of cyma recta with torus above and below is common as a base molding, e.g., *Corinth* II, nos. 217–220, fig. 98 (fragments from the theater).

[50] Strong, p. 148.

[51] *Corinth* I, ii, pl. V; Von Hesberg, *op. cit.* (footnote 18, p. 11 above), pl. 45:3. The motif was popular as a sima decoration in the later 2nd century in Rome (Strong, p. 148). Cf. also the sima of the Temple of Concord in Rome for an earlier example of its use (E. Nash, *Pictorial Dictionary of Ancient Rome* I, London 1962, p. 293, fig. 345). For treatment of the same motif in Greece, cf. W. Willson Cummer, "A Roman Tomb at Corinthian Kenchreai," *Hesperia* 40, 1971, pl. 42:b (cornice dated mid-1st to early 2nd century); *Corinth* I, iv, pl. 37:1 (crowning molding from the Fountain House in the South Stoa, dated to shortly before the middle of the 1st century after Christ).

[52] For the South Basilica, see *Corinth* I, v, p. 77, pl. 51:3. For dating of the Captives' Façade, see p. 11 above; for the sima, Von Hesberg, *op. cit.*, p. 225.

[53] *Corinth* I, ii, figs. 45, 53; P. Collart, *Philippes. Ville de Macédoine*, Paris 1937, pl. LXI:2–4. The blocks from the theater probably date to the second half of the 2nd century (Ginouvès, *Laodicée*, p. 89, note 1). For examples of the use of the twisted ribbon in Rome and Asia Minor, see Ginouvès, *loc. cit.*

[54] M. Wegner, *Ornamente kaiserzeitlicher Bauten Roms. Soffitten*, Cologne 1957, pp. 33–41, 74.

[55] Ginouvès, *Laodicée*, p. 92, note 2.

[56] The so-called Agoranomion, mid-1st century after Christ (J. Travlos, *Pictorial Dictionary of Ancient Athens*, New York 1971, p. 37); Monument of Philopappos, A.D. 114–116 (Stuart and Revett, III, chap. V, pl. VII; *Annuario*, n.s. 3–5, 1941–43, fig. 28, pl. XI; Kleiner, *loc. cit.* [footnote 21, p. 21 above]); the Library and Arch of Hadrian and Hadrian's aqueduct (Stuart and Revett, I, chap. V, pl. VIII; III, chap. III, pl. IV, chap. IV, pl. II); the Nymphaion in the Agora, mid-2nd century (H. A. Thompson, *Guide to the Athenian Agora*, 3rd ed., Athens 1976, fig. 77).

[57] The monopteroi of the Nymphaion of Herodes Atticus at Olympia (*Olympische Forschungen* I, Berlin 1944, pl. 38; *Olympia. Die Ergebnisse* II, Berlin 1892, pl. LXXXVI); the façades of the triumphal arches at Eleusis (G. Mylonas, *Eleusis*, Princeton 1961, fig. 60); the temples to Commodus at Corinth (*Corinth* I, iii, figs. 26, 32).

[58] *Corinth* I, iii, fig. 25, pl. 20:4. W.-D. Heilmeyer lists other examples of this type of capital from Greece (*op. cit.* [footnote 18, p. 11 above], pp. 76–77).

[59] Von Mercklin, *op. cit.* (footnote 46, p. 27 above), figs. 1065–1073.

[60] W. B. Dinsmoor, Jr., "The Monopteros in the Athenian Agora," *Hesperia* 43, 1974, p. 417, figs. 5, 6, pl. 88.

[61] *Corinth* I, ii, figs. 41, 44, 45, 53, 54, pls. III, V.

frieze of the block restored to the entranceway of the Bath (**92**), but it is much less elaborate with no small leaves at the bases of the palmettes and lotus.[62]

The final element of the façade belonging to the original construction appears to be the upper-order cornice. The diagonal console projecting from the inner angle can be paralleled in a mid-2nd-century building, although not in Greece, and the use of different motifs in the coffers of the cornice is common, at least in Asia Minor, from the mid-2nd-century onward.[63] The wind-blown rosette of **70** is Severan.[64]

The two unfinished capitals not assigned a position in the façade (**80, 81**) belong probably with late repairs to the structure.[65]

In conclusion, therefore, the original material from the façade seems to be Severan, a date which does not differ greatly from that assigned to some of the re-used material. The façade was therefore probably erected in the late 2nd or early 3rd century. Earlier material from another building or buildings was incorporated,[66] and repairs were made at a later date.

THE AREA AT THE BASE OF THE FAÇADE

The area enclosed by the projecting wings of the façade could not be cleared quite far enough to the west to provide a complete explanation of its different phases of construction. A totally different description may be necessary if the baulk of earth which now separates it from the tiled court is removed.

The Pool

At the base of the wall, but set out from it approximately 2.30–3.00 m., there was originally a pool with rectangular recesses echoing the plan of the walls (Pls. 42, 43). The evidence for the existence of the pool is slight, but it cannot be ignored. First, in contrast to the tiled court to the west, the floor of the area was originally paved with marble slabs, only two of which are preserved (Pls. 2:b, 40). These are approximately 0.14 m. lower than the paving of the tiled court and 0.43 m. lower than the level at the base of the northern wing of the façade. The slabs are bedded in a layer of coarse, white mortar, below which lies a layer 0.30 m. thick of waterproof mortar set on a packing of rough stones and brick fragments.

Secondly, there are the remains of vertical marble revetment and the bricks of the retaining wall for the higher ground level at the base of the façade wall. At approximately 2.90 m. from the northern and central walls of the façade, in two areas, two rows of bricks were found embedded in the mortar packing for the floor (Pl. 40). In front of them were preserved fragments of thin, white marble revetment, set upright (Pl. 3:a). The line of the bricks follows the plan of the piers of the façade, except that opposite the central part of the central wall the setback is only 0.26 m., which is less than the projecting dimensions of the piers. A similar shallow recess has been restored to the northern and southern walls of the pool. The junction of the two preserved sections of brick and marble at the northeast corner is not preserved.

By itself this evidence might only indicate that there was a platform at the base of the façade wall, but a section of marble revetment (dashed line on Pl. 40) with a length of 0.46 m., also set upright, is preserved at the very edge of the west scarp. The imprint of its further extent to the south is preserved for 0.28 m. in the coarse white mortar. The existence of vertical revetment at this point can only mean that a wall once ran in front of the façade. The evidence, therefore, of the bricks and revetment, the difference in paving material,

---

[62] For earlier use of S-scrolls in Corinth, cf. the Babbius Monument (*Corinth* I, iii, pl. 11). For the use of the same type of anthemion but on the sima, see Ginouvès, *Laodicée*, p. 106, note 2 (buildings in Asia Minor).

[63] For diagonal consoles, see footnote 32, p. 24 above; for different motifs in coffers, see Ginouvès, *Laodicée*, p. 112, note 2. Cf. also the coffers of a cornice fragment from the Severan Forum at Lepcis Magna (Lyttelton, *op. cit.* [footnote 4, p. 14 above], pl. 225).

[64] Ridgway, *op. cit.* (footnote 44, p. 27 above), p. 444.

[65] Since both capitals are unfinished, they are difficult to date.

[66] Since some of the re-used blocks are possibly Hadrianic but others seem to be later (see pp. 27–28 above), the re-used material probably comes from different buildings. Although there is evidence for an earlier building on the site (see p. 63 below), none of the re-used material in the façade can be assigned to that earlier building, nor is there evidence to show that there is an earlier phase of the Bath itself to which this material might belong.

and slight difference in level when compared to the tiled court to the west, all point to the conclusion that there was a pool in front of the façade separated from its base by a platform 2.30–3.00 m. wide, whose plan followed approximately the plan of the walls. The westernmost limit of the pool is given by the small fragment of revetment at the west scarp, which covered the eastern face of the pool wall. The parapet above may have been in openwork. One small fragment of an openwork parapet was found in the excavation of Room 5 (**86**).[67] A parapet of this kind has not, however, been added to the perspective drawing, Plate 43.

There are many parallels for the existence of a cold-water pool in the open court of Roman baths. In Corinth itself the bath north of the Peribolos of Apollo had a rectangular plunge in the open court, and a large pool in the courtyard served the early Imperial bath in the Gymnasium area.[68] In the Barbarathermen at Trier a pool is restored at the base of a façade which has rectangular and apsidal niches, and at Miletus in the Baths of Capito a pool was set at the foot of a semicircular façade whose purpose was to ornament the Baths.[69] Other examples show that an open-air pool was a common feature of the open court connected with Roman baths, and this supports the restoration of one in the open court of the Bath at Corinth.

Although the existence of a pool and its general extent may be restored with some confidence, the exact plan at its northeast and southeast corners is not known. The southeast corner has not been dug, and a foundation trench (Pl. 3:a) for a new room for the Bath, which was planned for this area, has destroyed the evidence in the northeast corner (see below).[70] The northernmost brick of the east wall of the pool, however, indicates that the wall continued north following the line of the façade wall and presumably meeting the northern wall of the pool at an obtuse angle (Pl. 42).[71]

The Foundation Trench

The foundation trench, equidistant from the northern and southern wings (Pls. 3:a, 40), was dug for an apsidal structure which was never built. The trench is 1.34 m. deep and runs for 6.72 m. in a curving line from the central wall of the façade at its northern end to the southwest where it disappears into the scarp. It reappears against the central wall at the southern end where the north edge of it was found in the 1970 test trench. The floor of the trench is of hard, yellow mortar which does not extend into the scarp, and a poros block, apparently a part of the general fill of the trench, is embedded in the floor. The trench has a width of 1.30–1.50 m., and when excavated it was filled with loose rubble. The south side at the east end where it meets the foundations of the façade wall had been cemented, forming a wall surface facing north with a length of 0.90 m. (Pl. 2:b). The cement extends onto the face of the foundations of the façade, blocking up the vertical impression from the wooden form (Pl. 4:c). Possibly the fill here below the original bedding for the pool was loose, and the cement face was added to make the side of the trench firm. The northern (outer) edge of the foundation trench at the east end, where it abuts against the foundations of the central wall of the façade, is in line with the vertical channel cut into the wall above at the northern end (Pl. 40).[72] Since the southern stretch of the trench has not been cleared, except for a very small section of the north side, we cannot be certain whether the outer edge there is also in line with the south vertical channel, but it seems likely. Possibly these channels were cut into the façade wall to ensure a firm bond with the brick facing of the new walls.

The purpose of the apsidal addition can only be surmised. Perhaps it was intended to hold a pool, opening off the west side of Room 3 of the Bath (Pl. 38).[73] The area was undoubtedly intended to be heated since Room 3 is heated, and the floor of the pool in front of the façade is about on a level with the hypocaust floor of

---

[67] A similar type of parapet is restored to the pool in the court of Peirene at Corinth (*Corinth* I, vi, p. 100, pl. XI).

[68] Williams, *Hesperia* 38, 1969, p. 63 (a plunge *ca.* 1.25 m. deep); Wiseman, *op. cit.* (footnote 2, p. 1 above), pp. 18–22 (a pool 1.58 m. deep at the sides and deeper towards the center). The pool at the base of the façade was shallow, only *ca.* 0.43 m. deep.

[69] Barbarathermen: Krencker, fig. 359; Baths of Capito: *Milet* I, ix, p. 23, pl. VIII.

[70] The southeast corner is unexcavated, but the evidence has probably been destroyed here also.

[71] The *natatio* of the Baths of Diocletian in Rome provides the best example of a pool with elaborate recesses which follow the plan of the walls of an ornamental façade (Krencker, fig. 412).

[72] See above, p. 15.

[73] For a large apsidal pool projecting from one wall of a caldarium, cf. the Baths at Trier (Krencker, pl. 2).

Room 3 (Pl. 39). Whether a pool or a heated room was planned, it was never constructed, for reasons connected with the later history of the area.

LATER HISTORY OF THE AREA

The walls of the façade show evidence of rebuilding and reconstruction suggesting that an earthquake damaged them. The greatest harm seems to have occurred in the southern wing. The lack of façade blocks found in front of this wall in the final destruction level indicates that this façade fell before the final destruction of the building.[74] In addition, at some earlier time the southern wing was extensively rebuilt.[75] The central wall of the façade also seems to have suffered, although not so severely that the wall itself had to be rebuilt. The niches and the spaces between the columns, however, were bricked up. The evidence for this later construction is well preserved on the southern pier of the central wall and in its niche, where the brickwork is preserved to a height of 1.05 m. above the top of the pier (Pl. 2:b). Remains of the construction could be seen on the northern pier of the central wall at the time of excavation. The construction was extended out to the very edge of the pier completely enclosing the column bases and the columns on their inner surfaces. The brickwork (Appendix I, Table 1:6) was presumably carried up to the entablature to support it. Whether the northern wing was also damaged is less clear. There was packing in the exposed apsidal niche, and there is still packing in the partially exposed rectangular niche to the west, but whether this simply raised the floor of the niches or filled in the niches entirely is not clear, nor is it possible to say whether the construction was carried out to the edge of the pier as it was on the central wall.

Although these repairs were made to the façade, it seems that the area was soon virtually abandoned. The marble paving of the pool was torn up, and the revetment on the podium was removed. During this period, presumably following the earthquake but possibly before, the foundation trench for the apsidal addition was dug. The plan was abandoned, however, and debris was allowed to accumulate in the area. After the debris had reached a height of approximately 0.80–1.00 m. at the base of the wall, sloping down towards the west, a barrel-vaulted service area was built against the central wall of the façade (Pl. 3:b). A rectangle of fill was dug out, and the service area was set on the bedding for the marble slabs of the pool floor.[76]

In the northwest corner of the excavated area of the façade, marble slabs were found, placed on a large accumulation of fill (Pl. 2:a). Their level is approximately 0.30 m. below the top level of the façade podium. When excavated, more were *in situ*, but several had to be removed to enable excavation of the northern part of the apsidal foundation trench. Originally the slabs extended to the west scarp, since in the course of the excavation a stone packing was found similar to that used beneath those slabs lifted during the excavation. Thus in their original state they formed a floor 3.15 m. wide along the northern wing, beginning at approximately 3.00 m. from the north angle. They are perhaps the paving of a courtyard for a house whose walls will be found in the unexcavated fill to the northwest.

The later history of the façade and of the pool is supported by ceramic evidence. The fill of the apsidal foundation trench dates to the late 4th century (Group 9), and the bulk of the pottery which accumulated over the area and over the trench dates to the late 4th and 5th centuries (Groups 10–12). This evidence suggests that the disasters which occurred in Corinth at the end of the 4th century[77] led to the abandonment of the plan to construct a new pool or room against the façade wall. It is not clear whether or not the damage to the façade by earthquake occurred before the foundation trench for the new addition was dug. Possibly the expansion of the building had commenced before the sequence of disasters struck Corinth at the end of the 4th century. Following these events, this area seems to have been virtually abandoned. Debris containing much material of the 5th century was allowed to accumulate over the tiled court to the west (Group 14),[78]

---

[74] See above, p. 17.
[75] See above, p. 16, and below, p. 55.
[76] For description of this service area, see below, p. 56.
[77] Earthquakes in A.D. 365 or 375 or both were followed in 395/396 by the invasion of Alaric and the Goths. For discussion of controversy over the date of Alaric's attack on Corinth, see James A. Dengate, "Coin Hoards from the Gymnasium Area at Corinth," *Hesperia* 50, 1981, p. 150, note 9.
[78] Although the lowest level of fill over the court is dated to the early 6th century by the pottery, the coins found there indicate

and the entrance there to the Bath may have been abandoned. This, together with the evidence from the façade area, suggests that during the 5th century, although the interior rooms of the Bath were probably still in use, little attention was paid to the appearance of the exterior on this side.

There is evidence for new activity in the 6th century, probably in the early part. Two drains and the service area were built,[79] and a quantity of ashy fill accumulated in front of the façade to a level just below the top of the podium. How much of this accumulation belongs to the period when the service corridor was in use is not clear. No hard strata were found above the level from which the service area was built, and once the fill in the area had accumulated to a certain height, use of the service corridor must have become extremely difficult, if not impossible. Presumably, however, it continued in use for as long as the pool in Room 3 was in operation. During this period some destruction of the façade continued: several blocks from the façade were found in these levels. The latest pottery from the accumulation belongs to the late 6th to early 7th century (Group 21). On this fill were laid the marble slabs found in the northwest corner of the area (Pl. 2:a). These seem to have had a short period of use, for over them and over the rest of the excavated area was found an earth fill which dated also to the late 6th to early 7th century (Group 23).

The final destruction of the façade was caused by an earthquake which brought down the walls of the building and with them the marble blocks which had not already fallen in the late 4th-century earthquakes and in possible early 6th-century damage. A thick layer of crumbled cement and brick fragments from the walls surrounded the fallen blocks and protected many of them from the lime kiln. The date of this disastrous earthquake is not precisely fixed but occurred between the late 6th or early 7th century and the 10th or 11th century. The material from the earthquake destruction debris (Group 33) is not informative for its date, since, although it contains some late Roman pottery, Byzantine wares of the 12th to 13th centuries were also found, and the group is, therefore, evidence only for the period when the area over the façade again began to be used.

---

that from the late 4th century onwards the court was apparently not being kept clean. Most of the coins are of the late 4th and 5th century; although the Bath had been in use during the 3rd century, there were no 3rd-century coins and not very many belonging to the first half of the 4th century.

[79] See below, pp. 56, 60.

III

THE INTERIOR OF THE BUILDING

THE MODERN VILLAGE STREET bounding the east side of the excavation runs through the middle of what must once have been one of the most imposing rooms of the Bath. This is Room 1, which is probably rightly named the *frigidarium*. From this room the heated rooms to the west were entered, Rooms 2 and 3, and doors to the north and south led out to the series of smaller rooms, Rooms 4, 5, and 7, the last two also heated (Pl. 38). Five service areas have been noted, and hypocausts have been discovered below Rooms 2, 3, 5, and 7.

ROOM 1

Description and Restoration

The axis of Room 1 lies approximately north–south. The room has been restored as cruciform in plan (Pl. 38), and the western arm of the cross has been fully excavated, except for two baulks of earth which were left against the walls to support the masonry. The central section of the room was cleared to expose a very small area of the parapet of a pool at the south end and approximately 0.80 m. (measured north–south) of a corresponding pool at the north. The total length of the room has not been cleared, but Ittar's plan (Pl. 37:a) shows that in 1802 the north wall was standing; from this plan the length of the room may be restored as 39.25 m. His drawing and the restored plan made in 1910/1911 (Pl. 37:b) give the room a width of 11.20 m. at north and south ends and of 20.20 m. at the widest part.

The floor of the room as cleared is constructed of marble slabs on a mortar bed. Two underlying floor levels were uncovered in a test area 2.00 m. square at the south end of the room against the west wall. Here the lowest level, a layer of mortar approximately 0.25 m. thick, was laid directly on earth, whose surface was covered by a layer of marble chips; no marble slabs were found. The second floor, a layer of mortar 0.07 m. thick, also had no flooring slabs preserved in the area cleared, but the imprint left by the wall revetment was observed along the edge of the floor at the base of the wall. The highest floor, which is the level found in the cleared area of the remainder of the room, consists of a layer of mortar 0.06 m. thick with the imprint of small rectangular slabs of marble still to be seen. The few fragments of these marble slabs still *in situ* indicate that a variety of stone was used. Plain white, *fior di pesco*, Proconnesian, and *lapis lacedaemonius* are preserved. One fragment is a re-used wall plaque with carved molding. At the south end of the room the imprint of the slabs shows that narrow bands of marble alternated with wider ones. One fragment of *lapis lacedaemonius* is *in situ* in one of the narrow rows, but in view of the variety found elsewhere in the floor of the room, it is not safe to assume that only this stone was used for the narrow bands.

In the center of the room lay a circular pool with a diameter (restored) of 6.50 m. (Pl. 38).[1] The highest floor level ran over this pool which when excavated was filled with destruction debris sealed by a layer of large tiles. The floor level to be associated with the pool is the middle one found in the test trench at the south end of the room and also in a small area cleared around the southwestern edge of the pool. The floor was apparently flush with the edge of the pool, for no trace of a parapet was found. The pool was almost one

---

[1] Less than a quarter of the pool could be cleared. Fill from the northern section could not be removed because scaffolding supporting the walls of the room is resting on it. Most of the pool extends eastward beneath the road which borders the excavation on that side.

If this pool is restored to the center of the room, a maximum width for the room of 15.25 m. results, and the northern and southern sections of the room must then be restored as 6.75 m. in width. These dimensions differ from those of the Ittar plan (Pl. 37:a), restored on the basis of the north wall of the room which in 1802 was preserved above ground level. The circular pool may, therefore, not lie in the center of the room.

Circular pools are not found very frequently in baths. See, however, the Baths of Caracalla (E. Brödner, *Untersuchungen an den Caracallathermen*, Berlin 1951, pl. 1); Aquae Sulis, England (B. Cunliffe, *Roman Bath* [Society of Antiquaries of London, Research Committee Report 24], Oxford 1969, fig. 45); small pools in baths in Germany (Krencker, figs. 351, 352:a, 354:a) and one in the bath at Aquae Flavianae, Algeria (Krencker, fig. 348).

meter deep and had a narrow bench or step running around the interior 0.46 m. below the edge of the pool. A thick mortar bedding was preserved on the walls of the pool and the bench; the impressions left by marble revetment were observed on the wall above the bench, but none was still *in situ*. The floor was constructed of cement and brick fragments covered by a layer of mortar which is partially preserved.

Of the pool at the south end of the room only a small section of the face of its parapet has been cleared. This stands to a preserved height of 0.05 m. at the west end, against the wall of the room. The pool at the north end, however, has been cleared for a width of 3.10 m. (Pl. 38). For neither pool is the full extent known. If they are restored as fully occupying the north and south ends of the room, they would be of considerable size, with a length of 9.45 m. and a width of 11.20 m. Although good parallels exist for large pools in *frigidaria*,[2] the possibility that they were small and placed only against the west wall of the room must also be considered. Room 3 of this building provides an example of this type of small pool (Pl. 55). With so little of the room at each end excavated no conclusive restoration can be made.

The parapet of the northern pool, 0.30 m. wide, is poorly preserved, but its height above the floor of the room may be restored as 0.30 m. from the remains of mortar on the wall. The parapet was constructed of bricks and mortar, and its restored height gives the pool a depth of approximately 1.38 m. A bench was set approximately 0.76 m. below the top of the parapet on the inside of the pool; it returns along the wall of the room, where it is narrower than below the parapet. The floor of the pool had none of its marble paving preserved when excavated, and no imprint of slabs in the mortar could be measured, but on the riser of the bench some of the Proconnesian marble revetment was still *in situ*.

In the western section of the room a drain or water channel (Pl. 38) was set in the floor, sloping from south to north and running from beneath the sill of the doorway in the south wall. Unexcavated fill both separates the two exposed portions of the channel and conceals its relationship to the north door. The extent cleared reveals that the channel is roughly cut in the floor for a depth of 0.25–0.30 m. Nothing is known of its function in the Bath, since so little of it has been cleared.

Except over distances of approximately 7.85 m. at the north and 7.05 m. at the south and for an area in the western section, the walls of the west side of the room have been cleared. Although the surface has been severely damaged in places and in others later repairs were made (Pls. 50–54), the west wall was originally symmetrical in elevation around its central axis, making restoration on paper possible.

The southernmost section of the wall (Pl. 50) is standing to a height of 7.86 m. It has been exposed over a length of 6.70 m. and is 1.10 m. thick (except at the north end, where it is enlarged into a pier measuring 2.30 × 1.50 m.). The wall is adorned by two niches, one within the other. The smaller, inner niche is rectangular in plan and 2.82 m. high. At 1.50 m. above the floor and approximately in the center of the back wall a hole 0.25 m. square is set into the face of the wall to a depth of approximately 0.81 m. Possibly a waterspout should be restored here.[3] The spring of the arch, constructed of voussoir bricks, begins 1.92 m. above the floor. The niche is set within what is in effect a larger but shallower niche, extending up the wall 7.64 m. and terminating in a rounded arch formed of voussoir bricks and rested on a course of bricks laid flat. The larger niche is set back only 0.14 m. from the face of the wall at the north, 0.075 m. at the south. On the south side the setback of the niche wall from the main wall is gradually reduced from the floor level upwards until, at 3.50 m., it merges into the main wall surface. In the main wall surface, 0.35 m. north of the larger niche and approximately 1.31 m. above the floor, a hole in the wall runs in diagonally for approximately 0.70 m. Its use is uncertain; it may be a scaffolding hole. Very little of the marble revetment of this wall remains *in situ*, but some evidence for the decoration of the smaller niche is preserved. On the soffit there is a small portion of mosaic bedding, and at the base of the niche in both corners two fragments of white marble

---

[2] Cf. the Thermae at Lambaesis, Algeria, where, in a cruciform *frigidarium* with a length of 32 m., two pools at each end of the room measure 6.50 m. each, occupying more than one third of the total length of the room (Krencker, fig. 295). In the Thermae at Lepcis Magna pools at each end of the *frigidarium* measure 10.00 m. each in length, occupying approximately one third of the length of the room (P. Romanelli, *Leptis Magna*, Rome 1925, pl. IV; Krencker, fig. 301). If restored as occupying each end of the room, the pools in Room 1 would together occupy a little less than half the total length of the room.

[3] The hole is larger than scaffolding holes found elsewhere in the building. It does not appear to extend further but may be blocked by fill. The various holes in the walls of this room do not appear on the elevations (Pls. 50–54).

revetment are still *in situ*. One small fragment of white marble is also preserved at the base of the wall north of the niches, and there is a small fragment of *lapis lacedaemonius in situ* over it. Clamp holes for the marble approximately 0.50 m. above the floor give the height of this first course of revetment slabs.

The corresponding section of wall at the north end of the room (Pl. 51) is standing less high, 6.16 m. as opposed to 7.86 m. Its thickness is 1.15 m. and its maximum exposed length 5.80 m. It may be restored from the plan made in 1802 when the wall was standing above ground for its full extent, approximately 13.75 m. (Pl. 37:a). The smaller, inner niche has the same dimensions as that at the south end and also has a hole in the center of the back wall (not shown in Plate 51), but the wall is not standing to a height sufficient to have preserved the large, shallowly recessed arch above. South of this niche, in the main wall surface, a hole in the wall corresponding to the one in the south wall is cut in diagonally, although only for approximately 0.45 m. White marble revetment is still *in situ* on the wall of the smaller niche at the south end, and a fragment of *lapis lacedaemonius* is preserved at the north end. A small number of fine, black-and-white stone mosaic tesserae on the soffit preserve evidence for one period of the inner niche's decoration. Clamp holes for revetment indicate that at another period the soffit was sheathed with marble. Evidence for two periods of decoration was also found on the wall just above the west bench of the pool. Two layers of mortar are preserved, of which the inner shows traces of burning. Three bronze pins *in situ* at the corner, approximately 0.55–0.60 m. above the floor, correspond in height to clamp holes found on the other walls of the room, and a small fragment of *lapis lacedaemonius* revetment is still *in situ* just north of the outer niche. Although the continuation of this wall further north was not exposed in the 1965–1968 excavations, it can be restored with three deep niches, two at ground level at each end, flanking a third set high in the wall in the center. All three were placed within shallower niches. This restoration is based on the plan made in 1802, when this north part was still standing above ground level. The plan drawn by Ittar is of the upper part of the wall and shows a central double niche placed between two shallow ones. Ittar indicates that the inner niche in the center was set high in the wall (Pl. 37:a).

The western arm of the room contains three doorways and was also adorned with a series of niches. The south wall of this section (Pl. 52), 4.35 m. long and 1.53 m. thick, is preserved to a height of 7.90 m. A line of beam cuttings from the construction of a modern house lies approximately 6.60 m. above the floor of the room. The doorway at the western end of the south wall is 1.60 m. wide and 2.32 m. high. At present its lower 1.30 m. is filled by a late wall constructed of field stones and fragments of brick and marble. A piece of the white marble doorsill, 0.56 m. in length, is still *in situ* at the eastern side. At the east end it is cut down for a length of 0.13 m. to accommodate a doorjamb. The lintel of the doorway is a shallow arch constructed of voussoir bricks, and above the lintel is a relieving arch. To the east of and higher than the doorway lies a badly damaged apsidal niche, with only a small section of its brick facing preserved. The niche is 1.05 m. wide and approximately 2.70 m. in height, with a depth of 0.40 m. Its base lies 2.80 m. above the floor of the room, and voussoir bricks form the face of the arch. Almost nothing of the decoration of this wall is preserved, although numerous clamp holes attest the use of marble revetment. Only two fragments are still *in situ*: a fragment of white marble at the west end and, at the east, a fragment of Proconnesian. No pattern can be discerned in the position of the clamp holes,[4] with the exception of a row approximately 0.54 m. above floor level, which corresponds to the holes found in the wall at the south and north ends of the room. In addition, a double row of holes above the doorway indicates the line of some form of decorative molding or narrow entablature.

The north wall of this western section of the room has the same length and thickness as the corresponding south wall but is in a much worse state of preservation (Pl. 53), and its doorway is totally blocked by undug fill. The lower arch over the door has been destroyed, but the placement of the eastern doorjamb could be measured at 2.12 m. from the east corner. The width of the door is restored on the plan (Pl. 38). The height of the apsidal niche is restored from the corresponding niche on the opposite wall, and it has the same width and depth. A double row of clamp holes in the niche approximately 2.00 m. above its floor indicates a string course at this point; over it is preserved a large rectangular hole. Two periods of revetment were found at the

---

[4] For restoration of revetment from spacing of clamp holes, cf. H. Schleif and R. Eilmann, "Die Badeanlage am Kladeos," *Bericht über die Ausgrabungen in Olympia*, IV, *1940 und 1941*, Berlin 1944, p. 60, fig. 28.

base of the wall, one laid over the other. The earlier, underlying revetment was Proconnesian marble, the later *lapis lacedaemonius*. A bronze pin 0.42 m. above the floor of the room indicates the original height at one period of one course of revetment at the base of the wall. This position is somewhat lower than that on the corresponding wall to the south.

The west wall of this section of the room (Pl. 54), although now in poor condition, must once have been imposing, with niches framing the entrance to Room 2 beyond. As now preserved, the wall is standing to a maximum height of 7.30 m., but its condition is so poor that fill had to be left against the central part and in the northwest corner to help support it. The wall measures 11.60 m. in length; at the north end it has a maximum thickness of 2.30 m., at the south a minimum thickness of 0.60 m. (Pls. 38, 54). The variation is caused by the difference in orientation of Room 1 from that of Rooms 2 and 3 to the west.

The entrance to Room 2 is not placed exactly in the center of the wall but lies nearer to the north end. It has a height of 2.30 m., measured at the north side, and a width of 2.20 m.[5] Because the wall widens to the north, the north jamb of the doorway measures 1.40 m., whereas the south measures 1.00 m. In the wall above the doorway is a relieving arch, of which little is preserved but enough to show that voussoir bricks were used.

All the niches in this end wall of the western arm are rectangular. The best preserved is that at the base of the southern part of the wall. It begins 0.24 m. from the south corner, and because the doorway is not centered in the wall, the niche lies further from the doorway than does the corresponding niche to the north. It is extremely shallow, being only 0.12 m. in depth. In height it measures approximately 2.30 m., and it has a width of 1.55 m. Its flat arch is formed of voussoir bricks. At one time the niche was evidently filled in, for the base of the niche is covered by a thick bedding of coarse mortar with some marble fragments in it. Fragments of white marble revetment are preserved on this mortar bedding. At 1.10 m. from the floor of the niche there are two large holes, measuring 0.15 × 0.12 m., which extend into the fabric of the back wall of the niche. The southern hole has not been cleared, but the northern one retains within the wall the impression from a cylindrical object, set horizontally, possibly a pole from the scaffolding used in the construction of the wall. The corresponding niche at the north end is obscured by fill and later construction, but its southern side could be located and its dimensions restored on the plan (Pl. 54).

Two tall, narrow niches set high in the wall flanked the doorway into Room 2, the southern one being set further away. Although damaged, their dimensions could be determined. They seem to have begun 2.80 m. above the floor, making the height of the niche 2.60 m. The width was 1.10–1.15 m. and the depth the same as that of the two niches at the lower level. Voussoir bricks were also used in the construction of the flat arches of the niches.

The north wall of the room is known only from the 1802 plan, from which the wall may be restored with a length of 11.20 m. and a thickness of 1.00 m. (Pl. 37:a). Approximately in the center, a space of 3.45 m. was recorded. This opening may indicate a window rather than a door. The room is provided with entrances to north and south in the western section of the room, and some lighting would have been necessary.

Many large fragments from the fallen vaulting of the room were found in the course of the excavation, but none were particularly informative for the restoration of the structure and shape of the roof. The form of the vaulting must be surmised from the ground plan, which suggests north–south barrel vaults over the arms of the cross, the main part of the room being covered by an east–west vault resting on the four piers at the corners. Since the curve of the lower vault of the west arm of the cross does not appear in the north and south walls of this section as preserved, it must have begun above 7.90 m., the maximum preserved height of the walls.

Room 1 has been so extensively robbed of its decorative marble that the over-all scheme has to be pieced together from the very fragmentary remains presented above. To the evidence *in situ* must be added that from the fill in the room. Green, blue, red, and orange glass tesserae were found, as well as a fragment of mosaic still attached to its mortar backing (Group 15). The types of marble revetment still *in situ* were well represented, and there were also fragments of *giallo antico*. *Rosso antico* seems to have been used for

---

[5] These dimensions differ from those of the plan drawn with the elevation of the wall (Pl. 54). That plan was made at a higher level before removal of fill against the west face of the wall enabled more accurate measurement.

revetment as well as for base moldings, for fragments were found in the fill. Small columns of *lapis lacedaemonius* were probably also part of the decoration.

Waterspouts and basins to catch water may be restored to the niches at the north and south ends of the room, but no fragments of these were recovered. Water for the pools may have issued from more elaborate fountains with such figures as Herakles and the Nemean Lion. A large fragment (**105**) of this group was found in Room 1. Of the other sculpture which must have decorated this room only small fragments are preserved. A small marble head of Pan (**106**), uncovered just above the floor at the north end, is one of the finest. In the south section were found a few other fragments which, since they were either directly on the floor or in the fill just above it, may also come from the sculpture in this room (Group 15).[6] Other fragments less certainly belong, since they were found in late fill or built into late structures over the room.[7] A fragmentary bearded head (**107**) was the best of these pieces.

CHRONOLOGY

Some evidence for the chronology of the various phases of Room 1 was discovered. A few fragments of pottery and one coin were found in the fabric of the fallen vaulting (Group 2). The coin dates to the 1st century B.C., the pottery from the 1st to possibly the 2nd century after Christ, providing a *terminus post quem* for the building of this room. Conclusive evidence comes from the circular pool which was filled with debris and sealed by the highest (third) floor. The latest material from this deposit (Group 8) was a coin of Valentinian II (A.D. 378–383), giving a date at the end of the 4th century or later for a reconstruction in the room, which involved the filling in of the pool and the laying of the third floor. The earthquake of A.D. 365 or 375, or both, may have damaged the room, damage which perhaps was intensified in the sacking of Corinth by Alaric in A.D. 395/6. Any one of these events, or perhaps all three together, may have made reconstruction necessary. On this evidence the construction of the pool and its associated floor level must be dated to sometime before the end of the 4th century, but whether the pool belongs with the original floor of the room has not been ascertained. Furthermore, we do not know whether the pools at the north and south ends of the room are part of the original plan or contemporary with one of the two later floors. The drain that runs through the western arm of the room appears to have been cut into the latest. After the final relaying of its floor Room 1 continued in use until the late 6th century, when together with the rest of the building it was abandoned. The marble was torn off the floor and walls, and a thick layer of debris accumulated. A child's grave was even found on the floor at the south end. With the exception of four Byzantine intrusions, the latest pottery and coins from the debris (Group 15) date from the late 6th to early 7th century.

ROOM 2

DESCRIPTION AND RESTORATION

Room 2 lies west of Room 1 but with its major axis approximately 13° to the northwest (Pl. 38). It was entered from Room 1 by a door set in a shallow apse in the center of the east wall, and two doorways in its west wall gave access to Room 3 beyond. Room 2 was subject to extensive reconstruction and repair; in its present state it is a narrow room measuring 13.20 m. in length with apsidal pools at the north and south ends. The room measures 4.05 m. in width at the south, increasing to 4.40 m. at the north. Its floor, preserved in entirety except for one area south of the north pool at its east side (Pl. 5:a), is supported on hypocaust columns. The floor of the hypocaust is concrete, and on this stand the columns, 0.755 m. high, all of which are apparently preserved. They are evenly spaced from east to west, but from north to south, as measured in only three of the rows, the spacing is not uniform (Appendix I, Table 2:26).[8] At the south end of the hypocaust there was perhaps a furnace or service entrance, indicated by a relieving arch in the back wall

---

[6] Although none of the sculpture found in the excavation may be definitely assigned to any particular room, all the pieces are mentioned in the discussion of the rooms in which they were found.

[7] Corinth inv. nos. S 2816 (snout of wild boar), S 2818 (foot), S 2825 (statuette of a youth), S 2829 (snake head). In the fill of the circular pool was found a hand (Group 8).

[8] Because of the narrow spacing of the columns no further measurements were taken.

of the south apse pool. At hypocaust level there appears to be no communication with the heated room, Room 3, to the west.

Four floors can be restored to this room. The earliest is constructed of two layers of bricks with a layer of mortar above. In the lowest layer the bricks are rectangular, approximately 0.30 m. wide from east to west, and are laid in continuous rows from north to south directly over the columns, leaving unbridged the north–south spaces between the rows of columns. The upper layer of bricks, 0.60 m. wide, is continuous over the whole area.[9] The mortar level above the bricks is 0.25 m. thick, and on this were laid white marble floor slabs which have been preserved by the mortar of a later floor laid directly on them. The edge of the lowest floor is preserved 0.54 m. south of the parapet of the north pool, where a vertical face can be seen in the break in the floor (Pl. 5:a). At the west side a trace of it can also be made out. This indicates the original northern extent of the floor and suggests either the position of the original north wall of this room, or that a pool parapet originally crossed the room at this point. Built into this floor level at the time of construction was a water channel which ran across the room at the north end (Pls. 5:a, 38). It may at one time have been connected with a channel in the floor of Room 3, but the junction, if any, has been destroyed. At the east end it follows the line of the eastern apse wall and passes through the doorway into Room 1, where presumably it emptied into a drain.

The third floor[10] of the room consists of a bedding of coarse mortar, 0.09 m. thick, laid directly over the first floor and covered with white marble slabs, a few small fragments of which are preserved. Some re-used material was apparently employed, for the imprint of a wall plaque with an elongated six-pointed design in relief, surrounded by a border of two lines, was found at the south end of the room (Pl. 6:a).[11] A second re-used slab to the west has left an imprint of parallel lines. At the north end of the room, north of the vertical edge marking the extent of the first floor level (see above), the mortar bedding of the third floor rests on a packing of brick fragments which separates the bricks over the hypocaust columns from the mortar of the floor. A small section of gray marble revetment is preserved upright in this part of the floor, set 0.341 m. from the parapet of the pool (Pl. 5:a). Its original height was 0.05 m. above the mortar of the floor, and when first excavated, slabs of marble were still *in situ* laid horizontally between this revetment and the parapet. The fourth floor level for the room is preserved in only one small area at the south end (Pl. 6:a). The construction is the same as that of the third floor, a mortar bedding, 0.09 m. thick, laid directly on the marble slabs of the floor below. No marble was found *in situ* on this floor.

That the two apsidal pools were not part of the original plan is shown by several details of their construction. The north pool could be more completely studied since the floor of the room is broken through just south of the pool at the east side. The pool was set off from the room by a parapet wall placed slightly in front of the apse. The gap remaining was then filled in with rubble and cement. The parapet wall rests on the floor of the hypocaust and incorporates one row of hypocaust columns. The construction at this level is rough, being a packing of stones, tile fragments, bricks, and coarse, white mortar as a foundation for the more regular construction of courses of bricks and mortar used for the parapet above (Appendix I, Table 1:7). The original height of the parapet above the floor of the room seems to have been 0.54 m., just to the bottom of a marble molding still *in situ* on the west wall of the room (Pl. 5:a). The parapet is not well preserved, however, especially towards the center where it is standing for only a few centimeters above the floor. Approximately 0.56 m. below the original top of the parapet, on the inside of the pool, was placed a narrow bench about 0.48 m. high. Several fragments of white and Proconnesian marble revetment are still *in situ* on the inner face of the parapet wall, two more fragments on the outer. The wall of the bench was also revetted with Proconnesian marble.

The pool itself measures 3.55 m. in width with a length from north to south of 1.40 m., excluding the bench. The surface of its floor must lie at approximately 0.54 m. above the floor of the hypocaust below. The

---

[9] This method of construction has a double effect. It provides more space in the north–south rows between the floor of the hypocaust and the floor of the room and lightens the weight of the floor. The system seems to have been quite sufficient; the floor in this room survived the best of all three suspended floors excavated.

[10] The second floor laid in this room is not now preserved. For the evidence that it once existed, see p. 42 below.

[11] For carved wall plaques with similar geometric designs, see Krencker, figs. 477–479, 481, 484, 486–493, 496, 501–503.

impression of the marble paving slabs remains in the mortar bedding, and there are fragments of Proconnesian marble still *in situ* at the base of the walls of the apse. The water from the pool was drained by means of a small outlet at the base of the wall. How the water was brought in we do not know.

The apsidal back wall of the pool, which is the present north wall of the room, is preserved to a height of approximately 3.00 m. above the floor of the pool. The foundations of this wall are visible in the service area below (Pl. 5:b). They have a maximum height of 1.80 m. and are built on a stone and mortar socle which projects 0.26 m. from the face above and is visible only on the west side. Above the socle the foundations are constructed of brick-faced cement and were built in three stepped sections with heights of 0.52 m., 0.42 m., and 0.88 m., from bottom to top. Each section is set back 0.10 m. from the face below in the place where it was necessary to leave a passageway open between the two parts of the service area. The setbacks gradually diminish from this point around the apse until the foundations present a smooth vertical face. Two different types of bricks were used in these foundations. Some of those in the uppermost section are similar to those in the main brickwork of the walls of the building above (Appendix I, Table 1:8).

Above the foundations the wall of the north apse is approximately 0.70 m. thick except at the west end where the apsidal shape is not maintained on its north (outer) face (Pl. 38). The western return of the apse does not bond with the west wall of the room, further evidence that the north apse is a later addition. Not enough fill, however, has been removed from the north face of the apse wall for the junction with the apse of Room 3 to be as easily observed. Two layers of mortar are preserved on the south face of the apse wall. A fine white mortar is covered by a coarse mortar with much ground brick, 0.05–0.06 m. thick in places. There are substantial remains of plain white and Proconnesian marble revetment still *in situ*, and the clamp holes for the revetment show that at the base of the wall tall, narrow plaques were used, 0.30–0.40 m. in width and with a height of 0.82 m. Above these came three courses of slabs with a height of 0.52 m. The junction of the marble of floor and walls of the pool, as well as the vertical junction of the walls with the bench, was sealed with mortar, a feature found in other pool construction in the rest of the building.

The back (north) wall of the pool once had a doorway set at an angle in it, evidence that a pool was not originally planned for the apse (Pl. 38). At present it is bricked up to a height of 1.63 m. above the floor of the pool.[12] The dimensions of bricks and mortar used in the packing and the treatment of the mortar are different from that used in the walls of the room (Appendix I, Table 1:9). Where the doorway is open above the packing a layer of coarse, reddish mortar, 0.10 m. thick, is preserved on the sides, the same as is found on the apsidal walls of the pool.

Although the south pool (Pl. 6:a) has no doorway in its back wall, and it was not possible to examine the construction of the parapet wall below the floor of the room, it, too, evidently belongs to a later phase of the room, for its parapet wall also lies slightly in front of the apse (Pl. 38), and the gap left between the wall of the room and the parapet has been carelessly filled in with mortar. The parapet is preserved to a height of 0.40 m. above the floor and perhaps should be restored to the same height as the parapet at the north end (0.54 m.), although there is no sign on the walls of the room that it was that high. White and *fior di pesco* marble revetment is preserved on the north face of the parapet, and fragments are still *in situ* on the inner face at the base and in the corners. Two layers of revetment were found here, the earlier layer being of white marble, the outer layer of white marble at the west and Proconnesian at the east.

As in the north pool a bench runs along the inner face of the parapet. It lies approximately 0.53 m. below the restored top of the parapet and was originally 0.57–0.60 m. high. At the west end it is poorly preserved. The construction is brick and mortar with a thick mortar bed for the marble revetment.[13] Two layers of revetment were still *in situ* on the bench, the upper of Karystian marble, the lower of Proconnesian. The mortar used is coarse and reddish, similar to that found on the north wall of the room. The wall of the bench was revetted with Proconnesian marble.

The floor of the pool lies approximately 0.60 m. above the floor of the hypocaust, and some fragments of its

---

[12] The outlet for the pool is in this bricked-up area. Doorways at an angle are not unusual in Roman bath construction. Cf. A. Lézine, *Carthage. Utique. Études d'architecture et d'urbanisme* (Éditions du Centre National de la Recherche Scientifique), Paris 1968, p. 142 and note 9.

[13] The brick dimensions were not obtainable because of the good preservation of revetment and mortar bedding.

paving in *lapis lacedaemonius* are still preserved. Water was probably brought in through one or both of two holes in the back wall, which lie 1.21 m. and 1.00 m. above the floor of the pool. How the pool was drained we do not know, since no outlet was found.[14]

The back wall of the pool, which is the present south wall of the room, is preserved to a height of approximately 4.10 m. above the pool floor. Its thickness is 0.65 m., and, unlike the wall of the north apse, it has the same thickness throughout. At about 1.80 m. above the floor of the pool the wall is broken through in a large area. Fragments of the wall revetment of Proconnesian marble survive at the base, laid on a thick bed of the same coarse mortar used on the wall of the north apse. This mortar covers most of the face of the wall, making it impossible to take adequate measurements of the brickwork.

The south apse wall also seems not to be part of the original plan of the room, for it does not bond with the original south wall on the west side. On the east the junction is obscured by mortar.[15]

The west wall of the room is preserved to a height of about 5.00 m. Its surface is much damaged, and there are a large break and a vertical crack through the wall south of the north doorway. A thick layer of the same coarse mortar found on the north and south apse walls covers much of the surface.

The doorways which open into Room 3 beyond are not symmetrically placed in the west wall, the north doorway lying closer to the north apse than the south one to the south apse. The south doorway, still partially blocked by unexcavated fill in Room 3, originally measured 1.63 m. in width and had a height of about 2.40 m. It was subsequently narrowed by 0.20 m. on the north by the addition of a pillar of bricks and mortar. The construction of the doorway at the top is the same as that of the south door in Room 1, a shallow arch with a relieving arch in the wall above. A fragment of a white marble doorjamb is still *in situ* against the south side of the doorway. The height of the north doorway is not preserved, but it, too, has evidently been altered, for at 2.00 m. from the center of the wall the original south side of the doorway is preserved. Two poros blocks, one on top of the other, were used to move the south doorjamb further north (Pl. 5:a). These are incorporated into a repair to the wall which extends through into Room 3. A fragmentary white marble doorjamb remains at the south side of the doorway, and the cutting for the north doorjamb is preserved in the mortar of the floor. The wall north of this doorway is not brick faced, and the surface is very rough. The original wall of the room was evidently cut back here when the north apse was inserted. In the hypocaust below, remains of either the original north wall of the room or of spur walls projecting from the east and west walls can be observed at both sides, at the west side preserved for approximately 0.60 m. A vent seems to have been originally built into the west wall. Its position lies now at the north side of the north doorway, and it was filled in when the doorway was altered. The original north side of the doorway would thus have stood further south.[16]

For knowledge of the decoration of this wall of the room we are dependent on small fragments of revetment. Three pilaster base moldings of *lapis lacedaemonius* are still *in situ*, two on either side of the south doorway and a third at the north side of the north doorway. They are partially covered by the third floor of the room and belong with the second phase when the apse walls were added and the north doorway in the west wall was altered. Impressions in the mortar bedding on the wall above the base moldings suggest that they once supported flat pilasters, 0.32 m. wide, which framed the doorways. A fragment of veneer, a pilaster capital (**94**), should possibly be restored to the north doorway. Its width at base can be estimated at approximately 0.32 m., and it was found at the north end of the room in fill south of the pool. Other evidence for the decoration of the west wall of the room is provided by the two small fragments of wall revetment at the north end above the pool parapet, both of grayish white marble. The surface of the wall is

---

[14] This has been noticed for pools in other baths in Greece. Cf. S. Charitonidis and R. Ginouvès, "Bain romain de Zevgolatio près de Corinthe," *BCH* 79, 1955, p. 107 and note 4.

[15] The original plan of the area south of Room 2 is reflected in the early plans of the building which recorded the upper levels of the walls, but Dinsmoor (Pl. 37:b) apparently saw more than Ittar (Pl. 37:a), since he drew an extension with curved back wall to the south where Ittar shows solid wall. The east wall seen by Ittar and Dinsmoor is still visible above the south apse wall (Pl. 10:a). At a lower level the original west wall of the area can be seen through the break in the south apse wall. It continues the line of the west wall of Room 2 south beyond the apse for 0.56 m. before it is joined by the wall of a vaulted chamber extending to the southeast. This vaulted chamber is probably a service area, but the land beyond the apse wall is private property, and it was not possible to investigate further.

[16] Since the wall above is not preserved (Pl. 6:b), there is no arch to help ascertain the original position of the doorway.

unfortunately too damaged to provide more information about the revetment from the pattern of clamp holes, but the re-use of a wall slab in the third floor of the room (Pl. 6:a) offers at least a suggestion for the earlier wall treatment.

The east wall of the room (Pl. 54) is standing to a height of approximately 6.90 m., with brick facing for a maximum height of 4.60 m. Most of the doorway and the wall to the south are obscured by unexcavated fill, but the plan shows that the entrance from Room 1 is set in the center of a shallow apse.[17] The lintel of the doorway was constructed of voussoir bricks, only traces of which remain, and there is a relieving arch in the wall above the apse.

At the north end of the room there is a narrow vent in the east wall (Pl. 5:a), which is fully preserved to a height of 2.60 m. and whose south side continues up to 5.80 m. The vent is 0.18–0.20 m. wide with a depth of 0.08 m. and at the level of the floor of the room and approximately 1.50 m. above has been blocked by coarse, white mortar. At the upper end it probably opened through the vault of the room.[18] In the lower part the bricks of the wall have been cut to form the vent. Higher up, however, the vent is built into the wall, although the brick courses on either side do not correspond. Although the junction is not completely clear, it must be here that the north apse was added onto the original east wall of the room. Because of fill in Room 1 to the east the vent could not be properly examined at a high level. Lower down, the vent is somewhat obscured by later blocking. The projecting remains of the wall preserved at hypocaust level (see p. 40 above) indicate that its south face was in line with the north side of the later vent.

The east wall has remains of three periods of mortar bedding for revetment. Above the north doorjamb and over the north end of the relieving arch are preserved two layers of a fine white mortar, and at the base of the wall there is a thick layer of coarser mortar which seems to be the same type as that which blocks the vent. Two fragments of bluish white marble revetment are still *in situ* with a floor slab of the third floor resting against them (Pl. 5:a).

The vault of the room was constructed of concrete with courses of bipedales at intervals of 0.55–0.75 m. The shape of the vault is partially preserved in the east wall (Pl. 54). From this evidence the room should be restored with a barrel vault rising to about 6.85 m. above the floor of the room. At each end there must have been a half dome over the pool, inserted beneath the original vault.

To the fragmentary evidence for the decoration described above must be added that of the fragments found in the fill of the room. Most of the revetment fragments were white, but there was some *fior di pesco* and *lapis lacedaemonius*. The only other architectural fragment of importance besides the pilaster capital (**94**) is a small epistyle-frieze block (**95**) which lay within the doorway to Room 1. Although there were no niches in the preserved standing masonry, one must assume that the room was also decorated with statuary which, in the absence of niches, stood on the floor on their own individual bases. In the south pool was found a marble head, a Roman copy of a Polykleitan original, and at the north end of the room a small fragment of a relief.[19]

Chronology

The history of Room 2 is a complex one of extensive reconstruction and repair. Four major phases have been distinguished. Originally the room was probably rectangular. Remains of either the ends of the north

---

[17] Setting a doorway in an apse is not unusual in Roman baths. The baths at Argos (R. Ginouvès, "Thermes romains," *BCH* 79, 1955, p. 324, fig. 36), the large North Baths at Timgad (Krencker, fig. 337), the Baths of Capito at Miletus (*Milet* I, ix, p. 24, fig. 29), and the Kaiserthermen at Trier (Krencker, pl. 2) have similar doorways. In the case of the Great Bath at Corinth the purpose was probably to mask the different axes of Rooms 1 and 2 (Pl. 38). As pointed out by Ward-Perkins in his discussion of construction at Lepcis Magna, the solution to the problem of differing axes in two adjacent buildings is to put the main door from one to the other at the base of a large semicircular exedra (J. B. Ward-Perkins, "The Art of the Severan Age in the Light of Tripolitanian Discoveries," *ProcBritAcad* 37, 1951, p. 276). Although the apse in Room 2 is not semicircular, the curved surface of the wall would help to mask the different widths of the doorjambs.

[18] For the use of the vents in walls of other baths in Greece, cf. Charitonidis and Ginouvès, *op. cit.* (footnote 14, p. 40 above), p. 109 and note 2; T. L. Shear, Jr., "The Athenian Agora: Excavations of 1968," *Hesperia* 38, 1969, p. 404.

[19] Corinth inv. no. S 2755 (head of Hermes), *BCH* 90, 1966, *Chroniques*, p. 756, fig. 9; Δελτ 21, 1966, Χρονικά, [1968], pl. 129:a; Mary C. Sturgeon, "A New Group of Sculptures from Ancient Corinth," *Hesperia* 44, 1975, pp. 290–292, no. 2, pl. 71. Corinth inv. no. S 2766 (archaistic relief fragment).

and south walls or of spur walls were apparently preserved at a high level and were drawn by Ittar and adopted by Dinsmoor (Pl. 37:a, b). Traces of these walls remain in the hypocaust below at west and east sides at the north end of the room. In this period there was a vent in the west wall of the room at the north end. If the edge of the first floor at the north end of the room preserves the original location of a pool parapet, then there was a pool at least at the north end of the room in this first period. If, however, we should restore the original north wall of the room at this point, then there must have been a hot-air space along the north wall, since the preserved north edge of the floor lies approximately 0.10 m. south of the projected line of the south face of the north wall. There was apparently no hot-air space along the east or west walls.

In the second period an apse was added at the north and at the south end of the room, with a doorway through to Room 4 at the north end. A vent in the east wall replaced the one in the west. At the south end of the room the apse was added either as a projection from the south wall, whose remains were incorporated as the east and west returns of the apse, or the apse was added on to existing spur walls. The north apse was built beyond the original north wall, or spur walls, perhaps because the service area below facilitated construction of the foundations. The spur wall, or the west side of the original north wall of the room, was cut back to the west wall. On the east side, however, extensive rebuilding was undertaken, although apparently at a high level there were still remains of the original construction here in Ittar's day (Pl. 37:a). A floor for the apsidal additions was laid level with the original floor of the room, as shown by the pilaster base molding *in situ* at the north doorway, which lies north of the edge of the floor of the first phase and is partially covered by the floor of the third phase. The floor of the second phase was presumably mostly removed when the pools were later inserted in the north and south apses, leaving only a section along the west side which preserved the pilaster base *in situ*.

In the third period the pools were inserted into the north and south apses, the parapet of the north pool, at least, being built over pre-existing hypocaust columns. The door to the north was blocked, and an outlet for the north pool was constructed there. A new floor for the whole room was laid, covering up the floor of the first period and, at least in the north end, filling in the area between the edge of the first floor and the parapet of the pool. At this time the revetment of the north, south, and west walls of the room was renewed, since the same coarse mortar bedding is found on all these walls as well as on the parapets of the pools. The vent in the east wall of the room was blocked before the third floor was laid but how much before is not clear, and they may both be part of the same modification to the room. That this turned Room 2 into a cold room is suggested for the room as a whole by the blocking of the vent, and the pool in the north apse was certainly a cold one, since there are no furnaces for the apse. Furthermore, the parapet wall rests on the floor of the hypocaust; the pool could not draw its heat from the hypocaust even if the room itself was heated. The pool area, however, could be heated by hot air circulating in the main area of the room. Until the area outside the room to the south has been cleared, we cannot know whether the furnace, suggested here by the relieving arch in the south-apse wall, remained in use during this third phase of the room. It must be significant, however, that there was no ash found in the hypocaust below as there was below the other heated rooms excavated, Rooms 3 and 5. The small section of the fourth floor found in this room seems to be unrelated to any other modification and represents the latest phase.

The first phase of Room 2 belongs with the original construction period of the building in the late 2nd or early 3rd century. The brickwork of the east and west walls cannot be separated from that of Rooms 1 and 3.

A date for the second phase when the apse walls were inserted is provided by a deposit (Group 3) from a lime-slaking pit found in the service area near the foundations of the north apse (see below, p. 57). This pit was presumably used to supply lime for the mortar used in the brick facing of the apsidal foundations. The two latest sherds (**130**, **131**) in the deposit, although not closely datable, belong to types of pottery which begin in the first half of the 3rd century, and the lime pit was sealed by an ash level whose latest material dates to the middle or second half of the 3rd century (Group 6). Furthermore, a date for the construction of the north and south apse walls of Room 2 should be expected to be fairly close to the construction date of the building, for although the brickwork of the south apse could not be measured because of the good preservation of mortar bedding for revetment, the brickwork of the north apse (Appendix I, Table 1:8) does not appear to differ greatly from that of the main building period (Appendix I, Table 1:1). This evidence indicates a date sometime in the 3rd century for the second phase of the room.

This dating is also supported by a small amount of pottery (Group 4), found within the hypocaust near the parapet wall of the south pool, which places the work in this area of the room in the mid-3rd century or later (**132, 133**). The work could, however, be either the building of the south apse or the insertion of the south pool in the apse in the third phase.[20] There is no other evidence for the dating of the third phase, nor is there any for the fourth phase when a new floor for the whole room was laid.

In the fill found over the destroyed floor of the room and in the pools there was much Byzantine contamination. But the pottery from the fill beneath a large fragment of fallen vaulting showed no Byzantine contamination and could be dated to the 6th century (Group 16). Room 2, therefore, was destroyed in the 6th century. The evidence suggests that a large fragment of vaulting fell comparatively early, but the absence of Byzantine pottery may be fortuitous. The remainder of the roof stood to a much later date as attested by the coins found in this room after removal of fallen vaulting (see footnote 16, p. 4 above).

ROOM 3

Description and Restoration

Room 3, the *caldarium*, has the same axis as Room 2 and is the westernmost of the three which form the nucleus of the building on this western side (Pls. 38, 39, 55). It has been cleared down to floor level only in the northern half, but the walls of the southern half were sufficiently exposed so that an accurate plan of the whole room could be made.[21] In plan, Room 3 is similar to the present form of Room 2 but larger, 8.90 m. wide with a length of 17.65 m. Its general state of preservation is not so good, since the floor of the room has collapsed in two large areas (Pl. 6:b), and the hypocaust columns are consequently less well preserved. It, too, was altered by the addition of pools. Three were found in the north half of the room: an apsidal one in the north apse, a rectangular one in the center, and a small pool against the west wall. Unlike Room 2 in its later phases, the walls were heated, as may have been the vault. A space, 0.07–0.10 m. wide, for the circulation of hot gases, separated the brick walls from a screen wall of bricks revetted with marble.

The floor of the hypocaust is composed of large tiles, 0.61 m. square, many of which are damaged. On them stand the hypocaust columns whose different shapes, dimensions, and spacing (Appendix I, Table 2:27–33) are evidence for the many repairs and alterations that were made to this room.[22]

There were furnaces for the heating of this room at the north end, one of which was later blocked up. The west pool, a later addition, was heated from a furnace in the west wall. The room may also at one time have drawn some of its heat from Room 5, which lies to the northwest. Between the common wall of the two rooms there is a passageway 0.56 m. wide (Pl. 38), once roofed by a brick arch, remains of which survive. This passageway was originally open only at hypocaust level.

In the floor of the room three periods could be distinguished. The earliest is that on the west side. Here the floor is 0.36 m. thick and constructed of pairs of large bricks, 0.06 m. thick, which span the hypocaust columns. On these were laid brick fragments set on end obliquely in a layer of mortar with a thickness of 0.20 m. Above is the mortar bed for the floor paving in white marble, a few fragments of which are preserved. The marble slabs did not abut directly onto the screen wall of the room: a layer of waterproof mortar, its top surface level with the marble of the floor, began at approximately 0.26 m. from the edge of the floor and, sloping up to the face of the screen wall, sealed the junction of wall and floor.

A shallow channel (Pl. 55) built into the floor lies at the base of the wall west of the apse. It slopes down to the east, and its purpose was presumably to catch condensation from the walls of the room. At the east end it

---

[20] The construction of both apsidal pools and the closing of the door in the north apse, which presumably barred access to rooms to the north, may belong with a contraction of the building for which we have the evidence of structures in Room 5 (see pp. 55, 59 below). This has been tentatively dated to the period following the catastrophes at the end of the 4th century. Possibly the construction of apsidal pools in Room 2 also belongs to that period.

[21] No discussion of the southern half of the room, however, will be attempted in the text. The approximately one and a half meters which still remain over the floor could not be removed because the south wall is damaged and further clearance would allow debris from the neighboring property to fall in. Many large fragments of fallen vaulting remain at this end of the room.

[22] The hypocaust has not been completely cleared. Only in areas where the floor of the room had collapsed and in a small section under the floor on the west side was complete clearance feasible.

abutted against the parapet of the north apse pool. The parapet preserves no trace of an inlet, but it seems probable that the channel emptied into the pool.

The floor on the east side of the room evidently belongs to a second period. For although its construction is otherwise the same as that on the west, its marble slabs ran right to the edge of the floor, and the mortar sealing at junction of floor and screen wall rests directly on the slabs. Fragments of the marble are preserved at the east wall, and four fragments of a narrow border of white marble are still *in situ* at the base of a bench which ran the length of the east side of the room (Pl. 55). From the imprint in the mortar the same border ran only partially across the room at the base of the outer step of the parapet of the north apse pool (Pl. 55). The imprint ends above the point where a change in the type of hypocaust columns begins (Appendix I, Table 2:29). Apparently columns and floor were rebuilt together on the east side of the room.

A second channel was built into the floor of the room on this east side. It runs to the east from the broken edge in the center of the room and ends within the doorway to Room 2 (Pl. 55). The channel is constructed of bricks and pink waterproof mortar; it was covered by the marble floor slabs as indicated by the imprint in the setting bed, and there seem to have been no intermediate cover slabs of tile. A patch of pink mortar on the west side of the large break in the floor of the room indicates the probable extent of the channel to the west. At its east end it may originally have emptied into the channel in the floor of Room 2, but the junction, if any, has been obscured by later floor levels in both rooms. Its purpose was presumably to catch dripping water from bathers.[23]

In the northwest corner of the room the third floor level covered up the channel at the base of the wall. This floor is preserved for approximately 0.90 m. and lies about 0.10 m. higher than the floor in the rest of the room. In the doorway in the east wall are further remains of the third floor level, which here has obscured the east end of the channel from the center of the room. In the northeast corner of the room remains of a lower floor can be seen below the upper at its east edge.

Of the three pools in the northern half of the room, the earliest is the rectangular one in the center (Pl. 7:a, 38). Part of the west and north walls is all that is preserved of this pool because its extent to the east was destroyed in the rebuilding of the floor on the east side. The north wall of the pool is preserved for only approximately 1.60 m. If the pool was centered in the room, the width may be estimated at 3.35 m. The west wall is preserved for a length of 2.25 m., but the pool probably extended further south.[24] The present depth of the pool is 0.31 m. It must originally have been shallower, since allowance should be made for a mortar bedding and marble revetment. Traces of this mortar can still be seen along the edges of the pool (Pl. 7:a), and the impression of the marble revetment slabs is still preserved on the walls.

The pool in the north apse extended out into the room for 1.68 m., including its parapet and outer step. The width of the pool proper from north to south measures 3.10 m.; its length is 5.75 m. It was closed off from the room by the parapet with a step on each side. No bricks of the outer step are preserved above the floor level, but the impression in the mortar from this outer step can be traced for 3.45 m. on the east side of the room. To the west there is no sign of it (Pl. 55). The parapet is largely missing, with only a few of the lowest course of bricks still *in situ* in the east-west section. At the east return, however, the parapet is better preserved, and around the apse it is well preserved. Constructed of bricks and mortar, it had a thick mortar

[23] The baths at Argos have a similar channel in the floor beginning in the center of the room. Ginouvès, *loc. cit.* (footnote 17, p. 41 above).

[24] A packing of bricks bonded with mortar, set diagonally and sloping down to the north, was used to fill in the preserved portion of the pool. (The packing along the west and north sides of the pool was removed in 1970 when some testing was done in this room, leaving a section along the broken east edge.) At 2.25 m. from the northwest corner the direction of the packing changes, and it slopes down towards the south (Pl. 7:a). The hypocaust columns to the south differ from the ones beneath the preserved part of the pool (Appendix I, Table 2:33). The columns immediately below the area where the change in the packing occurs have been rebuilt at the top with mortar joints, whereas in the lower part the joints are clay. Two square bricks cap each column instead of the one thick brick found on the round columns in the rest of the room. Since no south wall for the pool is preserved it seems probable that the southern part of the pool was destroyed, and so new columns had to be built and a proper floor for the room laid, instead of merely filling in the pool as at the north. The imprint of the marble slabs used to cover the area of the pool shows that the marble over the area to the south was laid at the same time: one large plaque lay over the junction of the rebuilt floor with the preserved area of the pool, at 2.25 m. from the northwest corner of the pool (Pl. 55).

bedding for white marble revetment, eight fragments of which are still *in situ* and which show the marks of the mortar sealing at the junction with the marble of the pool's floor. Two fragments of Proconnesian revetment are preserved at the east end on the wall of the parapet above the bench.

The floor of the pool has none of its marble preserved *in situ*, although the imprint of the slabs is clearly visible (Pl. 55). At the passageway through the wall to Room 5 the floor was constructed with a slight curve. Water from the pool was drained by means of a channel through the parapet around the north wall of the apse at a point just east of center. As now preserved, it is a semicircular, open cement channel.

The third pool so far excavated in this room is a small one placed against the west wall (Pl. 55). It has been only partially cleared for a length from north to south of 1.60 m. Its finished width from east to west, including the inner step, was 1.80 m. It was surrounded on all three sides by a parapet with a step on the outside; a narrow interior step ran along the east wall of the pool. The outer step is of the usual brick-and-mortar construction and was built together with the pool parapet (Appendix I, Table 1:10). The north and east parapet walls are preserved to a maximum height of approximately 0.50 m. above the floor; the west wall of the pool is built against the west wall of the room, where it is standing to a height of 1.325 m. above the floor of the pool. An arch with a height of 0.60 m. and a width at floor level of 1.00 m. is built into the back wall. The floor of the pool is covered by a layer of mortar and breaks off in front of the tunnel from the façade area. Remains of white marble revetment are preserved on the inside of the pool at the base of the walls and on the north wall at the junction with the bench along the east wall; on the exterior of the pool none of the revetment of the step was preserved, although there are several fragments of white marble on the wall of the parapet. As was usual, the joints of the pool were waterproofed with mortar, traces of which can still be seen.

The construction of the pool clearly indicates that it is later than the floor of the room, for its outer step is set directly on the marble of the floor. It was constructed together with a bench that is set against the west wall of the room and also overlies the original marble floor. This bench is largely constructed of re-used material consisting of fragments of round hypocaust tiles, bricks, and rough stones. Some white marble revetment fragments are also incorporated. The bench is preserved to a maximum height of 0.47 m. At 1.50 m. from the north wall of the room it has been totally destroyed for a length of 0.90 m.[25]

The bench along the east side of the room is set 0.53 m. in from the marble wall revetment. It is of different construction from the one on the west side, being built of regular courses of bricks and mortar (Appendix I, Table 1:11). The vertical faces are coated with a smooth layer of coarse, pink mortar. The preserved height of the bench is 0.30 m., and it extends north from the unexcavated fill for 1.75 m. The imprint in the mortar of the floor shows that it originally continued north, crossing in front of the doorway in the east wall and running over the channel in the floor (Pl. 55). At the north end it abutted onto the outer step of the north apse pool. One brick of the lowest course is preserved north of the channel.

The brick-faced walls of the room are standing highest in the south apse where they have an estimated height above the floor of 6.50 m. These walls were preserved above ground level in Ittar's day (Pl. 37:a), and part of the curve of the half dome over the apse still remains.

The east wall of the room, the party wall between Rooms 2 and 3, is standing to a maximum height of approximately 2.25 m. above the floor in the north half of the room. Above a height of 0.79 m. the wall has suffered extensive damage, but clear evidence of reconstruction and repair can be seen.[26] The wall has numerous clamp holes, but no discernible pattern could be measured with the exception of a row set approximately 0.75 m. above the floor to the north of the doorway.

The west wall of the room is almost totally obscured at the south end by fallen masonry and unexcavated fill. At the north end the wall is damaged from the level of the bench upwards but is standing to a height of approximately 1.80 m. above the floor. The northernmost of the three windows which pierced the wall was

---

[25] A length of 0.45 m. is now also missing, removed from the north end to uncover the channel in the floor.

[26] North of the doorway the wall has been repaired with a patch of bricks rising to *ca.* 0.79 m. above the floor (Appendix I, Table 1:12). South of the doorway the construction necessitated by the alteration of the doorway (see p. 40 above) can be clearly seen. A brick-and-mortar patch faces a very rough rubble-and-mortar construction at the corner, which extends onto the poros blocks in Room 2. South of this a second patch of bricks bonded with coarse, pink mortar is also part of the repair. The original south edge of the doorway can be seen here.

found partially blocked by large, rough stones. At 4.20 m. from the northwest corner of the room a vent with a width of 0.23 m. and a depth of 0.12 m. is lined with tiles (Pl. 55).

The north wall of the room, consisting of the apse and the walls to east and west, stands to a height of 2.86 m. above the floor of the pool. Its thickness is 1.66 m. Its surface is fairly well preserved except at the west and east corners of the apse and in the upper levels of the two east–west walls (Pl. 6:b). The apse wall has seven or eight scaffolding holes and many clamp holes for which there is no clearly discernible pattern.[27] Traces of burning are to be seen on the west wall of the apse, south of the break through to Room 5, and behind the apse parapet. There are two vents in this wall, one immediately south of the break, the other east of the central point of the apse (Pl. 55). The latter appears to be a later addition.

Two arches are built into the wall of the apse beginning at about the level of the pool floor, one over the passage between the hypocausts of Rooms 3 and 5 and one below the central vent. That over the passageway is preserved on both sides (Pl. 55), and there are traces of a second arch facing onto Room 5. The arch springs from two ledges formed by the walls of the passageway. The arch beneath the central vent has only nine of its bricks preserved at the base on each side. The wall has obviously been cut to insert this arch, which is clumsily built, and it is thus a later addition to the wall.

The inner screen wall of this room in its lowest course was constructed of large bricks (Appendix I, Table 1:13), laid parallel to the brick wall and resting on the hypocaust columns. One complete brick has been preserved by the bench on the west side of the room, others are still *in situ* against the parapet of the pool around the apse, and there are many fragments adhering to the edge of the floor of the room. Two types of screen wall were apparently used. *Tegulae mammatae* formed one type; none were found *in situ*, but 22 fragments of such tiles were found in the fill removed from over the floor (Group 17). The second type of screen wall is more unusual. The bricks of the screen wall were supported by iron clamps, and hollow terracotta tubes, through which the clamp passed, kept the bricks at the proper distance from the face of the main wall. Many fragments of these tubes were found (Group 17, and **113–115**). Where fully preserved, the largest measured 0.10 m. in length (**113**). This is the correct length for the air space in the west part of the north apse and the wall to the west. Some small tubes were also preserved in fill in the area of the façade to the west (**114**). In addition to the tube fragments, several fragmentary iron clamps were found (Group 17), but no fragments of bricks with a hole or a notch on the edge for the clamp have survived. This method of attaching the screen wall was also used in Roumania where similar tubes have been found, in one bath even *in situ*.[28] Other examples of these tubes have been found in the Corinthia, although not *in situ*.[29] The screen

---

[27] Many of the iron clamps are preserved in the wall, several of them wedged firmly into place by small marble chips. Since this wall had an inner screen wall (see below) and, therefore, no marble revetment laid directly against its surface, these marble chips or plugs could not have provided a key for the application of mortar bedding for the revetment, nor was the screen wall of a kind which required a mortar bed. For the reverse of this procedure, see McDonald, p. 146, pl. 130:a. Here a bronze wedge holds the marble plug in position, and the marble functions as a key for the mortar.

[28] I. Barnea, "Les Thermes de Dinogetia," *Dacia* 11, 1967, p. 234, fig. 15 for ones *in situ*; G. Popilian, "Thermele de la Slăvenie," *Apulum* 9, 1971, p. 632, fig. 4 for others found loose in fill, one with the clamp still in it. In the baths at Dinogetia the edges of the floor sloped up towards the walls as they do in Room 3, and the excavator concluded that the tubes were used only at this level and were designed to strengthen the sloping edge of the floor. Although it is possible that they were used only at one level, there does not seem to be any reason why they could not also be used higher up as well. Furthermore, since the sloping mortar which sealed the joint between wall and floor was laid against the marble and brick of the screen wall, it does not seem that this area would need any greater support than other areas of the screen wall. The method seems to be an improvement on the use of iron clamps alone, for the tube would hold the brick firmly at a fixed distance from the wall. In another version of this system, not apparently used in the Corinth Bath, terracotta nails were employed without an iron clamp. The iron clamp was the weak point since eventually it would rust away, causing the collapse of the screen wall. For an explanation of the use of terracotta nails in North Africa, cf. R. Cagnat and V. Chapot, *Manuel d'archéologie romaine* I, Paris 1916, pp. 220–221, fig. 115. Terracotta nails were also used in Pergamon; see W. Radt, "Pergamon 1979," *ArchAnz* 1980, p. 412. I am indebted to Mr. Popilian for the reference to the baths at Dinogetia.

[29] D. Pallas, Πρακτικά, 1955, pp. 212–214, figs. 5 and 6; Charitonidis and Ginouvès, *op. cit.* (footnote 14, p. 40 above), p. 112, fig. 9. Although not the same shape as the ones from the Bath at Corinth, they must have been used in the same way. The system is described in an early work. See Le Général Morin, "Note sur les appareils de chauffage et de ventilation employés par les Romains pour les thermes á l'air chaud," *Mémoires presentés par divers savants à l'Académie des Inscriptions* 8, ii, 1874, p. 365. He describes the tubes as used to support tubuli.

wall was revetted with white marble, fragments of which are preserved *in situ* at the base of the walls. A great many other fragments were recovered from the fill in the room. On the west side, and also in the area of the façade, were found several fragments with very large letters painted on them (**96, 97**). Unfortunately no complete words could be made out.

The plan of the room suggests that it should be restored with a central barrel vault with the axis north–south and half domes over north and south apses. The height of the vault was probably 11.13–13.35 m.[30] Two very large masses of fallen vaulting, as well as some smaller ones, were removed before excavation of this room was possible. The large ones fell from the north and south apses. The smaller ones presumably fell from the barrel vault. Although not much information was gained from the large fragments, the smaller ones in some instances preserved two finished faces and indicated that the thickness of the vault was approximately 1.60 m. Some information was also gained from them about the building method. Brick arches were apparently used to relieve the weight on the formwork during construction.[31] The formwork has left its impression in the concrete. In some of the fragments that were broken up, the impressions left by cylindrical rods, with a diameter of 0.11 m., were found set in the same plane as the bricks in the arches. Presumably these rods were of wood which has disintegrated; they cannot be considered vents for the escape of hot air, since, as shown by vents that have been preserved, these channels were larger and sometimes lined; the rods must rather have had a function in the construction of the vault.[32]

Some metal was also found within the concrete vault. A bronze clamp (**119**), braced in the wall by a bronze spike, was found in a fragment of fallen vaulting in the south end of the room. The clamp was at 45° to the face of the vault and did not project out from the surface. Several fragments from similar clamps and spikes were found both in this room and in others (Group 2). The other metalwork found, an iron shaft and crosspiece (**120**), was embedded in the concrete vault from the south apse. Fragments of another bar and of iron spikes were found in debris from the vault (Group 2).

Giuliani found impressions from similar metalwork in the vaults of the baths at Hadrian's Villa. Since they were all from rooms whose walls were heated, he postulates that the vaults were also heated and that the impressions were left by large metal clamps for suspension of the tiles that followed the curvature of the vault.[33] Giuliani's theory certainly seems tenable for Hadrian's Villa. In the Bath at Corinth, however, very large fragments of fallen vaulting were broken up, and no such regular arrangements of clamps was observed. The iron bar (**120**) did not extend anywhere near to the intrados of the vault. The bronze clamp (**119**) stopped just below the surface, although it could once have extended through, been cut off, and the surface refinished when the clamp was no longer needed. Perhaps at Corinth bronze clamps and spikes to brace them may have been used for fastening heavy architectural decoration to the vaults, such as large bronze or marble rosettes, rather than for provision of heated vaults.[34] The ironwork remains a mystery. The size of **120** makes it unlikely that its presence is accidental.

---

[30] The proposed height is calculated on the probable ratio of the width to the height of the room. A minimum ratio of 1:1.25 is suggested and a maximum of 1:1.50.

[31] For the use of brick arches, which were apparently rare until after Hadrian's time, cf. McDonald, p. 159.

[32] Similar impressions have been found in the vaults of other buildings, and C. Giuliani has offered a plausible explanation for them. He argues that they were set up to serve as guides in laying the vault, to delineate the curve of the extrados which always differed from that of the intrados ("Volte e cupole a doppia calotta in età adrianea," *RömMitt* 82, 1975, p. 340).

Vents for the escape of smoke were preserved in three fallen masonry fragments. One, lined with terracotta and with a diameter of 0.14 m., is preserved in a fallen fragment east of Room 4. Another with a diameter of 0.18–0.195 m. was found in the masonry removed from Room 2 (Pl. 49:d). A third is still to be seen in a fallen mass in Room 3; the vent is not lined but has a diameter of 0.35 m. For vents in other baths see J. B. Ward-Perkins and J. M. C. Toynbee, "The Hunting Baths at Lepcis Magna," *Archaeologia* 93, 1949, pl. XXXVII:d; Giuliani, *op. cit.*, p. 335; John J. Herrmann, Jr., "Observations on the Baths of Maxentius," *RömMitt* 83, 1976, pp. 412–413.

[33] Giuliani, *op. cit.*, *passim*. Iron bars were found in fallen fragments of the roof of the *frigidarium* of the Baths of Caracalla in Rome, and it has been suggested that they were used for hanging the flat ceiling from iron girders (R. Lanciani, *The Ruins and Excavations of Ancient Rome*, Boston 1897, p. 534). Vitruvius speaks of tiled ceilings suspended by an iron framework from the vault (v.10.3) but in reference to vaults made of wood.

[34] Iron clamps for applied decoration were noticed in the dome of the Pantheon (Licht, *op. cit.* [footnote 29, p. 23 above], p. 145). I would like to thank James Packer for his help with these problems.

The evidence for the decoration of Room 3 is not very extensive, and to the evidence *in situ* little can be added from that found in the accumulated debris in the room. In addition to fragments of revetment, one tiny fragment of stucco with a fluted surface and six mosaic tesserae (Group 17) were found. Very few marble architectural fragments were recovered. At the south end of the room high up in the fill were found column fragments of white marble and granite. In fill over the west pool an Ionic column capital was recovered and in the north apse two base moldings and a column fragment. The column is a small one in *lapis lacedaemonius*, the type found in every room of the building except Room 2. One of the marble base moldings is preserved in only a very small fragment.[35] That so little decoration has survived in so large a room is an indication of the thorough plundering of the building. No reconstruction can be attempted on the basis of this meager material. The room was probably decorated with sculpture. A fragmentary marble head (**108**) found in Room 3 was one of the few surviving in the building. The most interesting piece is from a group of Hermes(?) and a ram (**109**). All that have survived are the head and chest of the ram, his neck stretched up, and a fold of drapery; one fragment was found in the southeast corner of Room 5, the other in the north apse of Room 3.[36]

CHRONOLOGY

The sequence of repair and reconstruction in Room 3 begins with the rectangular pool in the center, the first feature for which we have evidence. This pool, however, seems not to have been part of the original design since the columns supporting the lower floor of the pool along the edge were apparently added to preexisting ones (Appendix I, Table 2:32). At this time there may have been a pool in the north apse as well, but if there was, it probably did not extend as far south as it does in its present condition. The evidence for this comes from the supporting columns beneath the parapet at the west side. There rectangular columns bonded with mortar were placed against round columns bonded with clay (Appendix I, Table 2:30). The two forms of column are therefore apparently of different periods, and this fact suggests that the southern part of the pool, where it extends into the room, may be an addition.

The second period is one of extensive rebuilding after a massive destruction which seems to have affected the east side of the room and possibly the south part below the unexcavated fill. Following the destruction, the west side of the central pool, which apparently had survived, was filled in, and a new floor with a water channel in it was laid on the east side of the room and to the south. Some of the hypocaust columns were rebuilt, too, and were bonded with mortar. At the same time the north apse pool was either built or extended further south into the room (see above). On the east where the destruction occurred, new columns were built, bonded with mortar (Appendix I, Table 2:29), and the parapet and outer step were constructed together with the floor of the room. On the west side of the pool the outer step was presumably laid on the existing floor slabs. This rebuilding must have been contemporary with or later than the alteration to the north doorway to Room 2, for the marble doorjamb of the new south side of the doorway and a cutting for the north doorjamb are set into the new floor on the east side of the room. The alteration to this doorway is connected with the extensive alteration in Room 2 when the north and south apse were added, reconstructions dating to the 3rd century on the evidence of pottery from a lime-slaking pit (Group 3) and from a deposit within the hypocaust of Room 2 (Group 4; see pp. 42–43 above). The reconstruction in Room 3 may date to this period also, but it seems more likely that it should be placed in a later period, perhaps following the earthquakes at the end of the 4th century (see p. 31 above). The use of mortar bonding for hypocaust columns is a later construction technique than the use of clay, at least in the Bath. Clay was still being used as the bonding material in the 3rd century as is shown by rebuilt hypocaust columns in the east side of Room 5 (see p. 54 below). The rebuilding of columns in Room 3 with mortar joints ought, therefore, to belong to a later period than the 3rd century.

The third period in Room 3 saw the building of the small pool and bench against the west wall of the room and the filling in of the channel in the floor at the west. The building of drains and service corridor against the exterior of the west wall (see pp. 56, 60 below) is connected with this pool. These structures can be dated

---

[35] Corinth Notebook 357, nos. 9a and b, 10a and b (column fragments), no. 31 (Ionic column capital), nos. 6, 7 (base moldings), no. 4 (column fragment in *lapis lacedaemonius*).

[36] For other fragments from this room see Corinth inv. nos. S 2855, S 2857 (arm fragments), S 2898 (leg[?] fragment).

to the early years of the 6th century (see p. 56 below), and therefore the pool and bench in Room 3 date to this period also.

There were thus three major periods in the room. For the less important change, the use of a different type of screen wall, we have no evidence. The iron-pin-and-tube system was in use in Roumania as early as the first half of the 3rd century[37] and could, therefore, have been used in Corinth in that period.

The final destruction of the room seems to have taken place in the late 6th to early 7th century. Pottery similar to that found in Rooms 1 and 2 was found in fill over the floor of Room 3 (Group 17). This fill was covered by a thick layer of crumbled mortar (Group 33). Unlike Rooms 1 and 2, the vaults of Room 3 appear to have succumbed early to an earthquake.[38]

ROOM 4

Description and Restoration

Room 4 lies north of Rooms 2 and 3 and east of Room 5, to which there was once access through a doorway now blocked (see p. 53 below). Room 4 has been cleared down to floor level in only a very small area (Pl. 9:a), since further clearance to the east was prohibited by a large mass of fallen masonry and by the danger of removing fill to the east of it. The limits of Room 4 have, therefore, been reached only on two sides, the northwest and the southwest, and the extent of even these walls has not been definitely established. The plan of the room as so far revealed is irregular, with the apses of Rooms 2 and 3 forming its southwest wall and one wall of Room 5 its northwest. The maximum length exposed is 7.25 m., the maximum width at floor level 3.20 m.

The floor is broken through in the west corner into the service corridor which runs beneath it (see pp. 56–58 below; Pls. 5:b, 38). The concrete vault of this corridor forms the floor of Room 4, and on the concrete was laid a layer of pebbles, coarse mortar, and tesserae, which constituted the bedding for a stone-mosaic floor in black and red with a white background. A large patch of mosaic with a design of ivy leaves in red[39] and a section of straight border in black is preserved at the north end of the cleared area. Another section, with a red border laid against the wall revetment still *in situ*, was preserved beneath a later wall, added across the triangular space formed by the junction of the walls of Rooms 3 and 5 (Pl. 38), just short of the doorway to Room 5. The tesserae of the floor are irregular in shape, measuring approximately 0.01–0.02 m. in width with a thickness of 0.02–0.025 m.

A tiled water channel set in this floor (Pl. 9:a) runs southeast from the northwest wall of the room for 0.30 m., then bends to the east and disappears beneath the mortar bedding for the mosaic. It extends to the west through the wall of the room for 0.32 m. at which point the rectangular channel is replaced by a terracotta pipe, which opened into Room 5.

The surface of the northwest wall of the room is badly damaged except where it has been protected by the later wall at the south end. The final 0.47 m. of the wall at the north end runs at an angle to the north, and the bricks are not bonded into the rest of the wall.

The southwest wall, which has been cleared to floor level only at the west end, there stands to a height of 2.75 m. above the floor of the room (Pl. 9:a). To the east it has been exposed around the north apse of Room 2, but only the uppermost part has been freed from fill. At the west end it is pierced vertically by a vent whose east side is damaged, but whose original width seems to have been approximately 0.55 m., its depth 0.35 m. At its base seven bricks of an arch over the service corridor below are preserved, partially hidden by

---

[37] Popilian, *op. cit.* (footnote 28, p. 46 above), p. 633. The baths at Dinogetia were built in the 4th century (Barnea, *op. cit.* [footnote 28, p. 46 above], pp. 248–249). The baths at Zevgolatio have been tentatively dated to the end of the 2nd or beginning of the 3rd century with a reconstruction in the late 4th (Charitonidis and Ginouvès, *op. cit.* [footnote 14, p. 40 above], pp. 119–120). The tubes were found in debris from the building, and there is no way of knowing to what period they belong.

[38] The half dome over the south apse of Room 3 remained standing for longer than the vaulting in the rest of the room. A Turkish bothros was found beneath the fallen masonry at this end of the room.

[39] Ivy as a design used in mosaic is found in Italy in the 2nd century. See M. Blake, "Roman Mosaics of the Second Century in Italy," *MAAR* 13, 1936, pls. 30:3, 31. An ivy-leaf mosaic in the Odeion at Argos dates to the end of the 3rd or beginning of the 4th century (Ginouvès, *Théâtron*, p. 121, fig. 54).

the later wall across the corner. At the top of the vent there is a horizontal hole through the thickness of the southwest wall.

The later wall which fills the angle has a length of 1.50 m., and its brick face, heavily encrusted with mortar, is preserved for a height of 1.20 m. The dimensions of bricks and mortar are the same as those in the other major walls of the building (Appendix I, Table 1:1).

A short stone-and-mortar wall projects from the southwest wall of the room just east of the vent (Pl. 9:a). It has been only partially exposed and rests on the concrete of the vault over the service area. Without further excavation to the east its purpose cannot be surmised.

The walls of the room were revetted with thin plaques of white marble, at least at the base. Two fragments are still *in situ*, one preserved by the later wall in the west corner, the other just north of the water channel in the floor (Pl. 9:a). The upper parts of the walls may once have been painted, since a small section of painted plaster was found on the wall just west of the blocked doorway through the north apse of Room 2. If this is still within Room 4, and that cannot be definitely established without further excavation, then the upper part of the walls in this section may be restored with what seem to be panels of dark reddish brown with a vertical border on the east of white, yellow, and black or dark blue. There are remains of a curving pattern in red.

This room provided numerous fragments of revetment, in a variety of marbles, many of which were found in the service area below. *Fior di pesco*, *giallo antico*, and Karystian marble were all found. Small column bases set on plinths were also recovered (**98**), as well as fragments of the small columns in *lapis lacedaemonius* that occur elsewhere in the building. Four pieces of stucco molding, one from a vault, were also found, and the room was apparently decorated with sculpture, represented only by fragments.[40]

Chronology

The evidence from the part cleared indicates that Room 4 was modified by the construction of a wall across the west corner, possibly to make the plan of the room more symmetrical,[41] quite soon after the construction of the building, since the brickwork of the addition is identical with that used in the original walls of all the other rooms. The building of this wall should probably be linked with that of the north apse of Room 2 whose brickwork is also close to that of the main building period. The wall in Room 4 should, therefore, be dated to the 3rd century.[42] Also during the 3rd century the floor of the room was damaged, for the water channel, which was out of use after A.D. 267 (Group 5; see p. 54 below), contained mosaic tesserae as well as pottery, and tesserae were used in the preserved bedding for the mosaic. At this time the door to Room 5 was closed (see p. 54 below), but Room 4 was evidently repaired and continued in use until the final abandonment of the building, for no levels datable earlier than the 6th century lay over the floor. It is possible, however, that before the final abandonment of the building, Room 4 had ceased to function as a public room, for the rubble-and-mortar wall partially exposed against the southwest wall does not rest on the mosaic floor but on the concrete of the vault of the service area. At the time this wall was built, therefore, the appearance of the room seems to have no longer been important. It was pillaged in the late 6th or early 7th century (Group 18) together with the rest of the building.

ROOM 5

Description and Restoration

Northwest of Room 3 lies Room 5, another heated room (Pls. 38, 39). Its north and west corners lie on private property and could not be excavated, but its full dimensions are known since small sections of the

---

[40] Stucco: Corinth inv. nos. A 605—A 607. Sculpture: Corinth inv. nos. S 2819 (foot on plinth), S 2821 (fragment of a togatus), S 2823 (male head), S 2826 (hand).

[41] The addition in the west corner corresponds to a short wall which must have linked the north apse of Room 2 to the west wall of Room 1 and which can be restored from the plan of the service area below (Pl. 38, represented by a dashed line). The plan of the southwest wall of Room 4 in its second phase thus formed two semicircles (the apses of Rooms 2 and 3) linked by a straight wall, with short, straight walls to east and northwest.

[42] For the date of the construction in Room 2, see p. 42 above.

northwest and northeast walls were fortunately just within the excavation. The room is rectangular in plan, measuring 12.00 m. from northeast to southwest and 10.45 m. from southeast to northwest, and was lighted by windows in its southwest wall.

The hypocaust of Room 5 shows signs of repairs both to its floor and to its columns. Different dimensions of tiles in different areas of the room indicate that the floor was repaired several times.[43] The hypocaust columns were well preserved in the west and north areas of the room; many were still standing to their full height even where the floor of the room above was not preserved (Pl. 8). In the south corner, however, the columns were missing in a large area (Pl. 38). Two types of columns were used (Appendix I, Table 2:34). The irregularity of the spacing of some of them,[44] combined with the differences observed in the floor of the hypocaust chamber, are of significance for the building history of this room. They indicate that an extensive repair was made to the southeast side with a patch set into the floor and new columns built. The columns in front of the eastern furnace flue were evidently badly damaged and replaced or strengthened; the walls in front of the western flue were presumably built when that flue was built or reconstructed (see footnote 65, p. 58 below).

At hypocaust level five entrances have been discovered. In addition to the two furnaces projecting into the northern part of the room, there was also an entrance to the hypocaust from the northwest, but until excavation has been undertaken outside the room, nothing more can be said about it. A fourth means of access, in the southeast wall of the room, had been bricked up (Appendix I, Table 1:14) and concealed by a mortar facing which covers the base of the wall (Pl. 8:a). The entrance, which does not appear on Plate 38, is located behind the fifth row of hypocaust columns counting from the northeast wall and seems to have been an arched opening with an original width of 0.78 m. and a height of 0.88 m., probably the remains of a furnace (see p. 58 below). The fifth entrance to the hypocaust is from Room 3 (see p. 46 above). In Room 5 the two ledges, from which sprang the arch opening onto Room 3, run through the thickness of the wall between the two rooms and are extended into the hypocaust in the form of two short spur walls, the southern one with steps built into its southwest side. These walls belong to a late period of construction.[45]

---

[43] Tiles 0.28 m. square pave the south corner of the hypocaust and the east corner beneath the preserved floor of the room. The paving is missing in an area *ca.* 3.10 × 2.50 m. northwest of two spur walls projecting from the southeast wall (Pl. 7:b). Tiles 0.56 m. square pave an area north of these two walls, 1.76 m. wide from northeast to southwest by *ca.* 2.00 m. and ending at the point where the floor of the room above is preserved. Tiles 0.29 × 0.30 m. pave the western side of the room. In its present state the hypocaust floor has a slight slope of 0.05 m. from southwest to northeast, and there is a slope down from the edge along the northeast and northwest walls of the room. The amount of slope seems too slight to be significant and may be due only to subsidence in the center. Although Vitruvius (v.10.2) specifies that the floor of the hypocaust should slope down towards the furnace, excavation has not shown that this was the general practice. It has been suggested that experience showed it to be unnecessary (A. Grenier, *Manuel d'archéologie gallo-romaine*, IV, i, *Aqueducs. Thermes*, Paris 1960, p. 237).

[44] The distance between the columns is regular, except in three areas: (1) Closest to the southwest wall of the room three northwest–southeast rows of columns are out of line with those further northeast (Pl. 38). (2) Along the northeast side of the room between two furnace flues there are three pairs of round columns spaced 0.42 m. apart. All are preserved to their full height, supporting the floor of the room and unexcavated fill above. The two southernmost columns are 0.88 m. in maximum height. They are constructed of eight round bricks on the usual square base with two square bricks above. On top of these are two rectangular bricks which occupy only the southwest half of the top of the column, thus providing a ledge to the northeast on which rest the large horizontal bricks of the floor above. The height of the hypocaust chamber here is lower than it would have been to the south, 0.75 m. as opposed to 0.88 m. Unfortunately, since the edge of the scarp lies directly above, we cannot know whether this difference in levels is reflected in the floor of the room. (3) East of the furnace flues, in the east corner of the room, there are twelve irregularly spaced columns. The southernmost row rests directly on the junction of two sizes of floor tiles (see the preceding footnote).

Square columns are found in the hypocaust in front of the two furnace flues. The columns south of the east wall of the east furnace flue have been fitted into a pre-existing scheme of round columns.

South of the western furnace flue two walls have been added to the hypocaust, one with a projection to the north. These walls incorporate round columns in their southeast ends and square columns in their northwest ends. Their purpose, like that attributed to short walls built inside the furnace of one of the rooms of the Terme del Foro at Ostia, was presumably to direct the smoke and gas stream from the furnace to the east side of the room (Thatcher, p. 213, note 107).

The structures in front of the western furnace flue show some, although not very severe, traces of burning; those in front of the eastern flue are very badly damaged by fire.

[45] The brickwork of these spur walls (Appendix I, Table 1:15) differs from the original brickwork of the room. In addition, the northern spur wall is set against the mortar facing which covers the base of the southeast wall of the hypocaust and conceals the blocked furnace entrance to the north. For further discussion of these walls, see footnote 66, p. 59 below.

The floor of Room 5 is preserved only in a strip 2.40 m. wide along the northwest wall and for a width of 1.70 m. along the northeast wall where it is partially under the scarp (Pl. 38). As preserved, the floor at the west measures 0.40 m. in thickness, that in the east corner 0.30 m. The construction on both sides of the room is of two layers of large bricks, 0.06 m. thick, which span the hypocaust columns. Above them is a layer of mortar, 0.14–0.16 m. thick, with bricks set vertically in it. The bricks in the floor to the west are arranged in large, irregular semicircles. In the floor to the north the mortar above is better preserved, and it is not possible to say whether the arrangement of bricks is the same. They do, however, appear to be set more obliquely in this section. Above the vertical bricks is a layer of mortar, 0.07–0.10 m. thick, with bricks embedded horizontally in it. No imprint of marble slabs is to be seen in the preserved sections of flooring, in contrast to Rooms 2 and 3, and it seems probably that the room was floored in mosaic. Two fragments of mosaic were found in the fill of Room 5 (Group 33), and the construction of its floor differed from that used in Rooms 2 and 3, where the upper layer with horizontal brick fragments was not used.

A space for the circulation of hot air separated the edge of the floor from the northeast, southeast, and southwest walls of the room;[46] along the exposed section of the northwest wall there is no hot-air space. The space along the southwest wall, as well as can be seen, measures 0.16 m.; along the southeast wall of the room it is 0.22 m. wide with some of the vertical bricks still *in situ*. Along the northeast wall it is only 0.10 m. wide, and the edge of the floor appears to have been cut; no bricks are *in situ* here.

Too little of the floor is preserved to retain traces of any pools that may have existed in the excavated portions, but there is evidence to suggest that at one time there was a pool somewhere in the room. The outlet through the southeast wall that connects with the channel in the floor of Room 4 would allow a flow from west to east (Pls. 9:a, 38). The outlet consists of a terracotta pipe built into the wall 1.30 m. from the north corner. It lies 0.74 m. above the floor of the hypocaust and is now covered by the mortar facing on the base of the wall. Its level above the floor is approximately the same as the height of the hypocaust columns between the furnace flues to the northwest,[47] and the columns and outlet probably should be considered as part of the same construction phase at a time when the floor of the room may have been lower. The floors of Rooms 4 and 5 would then have been on the same level; as now preserved the floor of Room 5 is higher. A lion's head spout (**99**), possibly from the wall of a basin, was found at the east side of the room, suggesting further that Room 5 was not a room with dry heat only.

The foundations of the walls of Room 5 are exposed in only one area. The southern end of the eastern face of the southeast wall is visible in the service area to the east of this room, under Room 4. The foundations here can be seen to consist of a rubble-and-mortar socle above which rises a well-built construction in *opus incertum*, forming the wall at hypocaust level. The same *opus incertum* construction within the hypocaust is visible in the southwest wall of the room where the mortar facing has fallen off (Pl. 8:b). The mortar facing here is fine and yellow in color, that on the southeast wall gray with ground-brick fragments in it. Above the *opus incertum* construction the walls are brick faced. Examination has shown a second period of construction: against the *opus incertum* is built the service area that lies below Room 4 (Pl. 38; see pp. 56–57 below), which can be seen to belong to the same construction phase as the brick-faced walls of the north apse of Room 3. These walls were constructed at the same time as the brick-faced walls of the remainder of the building, including the southwest and southeast walls of Room 5; the brickwork is the same, and no junction is visible. The upper section of the southeast wall of Room 5 (and presumably that of the southwest wall as well) is, therefore, later than the *opus incertum* of the lower part. It is probable that here is preserved part of an earlier building.[48]

The southeast wall of Room 5 above the foundations has been cleared for its full length (Pls. 7:b, 8:a). It stands to a maximum height of 3.30 m. above the floor of the hypocaust and has suffered extensive damage.[49]

---

[46] In the case of the southwest wall the hot-air space can be seen beneath unexcavated fill where it remains over the floor; no floor is preserved against the excavated portion of the southwest wall.

[47] See footnote 44, p. 51 above, under (2).

[48] This conclusion is supported by the different construction that can be observed in the foundations of the west wall of Room 3, where they were exposed by the apsidal foundation trench in a small area at the north end on the west face (see p. 14 above). They are of concrete with no aggregate of small stones showing (Pl. 4:c). Above these foundations the walls of Room 3 within the hypocaust are brick faced. For further discussion of the earlier building, see pp. 62–64 below.

[49] In addition to the break in the wall above the passageway between Rooms 3 and 5, there is a gap 0.76 m. wide caused by the

Besides undergoing repairs this wall was also modified. The doorway to Room 4 (Pls. 8:a, 38) was first narrowed from 1.53 m. to 1.27 m. by the addition of a brick pier against the northern jamb and later was completely closed (Appendix I, Table 1:17). The lowest of the brick courses filling the doorway are covered by the same mortar facing that closes off the drain outlet through the wall to Room 4. Numerous clamp holes were found in the brickwork of the doorway and the pier against its northern side; they were also found in the wall to the north, but no remains of clamps were found in the repairs to the wall, except for a large iron clamp still *in situ* at 1.51 m. from the hypocaust floor and 1.64 m. from the south corner of the room.

The southwest wall of the room (Pl. 8:b) is preserved to a maximum height of 3.00 m. above the floor of the hypocaust, although its surface is badly damaged in two areas. The wall was repaired in antiquity in three places (Appendix I, Table 1:18).[50]

The northwest wall (Pl. 10:b), which has been exposed for only a short extent, has a maximum preserved height of 1.23 m. above the floor of the room. The full thickness of the wall has not been cleared. It is constructed of stone blocks and brick-faced concrete (Appendix I, Table 1:19). The exposed section preserves the south side of a brick-built relieving arch with a layer of bricks outlining its outer circumference; those of the arch are flat, not voussoirs. Four stone blocks are built into this section of the wall, one of them the lintel block for the entrance at hypocaust level below. Four poros blocks were also found on fill over the floor directly in front of the wall. The difference in construction as compared to the southwest wall and the fact that there was no screen wall indicate that this section, at least, of the northwest wall is not original but belongs to a period of reconstruction.

The northeast wall (Pl. 8:a) has also been cleared for only a short extent above the floor of the room and has an exposed thickness of 0.50 m. The base is not in *opus incertum*, as were those of the southeast and southwest walls, but is constructed of bricks and mortar (Appendix I, Table 1:20) and was protected by a facing of mortar, traces of which survive. The base of the wall has a height of 0.735 m. and projects 0.16 m. beyond the face above. No clamp holes could be seen in this wall, and at the east end it was not bonded to the southeast wall of the room; a vertical layer of mortar separates the two, and the brick courses of the southeast wall continue north for approximately 0.19 m., where the core of the wall is exposed. This and the different brickwork indicate that the present northeast wall is not an original wall of the room.

A reconstruction of the screen wall is dependent on evidence found in the fill. An almost complete tubulus (**116**) and several fragments were found beneath the floor in the south corner.[51] A terracotta-tube fragment similar to those found in Room 3 and the projection from a *tegula mammata* tile were also found (Appendix III: Group 19). On the basis of this meager evidence it seems possible that all three systems were employed.

None of the decoration of the walls was preserved *in situ*, but many fragments of marble wall revetment were found, the majority white. Several architectural fragments were also found in the fill of the room. Base moldings in *rosso antico* and small columns in *lapis lacedaemonius* are evidence for a colorful decorative scheme.[52] Two white marble column fragments, an Ionic column capital,[53] and two coffered cornice fragments (**100, 101**) may also be part of the architectural details of this room, but three marble footing slabs from an apsidal latrine[54] serve as a reminder that quite large and heavy architectural fragments were moved

---

foundations of a Frankish wall. The brick surface of the wall has also been repaired in two large areas, one on each side of the passageway to Room 3 (Appendix I, Table 1:16).

[50] The original wall surface on either side of the repair at the western end is severely burned. The extensive damage to this and to the southeast wall was probably caused by soot fires, a common hazard in heated rooms. The Romans were aware of the danger. Proculus (*Digesta*, VIII.2.13) speaks of the illegality of placing tubuli against a party wall because of the danger of fire. Similar damage has been observed in other excavated baths; cf. the Terme del Foro at Ostia (Thatcher, p. 192, note 66). Lézine considered that the hot rooms of a bath had to be repaired every 30 to 50 years (A. Lézine, *Architecture romaine d'Afrique*, Paris 1961, p. 11). The three rows of hypocaust columns along the southwest wall of Room 5, which are out of line with those in the rest of the room (Pl. 38), presumably belong to a repair of damage resulting from a fire.

[51] The use of tubuli is apparently not common in Greece, but they have been found at Olympia (Schleif and Eilmann, *op. cit.* [footnote 4, p. 35 above], p. 69, fig. 35), Nea Anchialos (Πρακτικά, 1935, p. 68, fig. 19), and Zevgolatio (Charitonidis and Ginouvès, *op. cit.* [footnote 14, p. 40 above], p. 109).

[52] Corinth Notebook 357, no. 29 (*lapis lacedaemonius* column fragment). The base moldings are not numbered.

[53] Corinth Notebook 357, nos. 19a and b (column fragments), no. 30 (Ionic column capital, possibly 3rd century. Cf. Orhan Bingol, "Das ionische Normalkapitell in hellenistischer und römischer Zeit in Kleinasien," *IstMitt*, Suppl. XX, Tübingen 1980, pl. 19, nos. 118, 263, 288).

[54] Corinth Notebook 357, nos. 21a, b, and c.

to other rooms from their original position. Some large marble step blocks were also found[55] and several fragments of stone moldings once applied to a surface as decoration (Group 33). The room was presumably also decorated with sculpture, but only four fragments were found, one from a large draped figure (Group 33), another a fragment from a relief.[56] Two other pieces were built into late walls in the area at higher levels and thus may be from this room. Both are from draped figures, one seated (**111**), the other not further identifiable.[57]

Some evidence for the roof of Room 5 was preserved in the south corner where fallen fragments from the vault were found.[58] They had fallen face down towards the northwest in front of the southern end of the southeast wall of the room. Several fragments preserved part of a curve and were faced with brick (Pl. 49:a) (Appendix I, Table 1:21). Another fragment of masonry preserved two vertical faces and the curve of the vault. Its thickness was 1.02 m., and since that is only 0.13 m. less than that of the southwest wall of the room, and the shape of the masonry fragment is not suitable for the southeast wall at the southern end, it should be restored to the former. The room can, therefore, be restored with a barrel vault whose axis lay from northeast to southwest. The use of brick facing on the vault fragments indicates the seriousness of the damage to the eastern part of the room. The brick and mortar dimensions in the fallen fragments do not match the original brickwork of the walls. Brick facing was not used on the vaults over Rooms 2 and 3, and in all probability this situation prevailed in all the vaults of the original building period. In this case evidently extensive rebuilding was necessary, requiring the vault to be rebuilt with courses of brick.

Chronology

The building history of this room, as has been indicated, is one of many repairs and reconstructions. In the first period it was connected with Room 4 to the east and could be serviced or heated, also from the east, at hypocaust level. At this period the drain through the southeast wall at the northern end was still in use, and the floor level of the room may have been lower. Subsequently the east side of the room was rebuilt, although whether all the modifications noticed here were made at the same time cannot be stated. The entrance to Room 4 was closed as was the furnace entrance through this wall, and the base of the wall was faced, closing up the drain outlet. Since a setting line for hypocaust columns is incised in the new mortar facing (Pl. 8:a) we must assume that new columns were set; in addition, the hypocaust floor was repaired and a new floor to the room laid at the same time. A date for this reconstruction is suggested by the pottery (Group 5) found in the channel in the floor of Room 4 into which the outlet in the wall opened: no material later than A.D. 267 was found (**134, 135**).[59] The channel, therefore, was out of use after A.D. 267, and the major rebuilding in the east side of Room 5, which caused the abandonment of the channel, had taken place by this date, or shortly thereafter.

None of the other modifications to the room can be dated. The present northeast wall was probably built when the eastern furnace at that wall was closed and another built or rebuilt to the west (see footnote 61, p. 56 below; p. 58). Since, however, the service area has not been excavated, no date can yet be assigned to this rebuilding. The most that can be said is that the proportion of bricks to mortar in the northeast wall is approximately 1:1, which clearly represents a later period than the original brickwork of the building with

---

[55] Corinth Notebook 357, nos. 23a and b, 25, 26.
[56] Corinth inv. no. S 2892.
[57] Corinth inv. no. S 2814.
[58] All were measured, and one was preserved (Pls. 7:b, 49:a).
[59] This evidence suggests that the damage was sustained in the attack on Corinth by the Herulians. Until recently there was little archaeological evidence to indicate that Corinth was attacked. Only in the Sanctuary of Demeter and Kore and possibly in the South Stoa was there any sign of destruction which could be dated to this period. See *Corinth* I, iv, pp. 134, 136–138, 143, 151, 159; *Corinth* VIII, iii, p. 37; R. S. Stroud, "The Sanctuary of Demeter and Kore on Acrocorinth," *Hesperia* 37, 1968, p. 310; N. Bookidis and J. E. Fisher, "The Sanctuary of Demeter and Kore on Acrocorinth," *Hesperia* 41, 1972, p. 320. Excavations in 1981 have, however, added to the scanty evidence. The destruction by fire of a house east of the Theater has been dated to the middle of the 3rd century: C. K. Williams, II and O. H. Zervos, "Corinth 1981: East of the Theater," *Hesperia* 51, 1982, pp. 118, 133–134. The literary sources speak of an attack on Achaia (Aurelius Victor, *Caes.* xxxiii.3; Amm. Marc., xxxi.5.17; *Scriptores historiae Augustae Gallieni*, vi.1, xiii.8, *Claudius*, vi.2, ix.8; Zosimus, i.43), but only Synkellos says specifically that Corinth was sacked (382D; *Corpus scriptorum historiae byzantinae* XII, p. 717).

proportions of 2:1 (Appendix I, Table 1:1, 20). The northwest wall is also later, but its use of thicker bricks suggests that it is earlier than the northeast wall (Appendix I, Table 1:19). The repairs to the southwest and southeast walls have brickwork which is somewhat irregular because of the nature of the work; it does not seem at present that any date can be established for them from proportions of brick thickness to mortar.

The building of the projecting walls, one with steps, in the south corner indicates that Room 5 was abandoned as a public space and converted into a service area for Room 3, possibly in the late 4th century (see pp. 58–59 below). The pottery found in this corner, however, dated from the late 6th to early 7th centuries and could not be distinguished as earlier than that from the destruction fill in the rest of the room (Appendix III: Group 19). The final abandonment of the room is firmly dated to the late 6th or early 7th century by the material found over its destroyed floor and over the hypocaust floor (Appendix III: Group 19). The walls and vault of the room were destroyed by earthquake at the same time as Room 3 (Group 33).

[ROOM 6]

This area, thought to be an interior room of the building at the start of its excavation, is numbered 6 on the plans, Plates 38, 40 (see footnote 5, p. 14). It is discussed in Chapter II in connection with the Marble Façade and below with the first service area (pp. 56, 59).

ROOM 7

Description and Restoration

Room 7 corresponds to Room 5 in its relationship to the building as a whole, in that it forms the southwest wing of the building as Room 5 forms the northwest (Pl. 38). Much less of Room 7 has been excavated, however. Only 3.80 m. of the northwest wall of the room and 1.80 m. of the northeast have been exposed. In this corner there is a pool, two sides of which are preserved with a narrow parapet, set 0.15 m. from the walls of the room, providing space for the circulation of warm air (Pl. 9:b). The pool was revetted with grayish white marble, preserved not on the floor of the pool, where only the impressions of the slabs remain, but *in situ* all along the base and up the corner of the parapet. The mortar sealing the joints is particularly well preserved at this corner (Pl. 9:b). The hypocaust chamber below the pool could not be examined, but the tops of three hypocaust columns could be seen when the air space was cleared along the northwest wall.

The northwest wall of the room (the exterior wall of the building) is preserved to a maximum height of approximately 0.40 m. above the top of the parapet of the pool. At the southern end the brickwork is the same as that in the other walls of the building, but for approximately 2.00 m. at the northern end the wall has been repaired with square or rectangular bricks (Appendix I, Table 1:22).[60] This repair was made at the time the northeast wall of the room was widened (Pl. 9:b). The base of the latter projects 0.72 m. beyond the face above and is preserved to a height of approximately 0.44 m. above the parapet of the pool. The dimensions of bricks and the thickness of mortar are the same as those in the repair to the northwest wall, and the two sections of wall bond together. A horizontal channel is set across the top of the addition to the northeast wall. Its depth is 0.17 m., and it is set 0.06 m. into the wall behind. An iron pin is *in situ* at the back of the channel, and there is an iron pin in the wall above, 0.97 m. from the floor of the channel. A third iron pin is set 0.62 m. from the corner of the room at a height of 0.85 m. above the floor of the channel. The brick face of the upper part of the wall is preserved for 0.91 m., but the core of the wall remains to a greater height. The bricks are blackened as if burned. The screen wall of this room seems to have been held in place by the system of terracotta tubes, since three fragments were found in the fill (Group 20). The wall was revetted with white marble, one plaque of which was found behind the northeast parapet. Other fragments of white marble plaques were found in the fill, some with illegible dipinti in red paint (Group 20).

It is obvious that the pool is an addition to the room, put in when the northwest wall was repaired and the base of the northeast wall widened. This reconstruction took place concurrently with reconstruction to the exterior of the building, probably in the 4th to 5th centuries (see pp. 16, 31 above). The room presumably

---

[60] The mortar used appears to be the same coarse, white mortar employed as the bedding for the marble revetment of the pool.

went out of use at the same time as the other rooms in the building, that is, in the late 6th or early 7th century. Only one datable fragment of pottery, from the early 6th century, was found (Group 20).

SERVICE AREAS

Five areas have been discovered which are either service areas or possibly connected with service for the building. Only two of these have been excavated, and understanding of this aspect of the building is, therefore, incomplete.[61] On the exterior of the building to the west, against the central wall of the façade, one of the excavated service areas was built on the destroyed floor of the pool. It is a late addition, dating from the time when there was no concern for the appearance of the façade. The service area was a simple, barrel-vaulted structure projecting from the wall of the building (Pls. 3:b, 38) and open at the west end. Its walls are preserved to a height of 2.00 m.; its original height can be calculated, from a semicircular packing of stones in the wall of the façade and from the extension of the preserved section of vault, as approximately 2.39 m. The brick walls of the service corridor are preserved to their full lengths of 3.86 m. and 4.20 m. for north and south, respectively, the latter not fully cleared, and are 0.80 m. thick. The spring of the vault begins 1.04 m. above the floor, but on the exterior the wall continues vertically upwards to the level of the top of the façade podium (Pl. 39). The spring of the vault is set back from the interior face of the corridor wall for 0.10 m. The construction of the service area is of bricks and concrete (Appendix I, Table 1:23); the intrados of the vault was built of bricks set on edge, and the concrete aggregate consists of bricks and marble fragments. The exterior ground level in use with this service area was higher than that of the interior floor of the area which was formed by the mortar bedding for the marble floor slabs of the pool in front of the façade. A cornice block from the upper order (**72**), fallen from the façade, marks the junction with the higher ground level to the west of the service area and acted as a step block (Pl. 3:b).

Within the service area a platform, built partly of bricks and mortar, partly of large stones and fragments of brick and marble and measuring 1.10 × 1.17 m., was set in the northeast angle against the wall of the façade. Its preserved height is 0.45 m. A passage was cut through the wall of the façade to connect with the small pool built against the west wall of Room 3.

The date for the building of this service area is given by the pottery from the foundation trenches against the exterior faces of the corridor walls. These were dug in fill containing material dating to the late 4th and 5th centuries with four fragments which appear to be 6th and were considered intrusive (Groups 10, 11, 12). The pottery from the trenches themselves is dated to the early 6th century (Group 13).

The second service area excavated is that at a lower level to the north and northeast of Rooms 2 and 3, under Room 4. This consists of two vaulted corridors (Pls. 5:b, 38) which are evidently of two different periods of construction since their floor levels and orientations are different. At the junction of the two corridors lie the foundations for the north apse of Room 2 (Pl. 5:b), which almost completely block access from one area to the other. A passageway has been left which is only 0.60 m. wide and narrows to 0.12 m. at the base of the apse foundations.

The service area northeast of Room 3 (Corridor 1) lies beneath Room 4, and its vault forms the bedding for the mosaic of that room. The area is roughly T-shaped with the southwestern arm extending only as far as the north apse wall of Room 3 (Pl. 38). Originally at this point there may have been access to the hypocaust of Room 3, but this is now blocked by a rough wall which seems to be later than the original walls to the west and east and shows several periods of construction in itself (Pl. 10:c). The first stage may have been a stone-built socle with brick-built arch above and passageway through to the hypocaust of Room 3. This

---

[61] One of the five areas is separate from the building as now excavated. It consists of five vaulted chambers, possibly cisterns, which lie below ground level to the south on private property. Their connection with the building is not certain. A second area abuts onto the south apse of Room 2 and seems to be a late addition. The third unexcavated area lies to the north of Room 5 and can be entered through the west furnace flue in that room (Pl. 38). It shows several periods of construction, the latest of which is probably connected with the closing of the east furnace in Room 5 and the building or rebuilding of the furnace to the west (see p. 58 below). An Ionic column base found here (**102**) is identical to the one re-used in the colonnade west of the building (**90**).

was then roughly filled in, and later the wall above was twice rebuilt, the final stage perhaps coinciding with the building or rebuilding of the north apse pool in Room 3, for on it is laid the channel for drainage of the pool (Pl. 55).

Corridor 1 measures 7.80 m. in length from northwest to southeast and has a width of 3.15 m. Its height is 2.66 m. The area along the southeast wall of Room 5 has been cleared for only 3.00 m.[62] The service area is constructed with concrete barrel vaults set on brick-faced socles (Appendix I, Table 1:24). The concrete has an aggregate of large brick fragments, stones, and some marble fragments. The vault is preserved in entirety except for the area in the southwest corner of Room 4 (Pl. 9:a). The northwest wall of Corridor 1 is preserved only to the north of the bricked-up furnace entrance to Room 5 and can be seen to be 0.70 m. thick, laid against the foundations for the southeast wall of Room 5. The northwest end of the southwest wall of the corridor is exposed where it abuts against the foundations for the north apse of Room 3, with which it is not bonded in the lower part; two vertical faces can be observed. At a higher level, however, the concrete of the service area can be seen to be continuous with the foundations of the north apse of Room 3. Thus it seems that at this point earlier foundations have been re-used in the construction of the north apse of Room 3. They are similar to those re-used for the southeast wall of Room 5 on the northwest side of the service area.

The northeast wall of Corridor 1 at the southeast end abuts against the west face of a mass of masonry forming the north wall of the second corridor (Corridor 2), which lies further southeast. Two vertical posts from the formwork have left their imprint in the west face of this construction; the northeast wall of Corridor 1 is set against the imprint left by the northern post (Pl. 38).

Corridor 2 has a length of 3.55 m. and a maximum width of 2.60 m. Its height is 1.85 m., and its walls are not brick faced but of poured concrete. In its east wall the imprint of three vertical posts from the formwork are preserved; one of these does not continue down to floor level and thus does not show on the plan, Plate 38. The floor of this area is 0.35–0.40 m. higher than that of Corridor 1.

At the east end of Corridor 2 the service area continues north in a passageway 1.10 m. wide and with a height of 1.18 m. Only a small amount of fill has been removed here, exposing the passageway for 1.05 m. The floor of this area is 0.35 m. above that of Corridor 2. A small wall runs across the passage 0.80 m. from its mouth.

Some lime was found on the floor of Corridor 2, and in the floor of Corridor 1, against the northeast wall at the southeast end, a lime-slaking pit had been dug (Pls. 5:b, 38); this, when found, was filled with earth and pottery. Since it is set against the wall of Corridor 1, it was presumably not used to produce lime for the mortar in the brickwork of the walls of this corridor. The only other brickwork in the area is that of the foundations of the north apse of Room 2, and it was probably for this that the lime-slaking pit was dug.[63] It seems, therefore, that the sequence of construction is as follows: Corridor 2 is the earliest structure in the area. Its orientation and floor level are different from that of Corridor 1, and its north wall has been broken away and must once have continued further west. Furthermore, the northeast wall of Corridor 1 rests in an indentation left by the formwork for the mass of masonry which lies north of Corridor 2 and which seems to be part of its construction. In addition, the difficulty of access between the two areas indicates that they were not planned together. In a later period Corridor 1 was built together with the north apse of Room 3.[64]

An absolute chronology for the use of the service areas is established by the pottery found within the lime pit and over the floors of both corridors. The former (Group 3) suggests a date in the 3rd century for the building of the apsidal foundations (see p. 42 above). Within Corridor 1 no accumulation was found that antedates the lime pit, which was cut from the stereo level that forms the floor of the area. Above the lime pit an accumulation of ashy fill was found which contained pottery of the middle or second half of the 3rd

---

[62] Some fill was left over stereo at the northwest end of Corridor 1, and no fill was removed at the end of the northeast arm of the T. A baulk was left at the southeast end of Corridor 1 against the apsidal foundations (Pl. 5:b).

[63] For a description of these foundations, see p. 39 above.

[64] The fact that the brickwork of the walls of Corridor 1 does not resemble that of the walls of the building above has then to be explained on the grounds that old bricks were being used up. It would be expected that the thicker bricks of the service-area walls were earlier than the thinner ones of the major brickwork of the walls of the building above. A mixture of different thicknesses of bricks was used for the foundations of the north apse of Room 2 (Appendix I, Table 1:8).

century, as well as earlier material (Group 6). In Corridor 2 and the passageway to the north a fill (Group 7), in which the latest material was late 4th or early 5th century, was possibly dumped through the north passageway and had spilled out over Group 6 at the junction of the two corridors. Above these two deposits were found ash layers and over these in Corridor 1 a layer of blackened earth. The lower ash levels date to the first half of the 6th century (Group 31), the upper to the late 6th and early 7th centuries (Group 32), and there were also pieces of 3rd- to 5th-century date in both groups. This material gives some idea of the use of these two areas. During the 3rd century Corridor 1 was open long enough to allow the accumulation of approximately 0.60–0.80 m. of ashy fill, but Corridor 2 does not seem to have been much used. In the 4th century Corridor 2 was used as a dump, but Corridor 1 seems to have seen very little activity. This observation suggests a date at the end of the 3rd century for the closing of those entrances to the hypocausts of Rooms 3 and 5 which could be reached from this section of service area, for this evidence strengthens that of the blocked water channel in the southeast wall of Room 5 (p. 49 above). The outlet for the channel and the furnace entrance are covered by the same mortar facing. The deposit in the water channel (Group 5) suggests that the reconstruction in Room 5 had taken place by A.D. 267 or shortly thereafter (see p. 54 above). The entrance into the hypocaust of Room 3, which it is conjectured lay beneath the north apse of that room (Pl. 10:c), may, however, have been closed at a later period when Room 5 was converted into a service area, possibly at the end of the 4th century (see pp. 59–60 below). If, however, the entrance did remain open during the 4th century it seems to have been little used, for there was no datable accumulation of the 4th century within the corridor. Fifth-century deposits were also lacking. In the 6th century, however, different layers of ash could be distinguished in both Corridors 1 and 2 (Groups 31, 32). Since there was probably no access to a hypocaust during this period from Corridor 1, it is possible that the vault at the west end of Corridor 1 was already broken through by this time and that ash was being dumped in from above.

HEATING SYSTEMS

Our knowledge of the location of the furnaces for the different heated rooms of the Bath is even less complete than is that of the service areas. None of the four heated rooms so far discovered, nor their service areas, have been fully excavated. Room 2 has been cleared to the greatest extent, but if it had a furnace in its final stage, it evidently lay to the south of the room, an area which has not been investigated. Nothing can be said about the furnaces for Room 7 since such a small part of the room has been cleared. A little more, however, is known about Rooms 3 and 5. The latter has two furnaces at the northeast wall and had a third at the southeast. Of the two northern furnaces the easternmost projected into the room for 1.67 m., the longer one to the west for approximately 3.60 m. (Pl. 38). The construction of each is the same: vaulted tunnels formed of rows of bricks made in the shape of the vault and oval in cross section, resting on brick socles. The furnace at the east was blocked at the northern end by a brick wall presumably built when the service area to the north was reconstructed. This furnace was perhaps replaced by the one to the west, or, as the construction indicates, the western one may have been repaired when the eastern furnace went out of use.[65] That there was once a furnace at the southeast wall where there is now a bricked-up entrance (see p. 51 above) is suggested by the repair to the floor of the hypocaust which lies directly in front of it (see footnote 43, p. 51 above). The repaired area of floor is approximately the same length as the eastern furnace flue of the northeast wall, and the removal of walls would have necessitated the laying of new tiles. This third furnace went out of use in the second half of the 3rd century (see pp. 50, 54 above).

Three furnaces for Room 3 are known, and there must have been others located at the south end of the room. Beneath the north apse wall, in the center, the entrance to the hypocaust of Room 3, which is now

[65] The construction of the walls of the western furnace flue is visible in its southeast wall on the exterior. At the southern end, where it projects into the room, a clay coating covers the walls. This has been replaced at the northern end by a mortar facing. The use of a clay coating on the southern end of the furnace flue may indicate that this end of the flue is earlier than the northern end, since the use of mortar in the hypocaust of Room 3 is a later feature than the use of clay. Perhaps only the northern end was rebuilt when the service area was reconstructed. Heated rooms often had many furnaces in use at the same time. Cf. Thatcher, pp. 201, 212: three *praefurnia* each for two rooms and ten for a third in the Terme del Foro at Ostia.

blocked (Pl. 10:c), may once have been a furnace area. This supposition is supported by the existence of a furnace (see below), constructed in an alteration at the east side of Room 5, which presumably replaced the one beneath the north apse wall. Some direct form of heat for the north end of the room must have existed before the furnace in Room 5 was built, and the only possible source is from the service corridor to the north.

A furnace for Room 3, built into Room 5, is restored as the only possible explanation for the two walls, one stepped, which project into Room 5 on either side of the passageway through to Room 3 (Pls. 7:b, 38).[66] On these walls stood a boiler in which the water for the north apse pool was heated by the fire set directly beneath. The steps on the south side of the furnace walls provided access up to the boiler for maintenance and for turning the spigots which regulated the flow of water.[67] From the boiler hot water was fed directly to the pool. The temperature of the water was undoubtedly maintained by a *testudo alvei*,[68] placed over the passageway through the wall and supported by the projecting ledges in the passageway. Fragments of either the boiler or the *testudo alvei* may be preserved in some thick bronze fragments found in the destruction debris of Room 5 (Appendix III, Group 19).

The small west pool in Room 3 (Pl. 6:b) was served by a furnace inserted in a late phase in the wall of the room. The tunnel, cut through the west wall of the building below the marble façade (Pl. 3:b), opens at the west end into the service corridor and at the east into the pool in Room 3 and into the hypocaust below. The tunnel is 1.47 m. high and has a width at floor level of 0.50 m. The semicircular opening at the east end of the tunnel and the ledges in its sides indicate that there was a *testudo alvei* here, with its bottom slightly lower than the bottom of the pool, as in the Terme del Foro at Ostia.[69] The fire must have been placed directly beneath the *testudo*, and there seems to have been no separate boiler as there was for the pool in the north apse. Since the pool was small the *testudo* was apparently sufficient.[70] The square platform against the north wall of the service corridor may have held a water reservoir.

The furnace is dated by the service area which was constructed in the early 6th century (Group 13) and went out of use when the building was abandoned in the late 6th or early 7th century.

There is no firm evidence for the date when the furnace at the east side of Room 5 was established. Although the absence of distinguishable levels of 4th-century fill in the service area under Room 4 north of Room 3 suggests that access to the hypocaust of Room 3 from that area was closed at the end of the 3rd century, the reconstruction in Room 3 itself, which involved the building or rebuilding of the north apse pool, is probably later, because of the use of mortar joints for the hypocaust columns (see p. 48 above). The building or rebuilding of the north apse pool seems to have coincided with the final closing of access to the hypocaust of Room 3 from the service area, since the drain for the pool rests on the blocked-off area. With this access closed, the north apse pool could only have been heated by the furnace established in Room 5. If access was not closed at the end of the 3rd century, perhaps a more likely period would be after the disasters at the end of the 4th century (see footnote 77, p. 31 above). Because the conversion of Room 5 into a service area meant the loss of a large public room of the Bath, a time of reduced prosperity in Corinth, such as the 5th century, seems

---

[66] H. northern spur wall 0.86 m., L. northeast face 0.68 m., L. southwest face 0.81 m., Th. 0.96 m. H. southern spur wall 0.80 m., L. northeast face 1.06 m., L. southwest face 1.17 m., Th. at floor level 1.24 m. The stepped construction of the southern spur wall seems to be intentional. The steps are formed of roughly dressed poros blocks and one marble one; the mortar of the upper steps is smoothed onto the upper surface of the marble block which forms the lowest step, indicating that no other blocks were once built onto it. These steps can only have been used at a time when the floor of the room was missing in that area. When this south corner of the room was excavated no fallen flooring was found as it was in other areas of the room, and the hypocaust columns were totally missing (Pl. 38). A rough barrier with a length of 3.60 m., constructed of hypocaust tiles, a marble slab, a small column fragment, and stones, had been built over the remains of two hypocaust columns at 3.55 m. from the south corner of the room at a right angle to the southwest wall. West of the barrier, ash had been heaped up.

[67] For very similar remains, cf. the Lagerthermae at Lambaesis (Krencker, figs. 288, 289). Here similar structures with steps built into them were found outside the entrances to the hypocausts of three rooms. These are restored as the remains of furnaces above which stood the boilers.

[68] For a clear explanation of the working of the *testudo alvei*, see Ward-Perkins and Toynbee, *op. cit.* (footnote 32, p. 47 above), p. 177; Thatcher, p. 212, note 104.

[69] Thatcher, *loc. cit.* The Corinth Bath's *testudo* was a large one (W. 1.08, H. 0.87 m.).

[70] In the Hunting Baths at Lepcis Magna one of the three furnaces was apparently not supplied with a boiler, and the *testudo* alone was used. See Ward-Perkins and Toynbee, *loc. cit.* (footnote 32, p. 47 above).

probable.[71] Only one small piece of evidence, however, the presence of two fragments of mosaic flooring in the trench on the exterior of the façade (Group 9), indicates that this may be the correct date.

WATER SYSTEMS

The channels or drains built into the floors of the rooms have already been described. On the exterior of the building five drains have so far been discovered. Two drained to the west from the late service area built against the façade wall (Pls. 3:b, 38). The third borders the east edge of the tiled court (see p. 11 above) and at the north end empties into a fourth drain which runs to the west beneath the floor of the court. This in turn empties into the drain along the colonnade to the west (Pl. 38), which is the major drain so far uncovered. A marble statue support was found in it at the south end (**112**). The drain which runs to the west beneath the floor of the court originally began further east and presumably carried off the water from the pool at the base of the marble façade. Subsequently this drain was altered by the addition of a sluice to the south, which was in turn replaced by the drain along the east edge of the tiled court.[72] The two drains from the service area (Pl. 3:b) emptied into this one. The outlet for the southern of the two has been broken through the wall of the drain along the east edge of the court, indicating that it is a late addition to the water system in this area.

The colonnade drain and the drain beneath the court are contemporary with the building of colonnade and court. The sluice and the northern drain from the service area were probably built together. They are dated to the early 6th century by the pottery from the trench dug for the drain (Group 22). The drain along the east edge of the tiled court has brickwork similar to that of the late service area (Appendix I, Table 1:23, 25), and both probably belong to the same construction phase, also in the early 6th century but later than the sluice and the northern drain. The angle of the walls of the service area, which seems designed to include the northern drain, also indicates the same construction sequence. The building of the southern drain from the service area, the latest addition to the water system in this area, cannot yet be dated.

[71] Many buildings in Corinth were destroyed at the end of the 4th century (see footnote 3, p. 62 below). Only a few of these were rebuilt or refurbished. See, e.g., the Bema and the Central Shops and the North Market.

[72] Two of the cover slabs of this drain still *in situ* beneath unexcavated fill further south are of interest. One is an epistyle-frieze block, the other a block with the inscription GERMANICIF (H. of letter F 0.072 m.).

IV
CONCLUSIONS

CHRONOLOGY

A DATE FOR THE CONSTRUCTION of the main building on the site is based chiefly on the stylistic evidence of the façade, which suggests that the Bath was probably built at the end of the 2nd or early in the 3rd century (see above, pp. 28–29). Other evidence from within the building reinforces this date.[1] The most important evidence comes from the service area north of Room 3, where the lowest ash level (Group 6) indicates occupation in the 3rd century; the bulk of the material, which dates from the mid-3rd or second half of the 3rd century, must represent a cleaning of the hypocausts after a period of use. Of the architectural elements from within the building only the fragment of the veneer **94** provides any chronological evidence, suggesting a construction date in the second half of the 2nd century.[2] The Ionic bases **90** and **102** may date to the Severan period but could also be Hadrianic (see above, p. 12 and footnote 21). From the Lechaion Road entranceway the epistyle-frieze block **92**, possibly re-used there, may date to the Antonine period (see above, p. 11 and footnote 18). Other evidence suggests only a 2nd-century date for the building. Sherds from beneath the tiled court (Group 1) date to the late 1st or possibly early 2nd century, as do most of the sherds from crumbled masonry of the vaults (Group 2). This evidence provides a *terminus post quem* for the construction of the building, the date of which must be based on the stylistic evidence of the façade.

The subsequent history of the building is one of many repairs and remodelings. Sometime in the 3rd century, but probably not long after the original construction, Room 2 was altered by the addition of an apse at both the north and south ends, and the cross wall was added to the southwest corner of Room 4 (see above, pp. 42 and 50). Room 2 was further modified by the addition of pools at the north and south ends of the room, which seems to have become a cold one, but these modifications can not as yet be dated (see above, p. 42). Probably in the second half of the 3rd century the doorway between Rooms 4 and 5 was closed, and the water channel in the floor of Room 4 went out of use. At the same time the furnace at the southeast wall of Room 5 was removed, and the southeast side of that room was rebuilt (see above, pp. 54 and 58). It is not possible on the basis of the present evidence to say whether the remodeling in Room 2 took place at the same time in the 3rd century as that in Rooms 4 and 5. If all could be linked together as reconstruction after extensive damage to the building, then such damage might be attributed to the Herulians. As it is, only the evidence from the water channel in Room 4 (Group 5) has been tentatively associated with the Herulian attack (see above, footnote 59, p. 54). Possibly at the end of the 4th century, extensive reconstruction took place in Room 3 when the west side of the central pool was filled in, a new floor on the east side of the room was laid, and the north apse pool was built or rebuilt (see above, p. 48). At the same time Room 5 seems to have been converted into a service area for Room 3, replacing the one to the north of that room (see above,

---

[1] For difficulties in using the brickwork as a means of arriving at a construction date, compare the brickwork of Argos (Appendix I, introduction, pp. 86–87 below).

[2] Corinthian pilaster capitals of this type have an early history. Cf. H. Lauter, "Ptolemais in Libyen," *Jahrb* 86, 1971, pp. 152–153, fig. 4, here dated to *ca.* 40 B.C., and others quoted there. For examples from the end of the 1st century B.C., and mid-1st century after Christ, cf. V. Scrinari, *I capitelli romani di Aquileia*, Padua 1952, nos. 16, 26, and 27. The pilaster capitals from the North Gate of the South Market at Miletus, dated to the Antonine period, are also of this type, except that the helices do not spring from the volutes; *Milet* I, vii, figs. 118–120. (For a Hadrianic dating of the gate, see U. M. Strocka, *Winckelmannsprogramm* [*Archäologische Gesellschaft zu Berlin*], 128, *Das Markttor von Milet*, 1981.) The type lasts until a much later period. Cf. Scrinari, *op. cit.*, no. 73, end of 4th century.

The arrangement of the lobes of the acanthus leaf on **94** suggests a date in the mid-2nd or second half of the 2nd century. Cf. the pilaster capital from the exedra of Herodes Atticus at Olympia. *Olympische Forschungen* I, 1944, pl. 27. The absence of the chiaroscuro effect on **94** is explained by the thinness of the plaque, which necessitated shallow carving of the relief.

p. 59). Also at the end of the 4th century, or later, the pool in the center of Room 1 was filled in, the third floor of that room was laid, and the marble façade on the exterior of the building was damaged by earthquake (see above, pp. 37 and 31, respectively). The earthquakes of A.D. 365 or 375 or both and the invasion of Alaric and the Goths in 395/6 seem, therefore, to have been the cause of extensive damage to the building, as has been noticed for other buildings in Corinth.[3]

For the 5th century the history of the exterior of the building is clear, of the interior less so. On the exterior all interest in the appearance of the building on the west side was abandoned. The damaged architecture of the façade was simply buttressed, and the pool in front was destroyed (see above, p. 31). Perhaps at this time the lime pit was dug within the Lechaion Road entranceway at the west while debris was allowed to accumulate over the tiled court (see above, pp. 12–13). The building itself presumably continued in use during the 5th century. The pool in the center of Room 1 contains no material later than the end of the 4th century; because this dates the laying of the last floor in this room, it suggests that Room 1 continued in use in the 5th and 6th centuries, since if this room had been abandoned in the 5th century the floor would presumably have been pillaged for use elsewhere. It must be added, however, that less than a quarter of the pool has been cleared and that in future excavation later material may be found in its fill. The fact, however, that the marble façade was left in place and not pulled down for the lime kiln does suggest that the building continued in use.

In the early years of the 6th century the service area on the exterior was constructed; the pool and bench against the west wall of Room 3 were added (see above, pp. 56 and 60, and 48, respectively). The drainage system to the west underwent a series of modifications, and ash accumulated in the service areas north of Rooms 2 and 3 (Groups 31, 32) and on the exterior of the building (Group 21; see above, pp. 60, 58, and 32, respectively). Over the colonnade at the west side of the court a house and latrine were built (see above, pp. 12–13).

The building was abandoned by the late 6th century for a reason which cannot be connected with the earthquake that brought down the walls and vaults of many of the rooms. A layer of earth lay beneath this earthquake destruction debris and over the pillaged floors of the rooms. The latest material from the earth layers (Groups 15–20) comprised sherds dating from the late 6th to early 7th centuries and coins of Maurice Tiberius, A.D. 582–602. The latest material from the layers of ash found outside the service area built against the façade dates to the late 6th to early 7th century (Group 21). Presumably the ash was dumped there after cleaning out the hypocaust of Room 3. This evidence suggests that the abandonment of the Bath took place late in the 6th century. The building, therefore, seems not to have been affected by the earthquakes which occurred in A.D. 522 and 551 and to have continued in use despite the plague of 542 which killed half the population remaining after the earlier catastrophe.[4] Later in the century Corinth was attacked by invading tribes.[5] This must have caused the abandonment of the building which was then thoroughly pillaged. Finally an earthquake destroyed Rooms 4, 5, and 7, and most of Room 3. Above the destruction level, Byzantine deposits of the late 11th to mid-12th century were found. The earthquake thus occurred before this period and after the early 7th century. The vaults of Rooms 1 and 2 and the vault over the south apse of Room 3 appear to have survived to a later period.

An understanding of the history of the earlier building or buildings on the site has hardly begun. At the far west the walls of the entranceway belong most probably to an earlier shop constructed in the second half of

---

[3] Cf. the Bath North of the Peribolos of Apollo (Williams, *Hesperia* 38, 1969, p. 63), the Gymnasium and the bath in the Gymnasium area (Wiseman, *Hesperia* 41, 1972, pp. 4, 23), the Sanctuary of Demeter and Kore (Bookidis and Fisher, *op. cit.* [footnote 59, p. 54 above], p. 284, the Odeion (*Corinth* X, pp. 147–148), the Twin Basilicas and the Mosaic House (*Corinth* I, v, pp. 57, 77, 122), parts of the South Stoa (*Corinth* I, iv, p. 153), the Theater (*Corinth* II, p. 140), possibly the Captives' Façade (*Corinth* I, ii, p. 88) and Temple E (*Corinth* I, ii, p. 183), the Bema and Central Shops and the North Market (*Corinth* I, iii, pp. 131, 192).

[4] *Corinth* XVI, p. 8.

[5] The chronology of the invasions, as well as the extent of devastation, is the subject of controversy. It is generally agreed, however, that the first incursions took place *ca.* 580. For bibliography on this subject, see Robert L. Hohlfelder, "Migratory Peoples' Incursions into Central Greece in the Late Sixth Century: New Evidence from Kenchreai," *Actes du XIVe congrès international des études byzantines* 3, 1976, p. 334, note 5, and "Trans-Isthmian Walls in the Age of Justinian," *Greek, Roman and Byzantine Studies* 18, 1977, p. 178, note 33.

IDENTIFICATION

the 1st century and later converted into an entranceway for the Bath (see above, p. 11), but no date can be suggested for the earlier floor encountered in the colonnade (see above, p. 8). In the eastern part of the site, the foundations of the southeast and southwest walls of Room 5 belong to an earlier building, as probably does Corridor 2, the service area north of Room 2 (pp. 52 and 57). Other earlier rooms may lie to the north of the excavated area, thus partially explaining the different axes of Rooms 1 and 2 (Pl. 38).[6] No date for the construction of this earlier building can be given at present, although *opus incertum*, which was used in the foundations of the southeast and southwest walls of Room 5, occurs at Corinth in an early period.[7]

IDENTIFICATION

The chronology of the two buildings on the site is important for their identification. Pausanias, writing between about A.D. 155 and 170,[8] visited Corinth before the later building was constructed. Consequently it cannot be associated with either of the two baths he mentions by name, Hadrian's Baths and the Baths of Eurykles (II.3.5). The Baths of Eurykles, moreover, have now been identified with some probability as the Bath North of the Peribolos of Apollo,[9] and it seems unlikely that the earlier building on the site of the Bath on the Lechaion Road should be identified as Hadrian's Baths.[10] Since so little of this earlier building has

---

[6] If the location of Room 1 was decided by the existence of earlier rooms or buildings to north and south, and its axis possibly by a road at the east, then an explanation for the different axis of Rooms 2 and 3 can be suggested. The position of the Lechaion Road entrance at the west was apparently determined by the existence of earlier walls which were re-used (see above). If both entranceway and Room 1 had to be constructed in their present locations (whatever the reasons may have been), then in order to align the walls of the entranceway with the corners of the façade on the west exterior wall of Room 3, yet maintain symmetry within the building, Rooms 2 and 3 had to be placed at an angle to Room 1. If the plan of the building is redrawn with the major axis of Rooms 2 and 3 parallel to that of Room 1, when the corners of the façade are aligned with the walls of the entranceway the door into Room 2 from Room 1 is not centered in the east wall of Room 2 but lies at the north end. If the door is centered, the façade no longer has a proper alignment with the entranceway. The solution was to adjust the axis of Rooms 2 and 3. The angle of these two rooms, although obvious on the plan, perhaps would not have been noticed by those using the building.

[7] Cf. walls in the Central Shops, built probably in the 1st century (*Corinth* I, iii, pp. 112, 130, pl. 51:2); cross walls of the Northwest Stoa, constructed in the late 1st century (*Corinth* I, ii, pp. 114, 129, figs. 70, 77).

[8] See G. Roux, *Pausanias en Corinthie*, Paris 1958, pp. 27-29.

[9] These baths have long been thought to be the Baths of Eurykles. Reinvestigation showed that they are early Imperial in date, rebuilt in the third quarter of the 1st century and again probably in the 2nd century (Williams, *Hesperia* 38, 1969, pp. 62-63; 43, 1974, pp. 32-33). The most famous Eurykles was prominent in Sparta from after the battle of Actium in 31 B.C. until his banishment and death between *ca.* 7 and 2 B.C. See G. W. Bowersock, "Eurycles of Sparta," *JRS* 51, 1961, pp. 112-116. The excavation evidence does not at present indicate that the earliest phase of the Bath North of the Peribolos of Apollo is as early as the late 1st century B.C. There was, however, a 2nd-century Eurykles, C. Julius Eurykles Herculanus, who was a senator under Trajan and Hadrian and who died after A.D. 130 (Bowersock, *op. cit.*, p. 118; M. Woloch, "Four Leading Families in Roman Athens (A.D. 96-161)," *Historia* 18, 1969, p. 509; B. Forte, *Rome and the Romans as the Greeks Saw Them* [American Academy in Rome, *Papers and Monographs* XXIV], Rome 1972, pp. 264, 305). This Eurykles could have been responsible for a 2nd-century rebuilding of the Bath North of the Peribolos of Apollo. He could also have been the donor of an early building on the site of the Great Bath on the Lechaion Road. For complete sources on the Eurykles family see Alfred S. Bradford, *A Prosopography of Lacedaemonians from the Death of Alexander the Great, 323 B.C., to the Sack of Sparta by Alaric, A.D. 396*, Munich 1977, pp. 178-180.

[10] If the earlier building on the site was Hadrian's Baths, then its thorough destruction can only have been caused by an earthquake which must have occurred after Pausanias visited Corinth and before the late 2nd or early 3rd century. An earthquake in the mid-2nd century, attested in Sicyon (Pausanias, II.7.1), is not attested for Corinth and could not in any case have destroyed the Baths of Hadrian, since the earthquake occurred before Pausanias visited Corinth and the Baths of Hadrian were still standing at the time of his visit (Roux, *loc. cit.* [footnote 8 above]). There is moreover, another building in Corinth which, it has been suggested, may be the Baths of Hadrian. This lies north of the Theater and is unexcavated (H. S. Robinson, *The Urban Development of Ancient Corinth*, Athens 1965, pp. 29-31). Although some of the architectural material from the Lechaion Road Bath, namely the fluted columns from the upper order of the façade (**53-58**) and the two identical column bases from elsewhere on the site (**90, 102**), have parallels in the Hadrianic period, they can not at present be assigned to any building.

been uncovered, nothing conclusive can be said, and thus the identification of both the Great Bath on the Lechaion Road and the building which preceded it on the site must at present remain unknown.

SIGNIFICANCE OF THE EXCAVATION

The excavation of 1965-1968 has added to our knowledge of the topography of the Roman city east of the Lechaion Road[11] and shown that as it extended northward the road was still lined with shops, at least on the east side. In its size and magnificence the Roman Bath is an attestation of the prosperity of Corinth at the end of the 2nd or beginning of the 3rd century. Its construction in this period and its functioning in its original size until the disasters in the second half of the 4th century indicate the continued prosperity of the city during these years.[12] The history of the building during the four centuries of its existence augments the evidence found elsewhere in Corinth for the history of the city. Furthermore, the Bath has an importance not only for Corinth but also for more general implications concerning techniques of Roman construction in Greece. In addition, the "corpus" of Roman architecture in Greece has been considerably enriched by the architectural elements surviving from the Bath, particularly from the façade. In a more general architectural sense, the Bath is important for the history of Roman baths in Greece, since most of those published are built on a smaller scale. Of these the closest to the imperial type is Thermes A at Argos.[13] The Bath at Corinth appears to be even more extensive, which is not surprising in view of the importance of Corinth in the Imperial period as the capital of the province of Achaia.

[11] Recent excavation east of the Theater has uncovered a paved and colonnaded roadway that ran east-west connecting the Lechaion Road and the Theater. The road probably continued eastward after crossing the Lechaion Road and served as the southern boundary of the Bath (C. K. Williams, II and Orestes H. Zervos, "Corinth, 1981: East of the Theater," *Hesperia* 51, 1982, p. 128).

[12] Similar conclusions for the 3rd-century history of Corinth have recently been drawn from a study of the sculpture of that period (B. S. Ridgway, *op. cit.* [footnote 44, p. 27 above], pp. 443-447).

[13] R. Ginouvès, "Le bâtiment romain au sud du théâtre," *BCH* 78, 1954, *Chroniques*, pp. 173-175; "Thermes romains," *BCH* 79, 1955, *Chroniques*, pp. 323-328; P. Aupert, "Thermes A," *BCH* 97, 1973, *Chroniques*, pp. 490-500; *BCH* 98, 1974, *Chroniques*, pp. 764-774; *BCH* 99, 1975, *Chroniques*, pp. 699-703; *BCH* 100, 1976, *Chroniques*, pp. 748-750; *BCH* 101, 1977, *Chroniques*, pp. 667-671; *BCH* 104, 1980, *Chroniques*, pp. 689-691; *BCH* 105, 1981, *Chroniques*, pp. 901-902.

V
CATALOGUE

All dimensions are in meters. The diameter of the base of the capitals equals their resting surface. The following abbreviations have been used: H. (height), D. (diameter), W. (width), L. (length), Th. (thickness), p. (preserved), est. (estimated), max. (maximum), min. (minimum).

Inventory numbers in parentheses follow the catalogue numbers. The inventory numbers for architectural blocks stored on the site are field inventory numbers; see Corinth Field Notebook 357. Inventory numbers preceded by a letter of the alphabet are Corinth Museum numbers. Epistyle-frieze block **68** is numbered in both systems. Context material for the objects in the Catalogue is presented in Groups in Appendices II and III. The material is stored in Lots in Corinth.

Munsell soil-color-chart references have been given for the pottery and lamps only when the fabric is unfamiliar or unusual.

ARCHITECTURE

THE MARBLE FAÇADE

The following architectural blocks found in the façade area and inventoried in Notebook 357 have been omitted from the Catalogue: nos. 26, 44, 70, 75 (fragments of column capitals); nos. 84, 102 (large base and column fragment, found below the final destruction level); nos. 83, 100 (marble plaques).

THE LOWER ORDER

Supports

1 (89). Column base　　　　　　　　Fig. 1, Pl. 11

H. 0.223, D. top 0.535, weather line 0.50, D. lower torus 0.643. Upper torus battered, lower torus broken at front; large crack down one side.
White marble. *In situ* at north angle of façade.

Base with cyma recta between half round above and ovolo below.

Decoration (on front only): on lower torus, leaf frieze which runs from right and left towards the center; on upper torus, double guilloche. Lesbian leaf on cyma recta.

Empolion cutting (D. 0.04) and pour channel on upper surface; area around empolion cutting roughly cut away.

2 (90 a–c). Column base

H. 0.22, est. D. top *ca.* 0.53, est. D. lower torus *ca.* 0.65. Three joining fragments preserving three quarters of base.
White marble. *In situ* on south end of southern pier of central wall of façade.

Profile same as **1**. Decoration the same except that the leaf frieze on the lower torus runs to the right only and that there is a single guilloche on the upper torus.

Empolion cutting (D. 0.07) and pour channel partially preserved.

Fig. 1. Column base **1**. Scale 1:5

3 (46). Column base　　　　　　　　Pl. 11

H. 0.23, p.W. 0.46. Fragment preserving *ca.* one third of base. Upper torus mostly broken away.
White marble. Found on southeastern pier of northern wing of façade.

Profile same as **1**. Decoration (on front only): three rows of overlapping leaves on the cyma recta with tips of small leaves between the larger in the lowest row; guilloche on the lower torus, only faint traces of which are preserved. Decoration of the upper torus not preserved.

Pour channel preserved on upper surface.

4 (155). Column base　　　　　　　　Pl. 12

P.H. 0.10, p.W. 0.09, p.L. 0.18. Single fragment preserving lower torus and bottom of cyma-recta molding.
White marble. Found in Room 5, north of the façade.

From base with same profile and decoration as **3**. Guilloche on lower torus; on cyma recta, part of lower row of leaves preserved with tips of small leaves between the larger.

5 (47, 48). Column base

H. 0.22, p.W. 0.355. Two joining fragments from back of base. Complete profile preserved. Upper torus chipped.
White marble.

From base with same profile as **1**. Undecorated.

6 (57). Column base

P.H. 0.19, p.W. 0.365. Single fragment preserving lower torus and cyma recta from back of base.
White marble.

From base with same profile as **1**. Undecorated.

7 (32). Monolithic column shaft, unfluted Pl. 12

Est. D. base 0.505, est. D. bottom of shaft 0.43, D. top 0.45, weather line 0.41, D. top of shaft 0.372, L. 3.55. Most of base and part of upper molding broken away.
Karystian marble.

Small, shallow cutting in upper surface on axis of column for centering when cutting, or perhaps for a lead seal. For the latter see J. B. Ward-Perkins, "Nicomedia and the Marble Trade," *PBSR* 48, n.s. 35, 1980, p. 31.

8 (39). Column shaft, unfluted Pl. 12

D. base 0.50, D. bottom of shaft 0.448, p.L. 2.56. Base and two thirds of shaft preserved.
Karystian marble.

9 (33). Column shaft, unfluted

P.L. 1.07. Fragment preserving small area of base and one side of shaft.
Karystian marble.

10 (34). Column shaft, unfluted

D. bottom 0.46–0.47, p.W. top 0.425, p.L. 1.36. Fragment broken at both ends.
Karystian marble.

Back surface unfinished.

11 (68). Column shaft, unfluted Pl. 12

D. base 0.51, D. bottom of shaft 0.422, p.L. 2.21. Fragment preserving base; base chipped.
Karystian marble.

Back surface unfinished: claw chiseled for 0.78; remainder roughly picked with smoothed horizontal bands at intervals of 0.30 and 0.32.

12 (35, 54). Column shaft, unfluted Pl. 12

Max. p.D. bottom 0.41, D. top 0.41, weather line 0.385, D. top of shaft below molding 0.368, p.L. 2.50. Two joining fragments preserving top of shaft. Molding at top battered.
Red marble.

Surface smoothly dressed except for band 0.10 wide at top. Empolion cutting in top 0.04 × 0.04 with depth of 0.04.

13 (67). Column shaft, fluted

Est. D. base 0.50, D. bottom of shaft 0.434, p.L. 0.90. Fragment preserving part of base.
Giallo antico.

Rectangular dowel cutting in base (0.04 × 0.03).

14 (87). Column shaft, fluted

P.W. base 0.30, p.L. 0.48. Fragment preserving part of base.
Giallo antico.

The profile of the base differs greatly from that of **13**.

15 (56, 81). Column shaft, fluted Pl. 12

Est. D. top 0.436, est. D. top of shaft 0.38, max. p.D. shaft 0.412, p.L. 2.45. Two joining fragments preserving upper part of shaft and top.
Giallo antico.

16 (69). Column shaft, fluted

Est. D. top *ca.* 0.443, est. D. top of shaft 0.395, p.L. 0.74. Fragment preserving top of column.
Giallo antico.

Empolion cutting (D. 0.07) and hook-clamp cutting (p.L. 0.10). The surface around the empolion cutting has been roughly hacked away; the cutting for the hook of the clamp lies at the edge of the empolion cutting.

17 (59, 62, 79). Column shaft, fluted Pl. 12

Max. D. shaft 0.43, min. D. shaft 0.385, p.L. 3.10. Three joining fragments; top and bottom broken away.
Giallo antico.

18 (61). Column shaft, fluted

Max. p.D. 0.43, min. p.D. 0.41, p.L. 2.14. Fragment broken at both ends.
Giallo antico.

19 (60). Column shaft, fluted

P.W. 0.391, p.L. 1.69. Fragment broken at both ends.
Giallo antico.

Patch of coarse, white mortar in one flute.

20 (72). Column shaft, fluted

P.W. 0.452, p.L. 0.45. Fragment broken at both ends.
Giallo antico.

21 (64). Corinthian capital Pl. 13

H. 0.515, D. bottom *ca.* 0.39. Broken across right rear side of bottom. Three corners of abacus chipped.
White marble.

Unfinished at back. Top roughly picked with raised bearing surface in center 0.425 × 0.35, H. 0.015.

Acanthus leaves carved with five distinct lobes separated from each other by a short rectangular groove. Leaves deeply grooved with groove of the two upper side leaves continuing down to mark the stem of the leaf. Leaves of the upper row begin just below the tops of the lower row, but the stems of the leaves continue down to the lower zone by means of a slight triangular rib. Leaves of the upper row touch at their base above the leaves of the lower zone. Small, triangular cauliculi with a small boss at the bottom. From the calices rise the volutes and helices. Large, five-petaled flower, with wavy stem, on abacus. Lower part of abacus only very slightly curved.

Unfinished at back. Lower row of leaves begins slightly above bottom, leaving edge *ca.* 0.0025 high.

22 (77). Corinthian capital   Pl. 13

P.H. 0.43, D. bottom 0.388. Fragment preserving bottom, lower row of acanthus leaves, and part of upper row.
White marble.

From a capital similar to **21**. Small shallow cutting in bottom (cf. **7**).

23 (53). Corinthian capital   Pl. 13

H. 0.51, max. p.D. bottom 0.28. Battered and worn. Half of upper surface broken away; broken across bottom.
White marble.

Capital of same type as **59**. Two partially preserved dowel cuttings in bottom (0.04 × 0.02; 0.03 × 0.02). Rectangular cutting in upper surface at 0.215 from preserved edge (L. 0.16, W. 0.075).

24 (17). Corinthian capital   Pl. 13

H. 0.51, D. bottom 0.343. Battered and worn. Broken on upper surface and down one side.
White marble. Found in Room 5, north of the façade.

Capital of same type as **59**. Dowel cutting in bottom (0.04 × 0.025). Rectangular cutting in upper surface (p.L. 0.14, p.W. 0.08).

25 (98). Corinthian capital   Pl. 13

H. 0.52, p.W. bottom 0.24. Abacus and one side broken away. Small portion of bottom preserved.
White marble.

Capital of same type as **59**. In upper surface, rectangular cutting (L. 0.10, W. 0.05) and clamp cutting (L. 0.16) at a right angle to it; incised line parallel to front edge at *ca.* 0.09 from edge.

26 (104). Corinthian capital   Pl. 13

P.H. 0.24, p.W. top 0.50. Fragment preserving upper part of kalathos and two sides of abacus.
White marble.

From a capital of same type as **59**. On one side of the abacus, a five-petaled rosette, on the other a leaf. Upper surface dressed with a claw chisel; small, shallow cutting in center (cf. **7**) with four incised lines radiating from it.

Entablature

27 (51). Epistyle-frieze block   Pl. 14

H. 0.61, max. W. soffit 0.49, est. max. L. soffit 1.84. Soffit broken on right, part of crowning moldings above frieze broken. Back of block at left corner broken away.
White marble.

Two-fascia epistyle crowned by astragal and cyma reversa. S-shaped frieze above. On the soffit, overlapping leaf frieze in a narrow panel with incurved ends. Leaf frieze meets in center. Lower fascia of epistyle surmounted by a twisted ribbon, now much battered, apparently running from right to left. Second fascia crowned by a bead-and-reel with a Lesbian leaf on the cyma reversa below the fillet. Frieze carved with upright acanthus leaves alternating with water leaves. Acanthus leaves carved with four tips to each lobe. Above frieze a bead-and-reel surmounted by an egg-and-dart. Ends of block carved for a width of 0.27 measured on the soffit. Back roughly dressed and ends notched to fit the blocks set behind on each side. Upper surface at back roughly picked.

Cuttings. On the soffit, one dowel hole (0.045 × 0.025) preserved on left at 0.715 from center. On upper surface at back, two cuttings for hook clamps, which held the block in the wall, the one at right with iron clamp and remains of lead preserved; surface around clamp roughly cut away. Two cuttings, set diagonally in the notched ends, for clamps to the adjacent blocks.

28 (154). Epistyle-frieze block

Visible H. 0.32, max. W. top 0.46, visible L. 0.80. Molding along upper front edge broken.
White marble. Embedded in west scarp of excavation area at north end; left end exposed.

From projecting block. Moldings and decoration the same as **27**. Left end carved for 0.33 measured along top.
Cuttings. On upper surface, two clamp cuttings and remains of clamps which held the block in the wall.

29 (38). Epistyle-frieze block   Pl. 14

H. 0.62, W. soffit 0.265, p.L. 1.09. Right end broken away.
White marble.

From block set back in wall. Left end roughly cut down for width of 0.24 at top, 0.15 at bottom, to fit notch in block set forward on left. Moldings and decoration the same as **27**. The twisted ribbon runs to the right.

Cuttings. On upper surface, diagonal clamp cutting at left end.

30 (40). Epistyle-frieze block　　　　　　Pl. 14

H. 0.62, max. W. soffit 0.515, est. L. soffit *ca.* 1.87. Left end broken, right preserves notch for block behind. Crowning moldings of frieze broken away.
White marble.

From projecting block. Moldings and decoration the same as **27**, except that the twisted ribbon runs from right and left, meeting at the center of the block.

Cuttings. Dowel hole partially preserved on soffit at left at 0.64 from center of block. On upper surface, four cuttings for hook clamps which held the block in the wall.

31 (95). Epistyle-frieze block　　　　　　Pl. 15

H. 0.608, max. W. soffit 0.40, p.L. soffit 0.76. Right end broken, left preserves notch for block behind. Crowning moldings of frieze broken away at left end.
White marble.

From projecting block. Moldings and decoration the same as **27**, except for soffit which is carved with a guilloche.

Cuttings. Dowel hole on soffit at 0.20 from left end. Mason's mark B on soffit. Upper surface at left end cut down for depth of *ca.* 0.025, L. *ca.* 0.14. Iron pin, set vertically, preserved at 0.04 from edge. Diagonal hook clamp in upper surface at 0.15 from right end. Two hook-clamp cuttings for clamps which held the block in the wall.

32 (124). Epistyle-frieze block

H. 0.622, W. top 0.49, p.L. 1.08. Right front corner preserved, left broken away.
White marble. Partially exposed in find position against south side of service area.

From projecting block. Moldings and decoration the same as **27**. Right end carved for 0.26 measured along top.

Cuttings. On upper surface, two cuttings for hook clamps, the one on the left possibly recut; a third cutting in back below right upper cutting.

33 (97). Epistyle-frieze block

P.H. 0.37. Fragment preserving frieze.
White marble.

From an epistyle-frieze block similar to **27** but undecorated.

Cornice

34 (63). Geison block with dentils　　　　　Pl. 16

H. 0.40, max. p.W. 0.91, W. bed 0.575, max. p.L. 1.57. Right end broken; front edge broken away.
White marble.

Bed molding: dentils, set slightly above bed, surmounted by a fillet, an egg-and-dart, and a second fillet. Plain corona with face projecting slightly outwards, divided from the sima by a cyma reversa decorated with a Lesbian leaf. On sima, palmettes with a bead-and-reel below. At left end of block the moldings are cut to receive those on the adjacent block which was set forward. Upper surface dressed down for 0.01–0.02, leaving a raised band along front *ca.* 0.25 wide.

Cutting, partially preserved, on upper surface at left diagonal edge for hook clamp to adjacent block. Iron pin, for a repair(?), at left end of front face.

35 (71). Geison block with dentils　　　　　Pl. 16

H. 0.375, max. p.W. 0.57, max. p.L. 0.70. Fragment preserving bed molding. Both ends broken.
White marble.

From a geison block similar to **34**, but dart more finely carved.

36 (86). Geison block with dentils　　　　　Pl. 16

H. 0.38, p.W. 0.78, W. bed 0.47, p.L. 1.01. Right end and front broken. Bed molding preserved and part of left end at back.
White marble.

From a geison block similar to **34** but from a projecting block. Left end of block cut diagonally. Back roughly picked. Upper surface dressed down for *ca.* 0.01–0.02, leaving raised band along front 0.14 wide.

Clamp cutting at back on upper surface.

37 (107). Geison block with dentils　　　　　Pl. 16

Visible H. 0.245, W. 0.645, exposed L. 0.90. Left end broken; right end not completely visible.
White marble. Built into south wall of late drain in front of service area at base of façade.

From a geison block set back in wall, similar to **34**. The sima with palmette frieze and corona are visible. Upper surface dressed down for 0.04, leaving a raised band along front *ca.* 0.18 wide.

Diagonal clamp cutting for adjacent block in upper surface at right edge.

38 (160). Geison block (with dentils)　　　　Pl. 17

P.H. 0.165, p.W. 0.15, p.L. 0.21. Fragment from a top corner, preserving cyma reversa above corona, and sima above.
White marble. Found in Room 5, north of the façade.

From a projecting block. Moldings and decoration the same as **34**, but one side has a water leaf between two palmettes. Corner of the cyma reversa finished with a hanging palmette.

39 (114). Geison block with dentils

P.H. 0.35, p.W. 0.47, W. bed 0.28, p.L. 1.29.

Fragment preserving bed molding and small part of left end, cut diagonally.
White marble.

From a geison block set back in wall, similar to **34**. On upper surface, remains of mortar.

40 (123). Geison block with dentils

P.H. 0.30, p.W. 0.51, p.L. 0.62. Single fragment preserving four dentils and right end of block.
White marble.

From a geison block similar to **34**. Right end cut diagonally.

41 (152). Geison block with dentils

H. *ca.* 0.35, p.W. *ca.* 0.78, p.L. *ca.* 1.10. Right end broken; left end not visible.
White marble. Embedded in west scarp of excavation area at south end.

From a geison block similar to **34**. Two clamp cuttings are visible on the upper surface at the broken right end, one apparently to the rear, the second possibly set diagonally for the adjacent block. Distance from front edge *ca.* 0.39.

THE UPPER ORDER

Stylobate

42 (49, 52). Stylobate block   Pl. 17

H. 0.272, W. top 0.725, p.L. 1.96, est. L. top 2.00. Two joining fragments preserving complete block. Molding down left side and along top of left end broken away; left end battered, preserving only a small area of face.
White marble.

Projecting block with vertical front face crowned by cyma reversa which continues down the sides. Right end of block carved for length of 0.30, remainder cut diagonally and roughly picked; left end cut at right angle to front face. Back roughly picked. Upper surface dressed down along front edge and for two setting beds with setting lines (0.585 × 0.58), pour channels, and empolion cuttings. Empolion cuttings 1.39 apart (center to center) and at 0.31 from front edge.

Cuttings. On upper surface, one cutting to the back for hook clamp to fasten block to the wall. One cutting in each side for clamps to the adjacent blocks. Surface around right cutting roughly cut away.

43 (36). Stylobate block   Pl. 17

H. 0.285, W. 0.752, L. front 1.642. Complete block.
White marble.

Block set back in wall, similar to **42**, but with cyma-reversa molding only along upper front edge. Left end cut diagonally so that back of block is longer than front, right end cut at a right angle to front, with anathyrosis. Upper surface hammered in a band 0.22 wide along front edge. Setting bed at left (W. 0.68, L. at front 0.08, at back 0.17). Second bed partially preserved at right.

Cuttings. Cuttings for two hook clamps to adjacent blocks in upper surface, on left at 0.26 from front edge, on right at 0.27 from front. Some lead preserved. Right clamp possibly reset with smaller clamp; surface around cutting roughly cut away, and lead at end of cutting preserves imprint of hook of smaller clamp at a slight angle to original cutting.

44 (148). Stylobate block

H. 0.274, p.W. 0.41, p.L. 0.70. Fragment preserving part of right front corner.
White marble. Found on stylobate of colonnade at the west.

From a projecting block similar to **42**. On upper surface, part of setting bed (L. 0.61) and pour channel. Empolion cutting at 0.245 from front edge and 0.255 from right edge.

45 (42). Stylobate block

H. 0.28, max. W. 0.94, p.L. 1.23. Two joining fragments preserving part of front face and right end. Left end and right front corner broken.
White marble.

From a projecting block similar to **42**. Right end cut diagonally at 0.37 from front edge, measured along bottom. Upper surface preserves setting bed (0.52 × 0.57), empolion cutting (D. 0.08), and pour channel. Empolion cutting at 0.245 from front edge and 0.26 from end.

46 (65). Stylobate block

H. 0.285, W. 0.87, p.L. 1.23. Fragment preserving left end of block.
White marble.

From a projecting block similar to **42**. Left end cut diagonally at 0.32 from front edge measured along top. Top surface preserves irregular setting bed with empolion cutting (D. 0.065) and pour channel. Empolion cutting at 0.25 from front edge and 0.27 from end.

47 (74). Stylobate block

H. 0.285, W. 0.74, L. 0.745. Complete block.
White marble.

Block set back in wall, similar to **43** with cyma-reversa molding only along upper front edge. Ends cut at a right angle to front, with anathyrosis.

Cuttings. In upper surface, cuttings for two hook clamps in both sides at 0.38–0.40 from front edge. Surface around right cutting roughly cut away.

48 (80). Stylobate block

H. 0.286, p.W. 0.61, p.L. 0.33. Fragment preserving left-hand corner with cyma-reversa molding.

White marble.

From a projecting block similar to **42**. Left end cut diagonally at 0.35 from front edge measured along bottom. Top surface preserves setting bed with empolion cutting (D. 0.06) with remains of lead at 0.245 from front edge and 0.24 from left end.

49 (113). Stylobate block

H. 0.285, W. 0.59, p.L. 0.85. Fragment preserving part of front face and beginning of cyma-reversa molding.
White marble.

From a projecting block similar to **42**. Top surface roughly picked. Remains of empolion cutting at broken right edge.

50 (153). Stylobate block

H. 0.29, W. *ca.* 1.07, L. rear *ca.* 0.58, front *ca.* 0.51.
White marble. Embedded in west scarp of excavation area opposite northern niche of central wall.

L-shaped, projecting block with one carved face visible. Cyma-reversa molding along top and down left side. Left side of block not visible. Right side cut at a right angle to front face for 0.67 with anathyrosis for *ca.* 0.45. Remainder of block roughly worked and forming right-angled projection to right. Bottom surface flat and smoothly dressed.

Clamp cutting in upper surface at 0.32 from front edge, for adjacent block on the right.

Supports

51 (118). Monolithic column shaft, unfluted

Max. D. bottom of shaft 0.366 (measured at *ca.* 0.25 above base), D. top 0.352, D. top of shaft below molding 0.324, L. 2.75.
White marble. Found lying over drain at east edge of tiled court; base still embedded in scarp.

Back roughly picked. Roughly cut depression in top (0.20 × 0.22).

52 (99). Column shaft, unfluted

D. 0.366, p.L. 1.00. Fragment broken at both ends.
Fior di pesco.

53 (101). Column shaft, fluted   Pl. 18

D. bottom of shaft 0.405, min. D. top 0.39, p.L. 2.10. Broken at both ends, at bottom just above base.
Proconnesian marble.

From a column with arrises carved with fillet and astragal. At the base, the flutes are rounded with a hanging leaf between. Empolion cutting partially preserved, 0.04 × 0.04 with preserved depth 0.01.

54 (157). Base of fluted column

P.H. 0.175, est. D. shaft (where fluting is preserved) 0.41, p.W. 0.20, p.L. 0.22. Small fragment preserving part of base, three flutes, and part of a fourth; base molding broken away.
Proconnesian marble. Found in Room 5, north of the façade.

From a column similar to **53**. Base claw chiseled; dowel cutting partially preserved.

55 (156). Top of fluted column shaft   Pl. 18

P.H. 0.145, p.W. 0.065, p.L. 0.13. Small fragment preserving upper molding of column, top of one flute, and part of a second.
Proconnesian marble. Found in Room 5, north of the façade.

From a column similar to **53**. Small triangular leaf between flutes at top. Clamp cutting in upper surface partially preserved with small fragment of iron clamp.

56 (8). Column shaft, fluted

P.W. 0.21, p.L. 0.26. Small fragment preserving one end.
Proconnesian marble. Found in destruction debris in Room 5, north of the façade.

From a column similar to **53**. Preserved end cut straight.

57 (85). Column shaft, fluted

P.W. 0.21, p.H. 0.13. Small fragment broken at both ends.
Proconnesian marble.

From a column similar to **53**.

58 (88). Column shaft, fluted

Max. D. 0.35, min. D. 0.326, p.L. 1.94. Fragment broken at both ends.
Giallo antico.

From a column with fluting similar to **53**.

59 (78). Corinthian capital   Pl. 19

H. 0.45, D. bottom *ca.* 0.28 (originally *ca.* 0.325). Volutes broken away; abacus broken across left rear edge. Acanthus leaves battered.
White marble.

Acanthus leaves of second zone begin just below tops of lower zone. Above lower row of leaves, kalathos is summarily carved so that there is a noticeable ledge at this point. Above this ledge, cauliculi carved as plain rectangular protuberances. From these rise calices composed of two acanthus leaves; space between leaves carved as two triangles, one long one below, one short one above. Inside tip of inner leaf of each calyx touches a central leaf from which rises a wavy stalk for rosette or leaf on abacus. This central leaf rests on top of the leaf below. Abacus, where well preserved (see **26**), has only a slight curve; molding above flattened. Decoration on abacus either a rosette or a leaf. On one cap (**26**) both were employed. Helices in quite high relief with a definite spiral at their ends.

Bottom roughly cut back around front and sides to form smaller resting surface; dowel cutting in center (0.035 × 0.025); surface around roughly cut away. Upper surface dressed down leaving slightly higher area (W. *ca.* 0.045) along front edge and abacus with H. *ca.* 0.025 on front, 0.015–0.20 on sides. Hook-clamp cutting to rear (p.L. 0.135, W. 0.04) with some lead preserved.

60 (66). Corinthian capital Pl. 19

H. 0.43, est. D. bottom 0.34. Broken across bottom and partly up one side. Volutes and two corners of abacus broken away.
White marble.

Capital of same type as **59**. Dowel cutting in bottom 0.035 × 0.035. Upper surface dressed down leaving slightly higher edge along front; hook-clamp cutting to rear at slight angle (L. *ca.* 0.10).

61 (43). Corinthian capital Pl. 19

H. 0.448, p.W. bottom 0.34. Broken across bottom and up one side. Volutes and front edge of abacus broken away.
White marble.

Capital of same type as **59**. On two preserved sides of kalathos, no stalk for rosette or leaf on abacus. Dowel cutting in bottom 0.028 × 0.028; surface around cutting roughly cut away. Upper surface dressed down so that only lower fascia of abacus is preserved. Clamp cutting to rear in upper surface (L. 0.15).

62 (110). Corinthian capital Pl. 19

H. 0.485, D. bottom 0.30. Broken at bottom. Three corners of abacus broken away; ends of volutes of fourth corner also missing.
White marble.

Unfinished at back. Dowel cutting in bottom 0.03 × 0.03. Upper surface dressed down for 0.025 as bed for epistyle leaving higher area along front.

Entablature

63 (45). Epistyle-frieze block Pls. 20, 48

H. 0.47, W. soffit 0.525, L. soffit 1.74. Surface chipped. Crowning moldings partially broken away. Ancient repair (L. 0.325) to cyma reversa above frieze.
White marble.

Projecting block with three-fascia epistyle crowned by cyma reversa and fillet. S-shaped frieze. On soffit, overlapping leaf frieze in narrow panel with incurved ends; leaf frieze meets in center. Fascias and crowning molding of epistyle plain. On frieze, nine-petaled lotus-and-palmette, irregularly spaced and connected by S-scrolls whose ends curl in opposite directions. On left end of block, only half palmette carved. Above frieze, bead-and-reel and egg-and-dart moldings.

Ends of block carved for width of 0.29 at bottom to 0.34 at top. Back roughly dressed; ends notched to fit blocks set behind on each side. Roughly dressed raised band (W. 0.055) on soffit along back edge.

Cuttings. On upper surface, two cuttings for hook clamps in the notched ends and two in back edge, all at right angles to edge.

64 (106). Epistyle-frieze block Pl. 20

H. 0.475, W. soffit 0.515, est. L. soffit 1.66. Corners of block and crowning moldings chipped.
White marble.

Projecting block similar to **63** but frieze decoration more closely spaced and each anthemion carved with seven leaves or petals. Connecting spirals also differ from those of **63**. Adjacent ends curl in the same direction except beneath the fifth anthemion from the left end where the ends curl in opposite directions.

Cuttings. In upper surface, two cuttings for hook clamps in the notched ends and two in back edge, all at right angles to edge.

65 (151). Epistyle-frieze block

H. *ca.* 0.49, W. soffit *ca.* 0.53, exposed L. 1.26. Bottom edges broken away.
White marble. Embedded in east scarp of tiled court at north end; front face, right end, and top are not visible.

Projecting block similar to **63**, but frieze decoration, visible only on left end, incised rather than carved, possibly unfinished. Narrow panel on soffit undecorated. On upper surface, possible clamp cutting runs diagonally to left back corner of block.

66 (111). Epistyle-frieze block Pl. 20

H. 0.465, W. soffit 0.40, p.L. 1.00. Broken at both ends. Frieze and moldings above damaged.
White marble, discolored black.

From block set back in wall. Moldings and decoration similar to **64** with adjacent ends of connecting spirals of frieze curling in same direction, except in one instance where scheme of **63** was used. Soffit not decorated.

67 (76). Epistyle-frieze block

H. 0.465, max. p.W. 0.29, max. p.L. 0.24. Single fragment preserving part of soffit, face, and upper surface.

White marble.

From a block similar to **63** but undecorated. Diagonal clamp cutting in upper surface for adjacent block.

68 (A 987; 105). Epistyle-frieze block   Pl. 21

H. 0.46, W. soffit 0.535, p.L. 1.55, est. L. soffit 1.80. Re-used block cut down on top and with ends notched for use in the façade. Left end and almost half of back broken away.
White marble.

Projecting block similar to **63**. The wide spacing of the frieze decoration is close to **63**, but the number of leaves or petals in each anthemion and the arrangement of the connecting spirals resemble **64**, except at the right end of the front face where the adjacent ends curl in opposite directions.

Back of block carved with two-fascia epistyle: plain stepping crowned by plain cyma reversa and fillet. Lower fascia at left apparently unfinished. Figured frieze above (p.H. 0.18, p.L. 0.80): lower part of three standing figures preserved to waist and left leg of fourth figure at extreme left end of block. All stand with weight on left leg, right leg bent slightly at knee. Fifth figure partially preserved at far right. Of the three central figures, the one on the left wears a short tunic and a cloak whose fold hangs down on his left side. His right arm is by his side. The other two figures wear the toga. The one on the left has the right arm down and left raised, the one on the right has both arms stretched out towards the right and is holding an unidentifiable object in his hands. At the far right of the preserved face of the block can be seen the chest and right arm of the fifth figure, standing behind an unidentified object, perhaps an altar.

Cornice

69 (50). Console-dentil geison block   Pls. 22, 48

H. 0.335, H. face 0.32, max. W. 0.90, max. W. bed 0.51, L. 2.335. Parts of coffers at both corners missing, right end broken and crowning moldings mostly broken away.
White marble.

Projecting block. Dentils, set slightly above bed, surmounted by a plain fascia, from which sprang five consoles, four preserved; fifth partially preserved at right. Crowning molding for a sixth console projects diagonally from left corner of block. Consoles (W. 0.14, L. 0.225) impinge slightly on dentils; consoles carved on lower faces with acanthus leaves terminating in a scroll and on sides with an S-curve. Egg-and-dart molding crowning consoles interrupted at outside corners by small palmette and at inside corners by leaf. In square coffers between, carved rosettes of three different kinds with same type repeated at each end. Partially preserved coffer at far left irregularly shaped. Face of corona plain, surmounted by cyma reversa, carved with Lesbian leaf, and by fillet.

Left end of block carved for 0.34 from the front edge, measured along top. Right end preserves small portion of returning dentil fascia. Remainder of right and left ends and back roughly dressed. Ends mitered to fit adjacent blocks which were set further back. Upper surface dressed down for 0.035, leaving higher band 0.22–0.26 wide along front and left side.

Cuttings. On upper surface, two cuttings for hook clamps to fasten block to wall; third in diagonal left side at 0.42 from front edge; fourth cutting partially preserved in diagonal right side.

70 (37). Console-dentil geison block   Pls. 22, 48

H. 0.32, W. 0.775, W. bed 0.36–0.39, p.L. 1.74. Preserved are two consoles and extreme right edge of third along broken left end of block. One console an ancient repair. Lower surface of second broken away. Coffer between it and third console missing. Some dentils chipped; only a small portion of top front edge preserved.
White marble.

Block set back in wall. Moldings and decoration similar to **69**, but spacing between second and third console unusually large. Distance between two consoles on right 0.30, between second console and preserved right edge of console on left 0.655. Although the block is broken above, the dentils are well preserved and give no indication of the existence of an intervening console. The face of the fascia adjacent to the preserved right edge of the left-hand console is less carefully dressed, suggesting that this console projected diagonally. Consoles shorter and narrower than those of **69** (W. 0.122, L. *ca.* 0.22). Coffer and five-petaled rosette at right end of block mitered for the adjacent block. Wind-blown rosette in complete coffer. Upper surface of block very roughly dressed and slightly higher towards front.

Cuttings. Hook-clamp cutting in upper surface in diagonal right side at 0.28 from front edge (measured along diagonal side). Rectangular dowel cutting (0.08 × 0.025) at 0.50 from front edge and 0.98 from right side.

71 (58). Console-dentil geison block   Pls. 22, 48

H. 0.32, p.W. 0.47, max. p.L. 0.735. Two joining fragments preserving three dentils and a corner console; front face and right side preserved. Lower face of console broken at outer end.
White marble.

From projecting block. Console projects at 45° angle to outer corner of block. Small additional scroll carved on sides at inner end in compensation for greater length of console. Trapezoidal coffer carved with thunderbolt. Right side cut diagonally to back at 0.30 from front edge measured along top. Upper surface of block along front edge smoothly dressed and *ca.* 0.05 higher.

72 (103). Console-dentil geison block

H. 0.31, p.W. 0.79, p.L. 1.15. Broken in two fragments. Right corner of block preserved with parts of three coffers and two consoles.

White marble. One large fragment still built into south drain of service area against central wall of façade.

Projecting block similar to **69** with small, roughly carved molding, for a console on adjacent block, carved along diagonal right edge. Trapezoidal area at right end dressed flat without coffering but with battered rosette, possibly five-petaled, with elongated and indented center. Ten-petaled rosette (five large, five small petals) in coffer to left. Consoles longer and wider than those of **69** (W. 0.16, est. L. *ca.* 0.245). Right end of block has anathyrosis and is cut back diagonally at 0.25 from front edge measured along top.

Cuttings. In upper surface, one to back at 0.31 from back corner, one to diagonal right side at 0.22 from back corner (measured along diagonal edge). Vertical clamp cutting to bottom in back (L. 0.10) at 0.27 from rear right corner.

73 (138). Console-dentil geison block   Pl. 48

P.H. 0.30, p.W. 0.31, p.L. 0.99. Fragment preserving part of one console, traces of two others, and two coffers.

White marble. Built into steps of house constructed in the 6th century in the colonnade along the west edge of the tiled court.

From block similar to **69**, but consoles are slightly larger (W. *ca.* 0.145, L. not preserved) and sides of consoles are not decorated. Six-petaled rosette in one coffer; other coffer not visible.

74 (94). Console-dentil geison block

H. 0.32, p.W. 0.60, W. bed 0.32, p.L. 0.55. Fragment preserving dentils, parts of two coffers, and one console. Small section of mitered left side preserved.

White marble. Found built into a late wall over east end of tiled court.

From projecting block similar to **69**. Finished left rear face cut diagonally. Clamp cutting in upper surface to rear.

Unassigned Blocks

75 (96). Console block   Pl. 23

H. front face 0.42, W. front face 0.37, L. soffit 1.63, L. finished area 0.58. Complete block.
White marble.

Rectangular console block; rear end roughly dressed. On front face, torus with horizontal leaf frieze. On S-shaped frieze above, one acanthus leaf and half of two others with water leaves between. Large bead-and-reel molding and fillet above. On sides, fillet in shallow relief at top and bottom with intermediate S-scroll at front end. Leaf set in both corners of scroll. Hole pierced diagonally through lower left side of block in unworked area.

76 (112). Console block   Pl. 23

H. front face 0.395, W. front face 0.36, L. soffit 1.36, L. finished area 0.62. Complete block.
White marble.

Block similar to **75** but without diagonal hole through lower side.

77 (120). Rectangular block

H. 0.41, W. 0.37, p.L. 1.05. Broken at one end.
White marble.

One side smoothly worked with anathyrosis. On upper face, smoothly worked band (W. 0.07) along one edge; setting line. Remainder roughly picked. On lower face, smoothly worked band (W. 0.085) along one edge; remainder roughly dressed. Preserved end roughly picked.

In height and width this block is similar to **75**.

78 (119). Rectangular block

H. 0.38, W. 0.38, max. p.L. 1.00. Broken at one end.
White marble.

Roughly picked on ends, bottom, and one side. Other side preserves smoothly dressed band (W. 0.025) along one edge. On upper face roughly dressed band (W. 0.10) between two smoothly dressed areas (W. 0.20 and 0.07).

In height and width this block is similar to **76**.

79 (55). Column shaft with spiral fluting   Pl. 23

Max. est. D. 0.309, min. est. D. 0.298, p.L. 0.81. Two joining fragments, broken at both ends.
Gray-veined marble.

80 (11). Corinthian capital   Pl. 23

H. 0.40, D. bottom 0.265. Three volutes and two corners of abacus broken away.
White marble.

Unfinished column capital: volutes, helices, and acanthus leaves not completely worked; abacus partially carved with three steps; rosette on abacus missing some details; marks of drill and chisel evident.

Cutting with remains of lead for hook of hook clamp in upper surface at 0.02 from left edge (L. 0.05); small centering hole with lines (L. 0.175) radiating out to circular setting line.

81 (41). Corinthian capital   Pl. 23

H. 0.345, D. bottom 0.295. Three corners of abacus broken away; lower part of capital missing.
White marble.

Upper part of unfinished capital; back roughly picked. The lower part of the capital was carved from a separate piece. Bottom claw chiseled with no dowel cutting. Upper surface dressed down leaving a small raised area along the right edge; front edge broken away, but beginning of raised area along this edge preserved. Hook-clamp cutting (L. *ca.* 0.15) to rear.

82 (A 744 a). Revetment plaque with carved molding   Pl. 24

P.W. 0.18, p.L. 0.195, Th. 0.02. Single fragment preserving two edges. Back appears burned.

Fior di pesco. Found in debris in front of façade walls.

Complete profile preserved of two cyma-recta moldings, one reversed, separated by sunken band (W. 0.03). Back smoothed.

83 (A 744 b). Revetment plaque with carved molding

P.W. 0.24, p.L. 0.36, Th. 0.02. Two joining fragments preserving one edge. Back appears burned.

Fior di pesco. Found in debris in front of façade walls.

Cyma-recta molding and sunken band (W. 0.03) preserved along broken edge. Back smoothed.

84 (A 743). Revetment plaque with carved molding   Pl. 24

P.W. 0.125, p.L. 0.53, Th. 0.015. Three joining fragments, preserving one corner and part of cyma-recta molding.

Fior di pesco. Found in debris in front of central wall of façade opposite northern niche.

For complete molding see **82**.

85 (A 745). Revetment plaque with carved molding   Pl. 24

P.W. 0.205, p.L. 0.43, Th. 0.017. Three joining fragments broken all around. Back burned.

Fior di pesco. Found in debris in front of façade walls.

Single cyma-recta molding forming two right angles in opposite directions to the central line, perhaps from a meander.

86 (158). Openwork parapet   Pl. 24

P.H. 0.17, p.W. 0.073, p.L. 0.15. Single fragment preserving part of border and small section of openwork. White marble. Found in Room 5, north of the façade.

Border carved on both faces with plain fascia on outer edge and cyma reversa on inner. One face dressed down on outer edge in band (W. 0.03 with slight bevel to bottom W. 0.025, depth *ca.* 0.01). Right edge of cyma reversa on this face cut back for openwork. Left side of fragment roughly picked.

87 (7). Window molding   Pl. 24

H. 0.115, p.W. 0.175, p.L. 0.31. Fragment preserving left end at lower edge; upper left edge broken away. Right end and projecting ledge at back broken. White marble.

Front carved with plain fascia, cavetto, and cyma reversa. Moldings end at *ca.* 0.09 from left end of block; fascia less carefully dressed below, but surface of block is broken away. Back of block cut down for 0.073, leaving projecting ledge (H. *ca.* 0.04). Upper surface (W. 0.065) smoothly dressed. Bottom roughly picked except for one small area at back right edge of fragment; water-worn band (W. *ca.* 0.04) along front edge of bottom.

88 (146). Window molding

H. 0.115, p.W. 0.14, p.L. 0.42. Fragment broken at both ends; projecting ledge broken away; moldings chipped.
White marble.

Similar to **87**, but setting line on narrow (W. 0.06) upper surface 0.01 in from back. Bottom smoothly dressed except for narrow, water-worn band (W. 0.01) along front edge.

89 (159). Window molding

P.H. 0.095, p.W. *ca.* 0.26, p.L. 0.23. Fragment broken at both ends (?).
White marble. From marble pile in Room 5, north of the façade.

Similar to **87**, but hook-clamp cutting in molded face. Bottom smoothly dressed except for water-worn band (W. *ca.* 0.03) along front edge.

LECHAION ROAD ENTRANCE AND COLONNADE

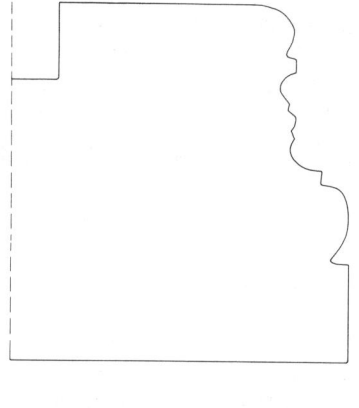

FIG. 2. Column base **90**. Scale 1:5

90 (149). Ionic column base on square plinth   Fig. 2

H. 0.17, total with plinth 0.235, D. 0.38.
White marble.

Ionic base with double scotia separated by fillet and astragal. Top of upper scotia in line with greatest diameter of torus above. Unfinished at back. Empolion cutting and pour channel.

This base is a mixture of the Greek and Roman Ionic forms, combining the double scotia of the Imperial Roman base and the Attic projection of the top fillet of the scotia. See footnote 21, p. 12 above.

An identical base was found within the Bath (**102**), and others of the same type, but of more careless treatment, were also found (e.g. **98**).

91 (122). Ionic column base on round plinth   Pl. 25

H. 0.23, total with plinth 0.30, D. 0.525, D. weatherline 0.505.
White marble. Two joining fragments.

Attic Ionic base with pour channel and empolion cutting.

Cf. *Corinth* I, i, p. 148, pl. XVII:C, D. For use of the Greek Ionic base in Corinth, see L. S. Meritt, "The Roman Ionic Base in Corinth," *Marsyas*, Suppl. I, *Essays in Memory of Karl Lehmann*, New York 1964, p. 302, and *eadem*, "The Geographical Distribution of Greek and Roman Ionic Bases," *Hesperia* 38, 1969, p. 195 and note 33.

After mid-1st century.

92 (91 a, b). Epistyle-frieze block   Pl. 25

H. 0.65, est. W. soffit 0.54, L. 2.75.
White marble. Two joining fragments preserving *ca.* one third of decorated face; large part of back missing. Crowning molding broken away.

Three-fascia epistyle, crowned by cyma reversa, S-shaped frieze above. Both faces of block carved, but decoration on one only. On soffit, overlapping leaf. Three fasciae of epistyle crowned by twisted ribbon which runs to the left, bead-and-reel, Lesbian leaf. Lotus and palmettes on frieze connected by spirals. Mason's mark Π on upper fascia of epistyle at right end.

Cuttings. Hook-clamp cuttings in middle fascia and in frieze at right edge of decorated face, two in back. Hook-clamp cuttings in top surface at each end of block at *ca.* 0.04 from decorated face.

93 (121). Geison block with dentils   Pl. 25

H. 0.25, W. 0.67, W. bed 0.457, L. 1.30.
White marble. One corner of corona broken away. Dentils chipped.

Dentils set slightly above bed. Plain bed mold above. Corona and crowning moldings plain. Ends roughly dressed.

For two other geison blocks of similar dimensions, see Notebook 357, nos. 126, 134. One of these fragments was used as a cover slab for the drain of the later latrine.

ROOM 2

94 (A 686). Revetment plaque   Pl. 26

H. 0.295, max. p.W. 0.205, est. W. at bottom 0.32, Th. 0.023. Group 16.
White marble. Right side missing; mended from two fragments.

Corinthian pilaster capital with helices starting from the volutes and without calices and cauliculi. Apparently only three acanthus leaves, since there is not sufficient room on the preserved portion for a leaf of the lower row. Volute and helix slightly concave. Five-petaled rosette with two small leaf tendrils between volute and helix. Similar rosette, partially preserved, on abacus, which is slightly concave. Back smoothly dressed with slightly higher band down one side (W. top 0.105, bottom 0.085).

95 (116). Epistyle-frieze block   Pl. 26

H. 0.31, W. 0.22, p.L. soffit 0.30, upper surface 0.55.
Fine-grained, pinkish marble. Right side broken away.

Three-fascia epistyle separated by plain astragals and crowned by cyma reversa decorated with Lesbian leaf. Frieze carved with lotus and palmettes connected by spirals. Crowning moldings: bead-and-reel and egg-and-dart. Preserved side also decorated. Two holes in egg-and-dart filled with hard cement, some cement on finished end.

Cuttings. Hook-clamp cutting on upper surface at back edge at 0.17 from right side. Cutting in soffit.

ROOM 3

96 (A 741 a). Revetment; dipinti   Pl. 26

P.H. 0.32, p.W. 0.26, Th. 0.024. P.H. letter 0.20. Group 17.
Fine-grained, gray marble with veins of mica. Mended from five joining fragments, preserving part of right edge.

Preserved are parts of two letters in red paint: Ϙ Ι
Abbreviation sign above.

97 (A 741 c). Revetment; dipinti   Pl. 26

P.H. 0.35, p.W. 0.27, Th. 0.02–0.025. P.H. letter 0.15, vertical spacing between lines 0.11. Group 17.
Greenish gray marble. Mended from six joining fragments, preserving part of right edge.

Parts of two lines of letters preserved in red paint: N Α / T
Coarse mortar along preserved edge in band 0.025 wide.

For other fragments of revetment with dipinti, see Groups 17 and 20 and Lot 5116.

ROOM 4

98 (150). Ionic column base on square plinth   Fig. 3

H. 0.205, p.W. base 0.17, L. base 0.29, est. D. 0.22.
White marble. Broken in half from front to back; left side preserved.

Ionic base with double scotia separated by astragal and fillet. Top of upper scotia in line with face of torus above. Small dowel hole in upper surface. Unfinished at back.

Careless treatment of same type of base as **90** and **102** (cf. Fig. 2). Several other similar bases were found in Room 4 and the service area below.

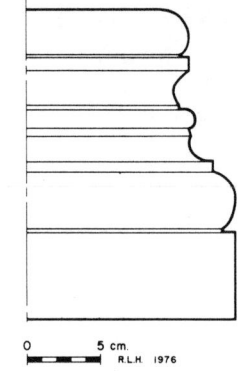

FIG. 3. Column base **98**. Scale 1:5

ROOM 5

99 (A 593). Lion's head waterspout   Pl. 27

P.H. 0.24, p.W. 0.20, Th. 0.052. Group 19.

Coarse-grained, grayish white marble. Broken on all four sides. Lower jaw and nose of lion missing.

Head of lion in low relief. Hollow in back, opening through mouth of lion. Back flat.

Fragment of veneer from wall of basin.

100 (24). Coffered cornice   Pl. 27

H. 0.09, p.W. 0.30, p.L. 0.31.
White marble. Broken at both ends and at back; parts of two coffers preserved.

Coffers with plain cyma reversa and rosette in center; five-leaved palmettes in corners. Bead-and-reel around coffers. On face acanthus scroll with small rosettes; plain fillets above and below.

101 (A 594). Coffered cornice   Pl. 27

H. 0.085, p.W. 0.10, p.L. 0.368.
White marble. Broken at both ends and at back.

Similar to **100**, but design on front face better preserved.

SERVICE AREA NORTH OF ROOM 5

102 (142). Ionic column base on square plinth

H. 0.175, total with plinth 0.235, D. 0.38.
White marble. Upper torus and plinth chipped.

Ionic base with double scotia separated by astragal and fillet. Top of upper scotia in line with face of torus above. Unfinished at back.

For identical base see **90** (Fig. 2).

SCULPTURE

COLONNADE

103 (S 2905). Relief plaque with four-horse chariot   Pl. 28

P.H. 0.83, p.L. 1.26.

White marble. Broken diagonally across right side. Heads and forequarters of three horses preserved; head of the fourth worn. Horses' front legs mostly broken away.

Publication: *Archaeological Reports*, 1969, p. 10, fig. 9; *BCH* 94, 1970, p. 953, fig. 137; *Hesperia* 50, 1981, p. 435, note 52 (mentioned).

The horses race to the left. The position of the four heads is the same with no attempt at variation. Manes carved in short parallel lines; sinews and bones of front legs well indicated. Reins carved where they lie on the horses' necks. Cyma-reversa molding at top of plaque. Incised line down left side of front at 0.02 from edge at top, widening to 0.045 at bottom. Back roughly picked.

Left side at back cut down for width of 0.055 to give edge with thickness of 0.05–0.052.

Cf. two similar reliefs from Cyprus, dated to the 2nd century (*Archaeological Reports*, 1957, p. 29, fig. 1 and V. Karageorghis, "Chronique des fouilles à Chypre en 1973," *BCH* 98, 1974, p. 844, fig. 39; *AJA* 80, 1976, p. 365, no. 5, fig. 21, listed there as Hellenistic).

104 (S 2906). Relief plaque with four-horse chariot   Pl. 28

H. 0.97, p.L. 1.53.

Fine-grained, white marble. Broken on right side, chipped on left. Surface of relief defaced. Top and bottom molding partially preserved.

Relief from same frieze as **103**, preserving four horses galloping to the left. Two sets of reins, charioteer's whip and part of his hand are preserved at upper right edge. Hole with incised line around it below lead horse. Clamp cuttings in upper surface of relief. Back roughly picked and water worn. Left side at back cut down for width of 0.055 as on **103**.

For parallels see **103**.

ROOM 1

105 (S 2828). Fountain group of Herakles and   Pl. 29
the Nemean Lion

P.H. 0.54, p.W. 0.35, p.Th. 0.37. Group 15.

White marble. Fragment broken at top and bottom and on statue's right side.

Lion with head turned to front, left paw partially preserved; left arm of human figure preserved, grasping lion around neck. Along back of lion a roughly cut channel, which ends in the lion's mouth, once held a metal water pipe.

The subject of Herakles and the Nemean Lion is recognised from a very similar group, also used as a fountain, found at Isthmia (O. Broneer, "Excavations at Isthmia, 1959–1961," *Hesperia* 31, 1962, pp. 18–19, no. 2, pl. 9:a). Another, also from a bath, was excavated at Argos (J. Marcadé, "Sculptures argiennes (III)," *Études argiennes* [*BCH*, Suppl. VI], Paris 1980, pp. 157–158, no. 184). The group ultimately derives from a Hellenistic original in which the head of the lion is turned to the rear. The scheme with the lion's head to the front is a variation found in other examples and not just in ones adapted for use as water fountains. See E. Künzl, *Frühhellenistische Gruppen*, Cologne 1968, pp. 70–75; for the variations, pp. 72–73, notes 8–10.

106 (S 2815). Head of Pan   Pl. 29

P.H. 0.138, p.W. 0.10. Group 15.

Fine-grained, white marble with mica. Broken at back and on top of head; nose and most of beard missing.

Publication: G. Daux, "Chronique des fouilles 1966," *BCH* 91, 1967, p. 635, fig. 4.

Head from a statuette of Pan with deep-set, slanting eyes and thick curving lips. One pointed ear preserved. Hair and beard are indicated by shallow carving.

For similar figures of Pan, see A. K. Orlandos, Πρακτικά, 1935 [1936], p. 79, fig. 7, dated 2nd century; Semni Karouzou, *National Archaeological Museum, Catalogue of Sculpture*, Athens 1968, nos. 251, 252.

107 (S 2749). Male portrait[1]   Pl. 29

P.H. 0.12, p.W. 0.081.

White marble with some mica. Fragment preserving lower left side of face; cracked diagonally across cheek and chin.

Lower part of left side of face of man with beard and moustache. Skin below corner of mouth shaved. Beard and moustache delineated with short chisel strokes.

Cf. H. P. L'Orange, *Studien zur Geschichte des spätantiken Porträts*, Rome 1965, no. 14, figs. 42, 44; no. 18, figs. 51, 52.

Date: Tetrarchic period.

ROOM 3

108 (S 2824). Head   Pl. 29

P.H. 0.243, p.W. 0.14, p.Th. 0.17.

White marble. Fragment broken at neck and from back of neck on left side across to right ear. Face also missing except for left ear, left cheek, outline of chin, and part of right ear.

Head of boy or man from life-size statue. Loose curls of hair brushed in alternating directions in rows on temple and head above, in less orderly arrangement on back of head. Ear deeply carved.

109 (S 2853). Head and chest of ram   Pl. 31

P.H. 0.575, W. 0.23. Groups 17 and 19.

White marble. Two joining fragments. Head battered.

Head and chest of ram with neck stretched up and head turned slightly to its right. Right horn and ear carved in high relief, fleece roughly indicated. A fold of drapery is preserved on ram's right side.

Possibly from a group of Hermes and a ram. Cf. S. Reinach, *Répertoire de la statuaire grecque et romaine* II, Paris 1897, p. 151, no. 8. Pausanias (II.3.4) describes a bronze group of Hermes and a ram set up on the Lechaion Road. For representations on coins, see F. Imhoof-Blumer and P. Gardner, *A Numismatic Commentary on Pausanias*, London 1885–1887, p. 23, pl. F:110, 111.

FAÇADE AREA

110 (S 2900). Head   Pl. 30

P.H. 0.15, W. 0.097, Th. 0.092. Group 21.

Fine-grained, white marble with veins of mica. Broken at neck; point and fold of cap which hangs down right side of head at back is broken off; nose, right cheek, mouth, and forehead battered. Marble discolored at back.

Youthful head from a statuette in the round. The head is turned to the viewer's left and wears a soft cap. Falling from beneath the cap, locks of hair lie low on the neck.

The headdress is perhaps a Phrygian cap with the point broken off. In this case the statue may be a representation of Attis or Ganymede. For Attis, see Reinach, *op. cit.* (under **109**), pp. 471–472; Th. Macridi-Bey and Ch. Picard, "Attis d'un Métrôon(?) de Cyzique,"

---

[1] Catherine de Grazia, *Excavations of the American School of Classical Studies at Corinth: The Roman Portrait Sculpture*, diss. Columbia University, 1973. The references are taken from her no. 48.

BCH 45, 1921, pp. 456–468. For Ganymede, see Reinach, *op. cit.*, pp. 473–475; G. Iacopi, *L'Antro di Tiberio a Sperlonga* [Istituto di Studi Romani, *I monumenti romani* IV], Rome 1963, figs. 109–111; J. Marcadé, "Sculptures argiennes," *BCH* 81, 1957, pp. 445–448, figs. 25, 26.

ROOM 5

111 (S 2767). Seated figure   Pl. 30

Max. p.H. 0.72, max. p.W. 0.49, p.Th. 0.33.
White marble with veins of mica. Two joining fragments.

From a draped figure seated on a stool, of which the seat and one leg are preserved.

COLONNADE DRAIN

112 (S 2899). Statue support (?)   Pl. 30

H. 0.78, W. bottom 0.335, L. bottom 0.415. Group 26.
Fine-grained, white marble with some mica. Fragment preserving right side of bust and most of back. Left side hacked away. Surface badly worn and pitted.

Bust of bearded man with long hair which hangs down his back. Shoulders and chest roughly carved. The head is turned slightly to the viewer's left. A fold of drapery of some kind hangs down the right side of the figure's head and over its back. Although broken away on top of the head, the drapery seems to have continued across the top.

The bust is presumably a statue support. For a similar type of support, in this case only a head, cf. Reinach, *op. cit.* (under **109**), ii, p. 796.

TERRACOTTA

ROOM 3

113 (FM 88). Tube from heating system   Fig. 4, Pl. 31

D. 0.062 and 0.055, L. 0.10. Group 17.
Dark brown, gritty clay, blackened on exterior. Mended from three fragments.

Hollow cylinder flaring at one end.

114 (FM 92). Tube from heating system   Fig. 4

Est. D. 0.04 and 0.06, L. 0.065. No pottery group.
Coarse, reddish brown clay. Fragment preserving both ends.

From a hollow cylinder with an everted lip at one end.

115 (FM 91). Tube from heating system   Fig. 4

D. 0.071, p.L. 0.06. No pottery group.
Coarse, red clay. Fragment preserving one end.

From a hollow cylinder with a thick flaring end. For other tubes, see Groups 17, 33, and FM 90 in the Corinth Museum.

ROOM 5

116 (FM 79). Tubulus   Pl. 31

H. 0.345, W. 0.105, L. 0.31. Group 19.
Reddish buff clay, blackened by fire. Mended from several pieces. Half of one face and of one side missing.

A rectangular tube, open at top and bottom, with two oval vents in the narrow sides.

117 (FP 203 a). Stamped tile   Pl. 31

P.W. 0.20, p.L. 0.12, Th. 0.025, H. letters 0.025. Group 19.
Orange clay. Broken and mended from two fragments.

Part of the stamp preserved: COL.IVLC.   For

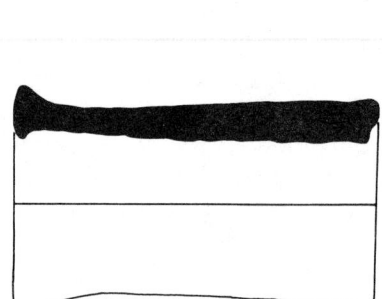

113

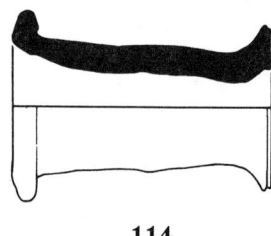

114

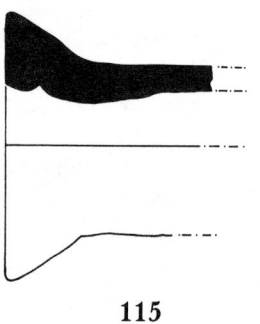

115

Fig. 4. Terracotta heating tubes **113**–**115**. Scale 1:2

other similar stamped tiles from Corinth, cf. *Corinth* X, fig. 135:a; *Hesperia* 36, 1967, pp. 12, 38, 427, fig. 20, pls. 6:d, 91:f; *Hesperia* 38, 1969, p. 101, pl. 30:q. The use of Latin letters is an indication of early date (*Corinth* X, p. 139; *Corinth* VIII, iii, pp. 18–19).

118 (FP 203 b). Stamped tile   Pl. 31

P.W. 0.18, p.L. 0.19, Th. 0.025. Group 19.
Orange clay. Fragment broken all around.

Part of the stamp preserved:

.. L.COR.AL.

The O and R are connected by a short horizontal stroke. The final L is stamped at a higher level than the remainder of the stamp.

The letters AL at the end are probably the abbreviation for the name of the manufacturer. Cf. *Corinth* X, p. 136, note 1.

METAL

ROOM 3

119 (MF-68-47). Spike and clamp   Pl. 32

Spike: L. 0.34, Th. 0.017 tapering to 0.011. Clamp: W. 0.024, p.L. 0.295, Th. 0.0175. Group 2.
Bronze. Clamp broken at one end.

Clamp with round head pierced by square hole. Tapering spike cut diagonally at large end.

For seven fragmentary bronze spikes, see Group 2.

120 (MF 12658 a, b). Shaft and crosspiece   Pl. 32

Shaft: W. 0.045, p.L. 1.44, Th. 0.042. Crosspiece: p.L. 0.19, Th. 0.035–0.04. Group 2.
Iron. Shaft mended from two fragments. Corroded.

Shaft with wedge-shaped crosspiece driven through at a right angle.

For other fragments of crosspieces and shaft, see Group 2.

POTTERY

COLONNADE

Fig. 5. Late Roman C bowl **121**. Scale 1:2

121 (C-68-79). Bowl with thickened rim, Late Roman C[2]   Fig. 5

H. 0.05, D. 0.163. Group 26.
Hard, red, homogenous fabric with a few white inclusions; dull red glaze, much worn. Complete profile; two thirds of bowl preserved; broken and mended.

False ring foot. Four concentric rings on floor; two shallow grooves around inside of rim; exterior grooved below rim.

The fabric, technique, and ring foot of this bowl are all closely paralleled in Late Roman C ware. The shape appears to be transitional between Forms 1 and 3 (Hayes, pp. 325–327, 329).

Another example of the same shape from Group 26 is stored in Lot 5140.

First half to middle of 5th century.

122 (C-68-99). Stamped base   Pl. 32

Max. dimension 0.115. Group 26.
Hard, light reddish brown (Munsell 5YR 6/4) fabric with flecks of mica and white inclusions, some of which have burned out; reddish yellow slip (Munsell 5YR 7/6). Single sherd preserving half of flat base and oblique lower wall.

Some paring in concentric bands on exterior and interior. On interior within circular groove, double-ribbed Greek cross with triangular pendants.

The fabric of this fragment cannot yet be classified. For same general type of decoration, cf. *Antioch* IV, i, fig. 34, center (Hayes, p. 365, motif 70).

123 (C-68-105). Plate, African Red Slip Ware   Pl. 32

P.L. 0.102, p.W. 0.06. Group 26.
Hard, red, micaceous fabric with some white inclusions. Single fragment from floor of plate; broken all around.

From plate with flat floor. Stamped decoration of eight-petaled rosettes within triple groove; central circle with dot.

The decorative motif is generally similar to Hayes, motifs 56–59 (p. 238, fig. 41), but these are not listed as occurring on this shape of plate.

124 (C-68-104). Bowl, Asia Minor "Light-Coloured" Ware   Pl. 32

---

[2] For renaming of Late Roman C Ware, see Hayes, *SLRP*, p. 525.

P.L. 0.166, p.W. 0.14. Group 26.

Slightly gritty, very hard, pale brown fabric (Munsell 10YR 8/4) with flecks of gold mica; light red to reddish brown glaze (Munsell 2.5YR 6/8–5/4) with metallic sheen. Fragment preserving full profile; center of floor missing.

Broad bowl on ring foot with flanged vertical rim. Two bands of multiple rouletting on floor, one over foot; circular groove in floor. Two bands of notched rouletting on exterior of rim.

Cf. Hayes, p. 409, fig. 92:1; Hayes, *SLRP*, p. 534.

Second half of 5th century.

125 (C-68-33). Storage jar; dipinto   Pl. 33

P.H. 0.168, p.W. 0.16. Group 26.

Coarse, red fabric with white inclusions and flecks of mica; buff slip. Fragment preserving neck, part of shoulder, and strap handle.

Body spirally grooved. On shoulder, dipinto in red paint.

126 (C-68-47). Storage jar; dipinto   Pl. 33

H. 0.14, D. mouth 0.087. Group 26.

Moderately coarse, white fabric with some inclusions, a little mica. Slipped. Four joining fragments from shoulder, neck, and part of one handle.

Faint wheel ridging on shoulder; grooved handle; slightly flaring lip. Illegible dipinto in red paint on shoulder.

127 (C-68-347). Storage amphora, red slipped   Pl. 33

P.H. 0.262, D. rim 0.108. Group 26.

Soft, reddish yellow clay (Munsell 5YR 7/6) with flecks of mica; light-red to red slip (Munsell 10R 6/8–5/8). Fragment mended from ten sherds. Partial profile preserved. Large chip in lip and one handle; smaller chips in handle and slip.

From an amphora with ovoid body, short, narrow, concave neck; outward-thickened and squared rim with slight groove around inside at top. Ridged handles from neck to shoulder.

Partial red slip ending below shoulder.

Late Roman, 4th–6th century.

128 (C-67-62). Storage amphora   Fig. 6, Pl. 34

H. 0.46, D. 0.34. Group 29.

Coarse, pinkish buff fabric. Mended; a few body fragments missing.

Rounded base with small projecting toe. Ovoid body. Broad neck tapering up to flaring rim and rounded lip. Handles oval in section. Spiral grooving, slightly flattened, on shoulder and upper third of body.

Cf. G. F. Bass, "Underwater Excavations at Yassi Ada: A Byzantine Shipwreck," *ArchAnz* 77, 1962, cols. 552–

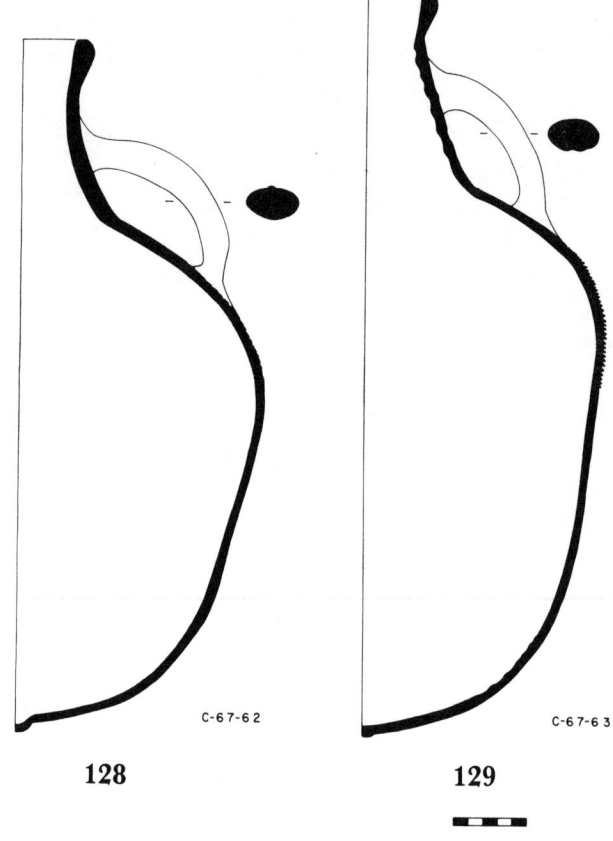

Fig. 6. Storage amphoras **128** and **129**. Scale 1:5

553, fig. 6:a; J. W. Hayes, "Excavations at Saraçhane in Istanbul," *DOPapers* 22, 1968, p. 215, no. 8.

Late 6th–early 7th century.

129 (C-67-63). Storage amphora   Fig. 6, Pl. 34

H. 0.49, D. 0.315. Group 29.

Coarse, reddish buff clay, some fragments burned. Mended; large sections of body and shoulder missing.

Round base with small knob. Broad neck tapering up to flaring rim. Handles oval in section. Spiral grooving, slightly flattened, on shoulder and upper part of body.

Cf. Hayes, *loc. cit.* (under **128**), no. 3; I. Barnea, "L'incendie de Dinogetia au VIe siècle," *Dacia*, n.s. 10, 1966, p. 254, fig. 12:7 (Dinogetia was destroyed in 559, *op. cit.*, p. 258); *Histria* 1, 1954, p. 455, fig. 383; G. Daux, "Chronique des fouilles," *BCH* 89, 1965, p. 947, figs. 22, 23 (deposit dated to the end of the 6th—beginning of the 7th century); *Kythera, Excavations and Studies Conducted by the University of Pennsylvania Museum and the British School at Athens*, J. Coldstream and G. L. Huxley, edd., London 1972, nos. 49–52, 55, fig. 52, pl. 49 (late 6th—early 7th century).

Late 6th–early 7th century.

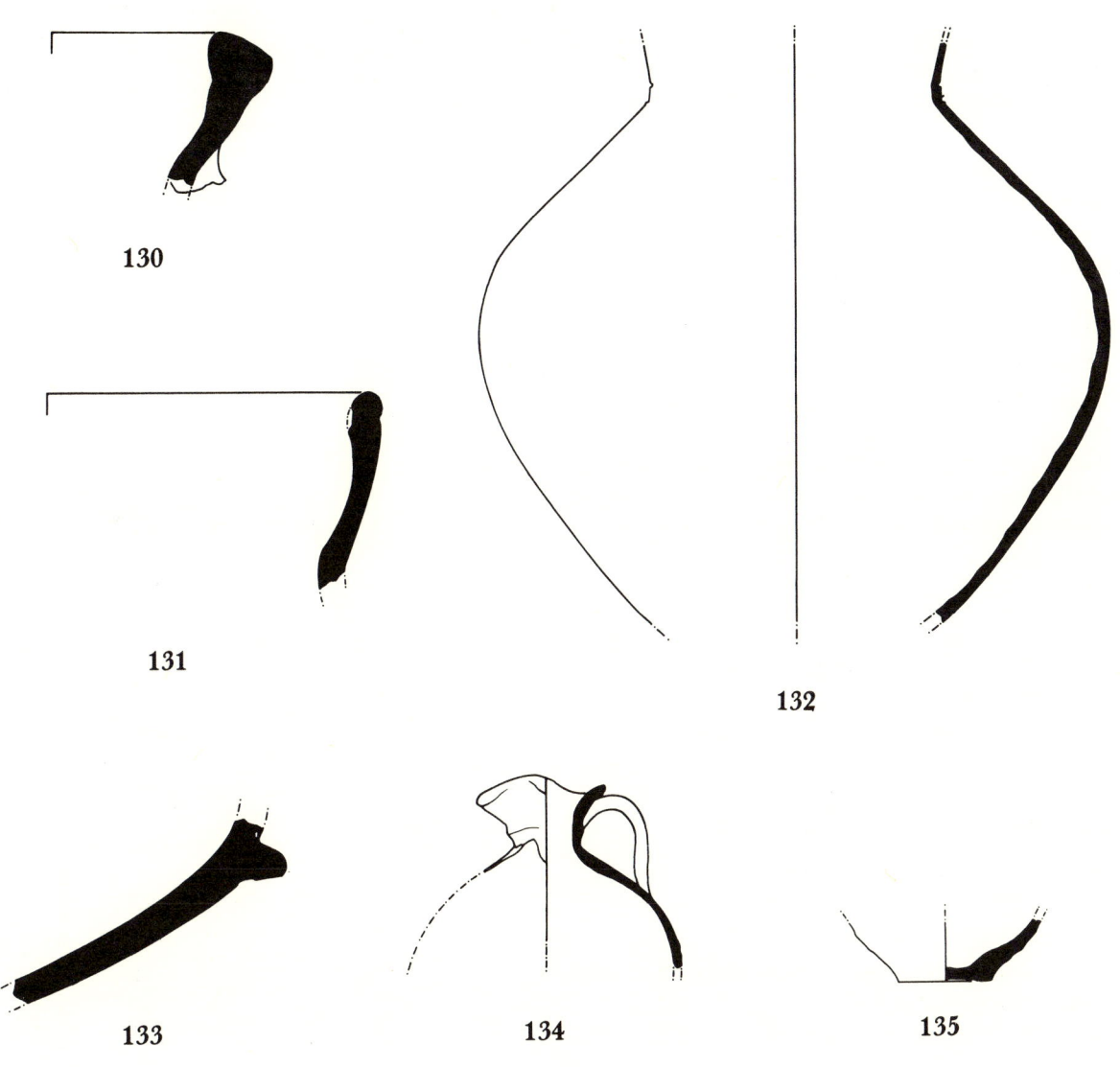

Fig. 7. Pottery: **130–135**. Scale 1:2

SERVICE AREA NORTHEAST OF ROOM 3

130 (C-66-243). Rim fragment from amphora   Fig. 7
P.H. 0.045, est. D. rim 0.115. Group 3.
Hard, gritty, orange-buff clay; slipped. Fragment of rim, preserving the attachment point of one handle.

From an amphora with ovoid body, narrow neck, and flaring rim; lip curves inward at top. Rim slightly ridged on exterior.

From an African amphora of a type exported from before A.D. 200 until the 4th century. Cf. *Agora* V, J 50, dated late 2nd to early 3rd century; *Studi Miscellanei* 21, *Ostia* III, ii, A. Carandini and C. Panella, edd., [Rome 1973], pp. 575–576, 629, figs. 25, 26.

131 (C-66-244). Flanged bowl, Athenian ware   Fig. 7
P.H. 0.055, p.W. 0.46. Group 3.
Soft, yellow buff clay with fine light and dark inclusions; matt, yellow brown glaze on interior fired dark brown on exterior. Fragment from rim.

From a bowl with vertical rim and groove just below lip on exterior.

Cf. *Agora* V, K 42, mid-3rd century; **131** is from a similar bowl. These were made in Athens beginning in the first half of the 3rd century and continuing until the 5th.[3]

---

[3] The life of these bowls is longer than indicated in *Agora* V. For further discussion see the publication of the Roman coarse ware from the Athenian Agora, in preparation by Barbara Johnson.

ROOM 2

132 (C-68-337). Jug   Fig. 7
P.H. 0.16. Group 4.
Hard, red, gritty clay. Fragment from body and base of neck.

From a globular jug with two grooves around base of neck, single groove around shoulder.
Cf. *Agora* V, K 82, K 83, mid-3rd century.

133 (C-68-338). Flanged bowl, Athenian ware   Fig. 7
P.H. 0.087, p.W. 0.08. Group 4.
Hard, pinkish orange clay; dark brown, slightly lustrous glaze. Fragment.

From a basin with flange on exterior, groove beneath flange.
Cf. *Agora* V, K 29–31, mid-3rd century; Hayes, p. 407.
For date, see **131**.

ROOM 4

134 (C-66-245). Miniature jug   Fig. 7
P.H. 0.061. Group 5.
Hard, fine, buff clay; dull, dark brown partial glaze. Fragment from neck and shoulder.

From a trefoil-mouthed jug. Wheel ridging on body below shoulder. Strap handle from mouth to shoulder.
Cf. *Agora* V, K 69, mid-3rd century. The fabric of the Corinth example is much finer and thinner.

135 (C-66-246). Miniature cooking pot   Fig. 7
P.H. 0.019, D. base 0.022. Group 5.
Dark gray clay. Base fragment.

From a miniature cooking pot with flat base, slight wheel ridging on body.
Cf. *Agora* V, K 97, mid-3rd century.

ROOM 5

136 (C-65-152). Bowl or dish, African Red Slip Ware   Pl. 34
Max. p.W. 0.083, max. p.L. 0.07. Group 19.
Red clay; dull red glaze on interior. Fragment from base.

Ring foot. Stamped decoration, on interior, of a saint with right arm raised, left holding cross; double groove around stamp. Cf. *Antioch* IV, i, fig. 32:1; Hayes, p. 266, type 239, B for decoration. For vessel form, cf. Hayes, form 104.

Second or third quarter 6th century.

137 (C-65-153). Amphora; graffito   Pl. 34
P.H. 0.07, p.W. 0.075. H. of letter 0.019. Group 19.
Gritty, reddish orange clay, unslipped. Fragment from shoulder.

Wheel ridged. Graffito: K A. Perhaps the number 21. Cf. *Agora* XXI, F 297; I 6.

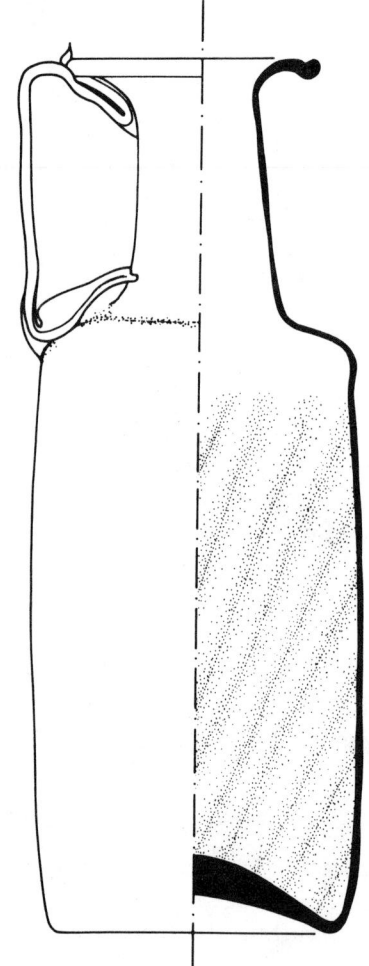

Fig. 8. Glass one-handled jug **138**. Scale 1:2

GLASS

COLONNADE

138 (MF-68-33). One-handled, four-sided jug[4]   Fig. 8, Pl. 33

H. 0.235, W. base 0.08, D. rim 0.072. Group 26.

Dark bluish green glass with many bubbles of different sizes, some very large. Slight traces of weathering. Mended from many pieces; fragments of body missing.

Concave base with pontil mark. Four-sided body. Cylindrical neck tapering upward to outturned rim, which is rounded off; slight groove around rim on top. Flat strap handle, unribbed, and attached under rim and at shoulder, folded twice (upward and downward).

Body both inside and out covered with sloping corrugations which were achieved by optic blowing. Corrugations on inside deeper than those on outside.

Rectangular jugs of this shape are common throughout the first four centuries after Christ. Cf. D. B. Harden, *Roman Glass from Karanis*, Ann Arbor 1936, Class XI C, nos. 749–764; idem, "The Glass," in *Camulodunum*, C. F. C. Hawkes and M. R. Hull, edd. [Society of Antiquaries of London Research Committee, Report 14], 1947, p. 306, no. 98; C. Isings, *Roman Glass from Dated Finds*, Gronigen 1957, Form 50b; O. Vessberg, "Glass: Typology, Chronology," *Swedish Cyprus Expedition*, IV, iii, *The Hellenistic and Roman Periods in Cyprus*, Stockholm 1956, pp. 148–149, 200–201, type A IV. The technique of optic blowing seems, however, to be late, occurring in Iran from the 5th century onwards. See C. J. Lamm, *Glass from Iran*, Stockholm 1935, p. 10 for explanation of the technique, pls. 18–20 for examples.

LAMPS

ROOM 5

139 (L 4375). Corinthian lamp   Pl. 35

W. 0.067, L. 0.087. Group 19.

Reddish brown, micaceous clay with white inclusions. Intact.

Disk with chi-iota monogram, framing ring. Herringbone rim. Solid handle with ladder pattern on top, punched at base. On base, within double circle:

XIO NHC

Cf. Garnett, pl. 43:14. Derived from Attic lamps of the Chione workshop. Cf. *Agora* VII, pp. 55–56. The series of Corinthian lamps with this signature dates from the mid-5th to mid-6th century.

Mid-5th to mid-6th century.

140 (L 4455). Corinthian lamp   Pl. 35

W. 0.08, L. 0.105. Group 19.

Dark reddish brown, micaceous clay with white inclusions. Intact.

Disk with rosette; herringbone rim. Solid handle with triple groove on upper surface, double on lower. On base, within double oval groove, signature ΔIO NYE with branch.

Derived from Attic lamps from the shop of Διονυσιά. For the Attic shop, cf. *Agora* VII, pp. 25, 31.

141 (L 4361). Attic lamp   Pl. 35

W. 0.06, p.L. 0.115. Group 19.

Reddish yellow clay with white inclusions, slipped. Nozzle missing; wick hole burned.

Oval disk with channel to neck, hole in channel, cross with flaring bars. Rim: raised branch. Knob handle. Circular base ring with ridge to handle.

Cf. *Agora* VII, no. 2591.

6th century.

COLONNADE

142 (L 4515). Corinthian lamp   Pl. 35

W. 0.065, p.L. 0.085. Group 26.

Reddish clay with white inclusions, fired buff on surface. Traces of burning on upper surface. Nozzle missing.

Disk with channel to wick hole, jeweled cross; row of concentric circles on rim. Pointed knob handle. Base: circular base ring with ridge to handle; small rings within.

On the basis of fabric and technique this lamp belongs with other Corinthian imitations of North African lamps. For discussion of these, see Garnett, pp. 178–184, 195–197.

6th century.

143 (L 4513). Attic lamp   Pl. 35

W. 0.09, L. 0.09. Group 26.

Light reddish buff, micaceous clay. Handle chipped, otherwise intact. Wick hole burned.

Disk with small rings between rays; framing ring.

---

[4] I am indebted to D. B. Harden and G. D. Weinberg for help with this jug.

Rim: dolphins, circles, conventional ivy patterns; wick hole. Small knob handle. Base ring.
Cf. *Corinth* IV, ii, no. 1502.
Second half 6th century.

144 (L 4514). Corinthian lamp   Pl. 35
W. 0.081, L. 0.11. Group 26.
Red, micaceous clay with white inclusions. Filling hole chipped, wick hole burned.

Disk with rosette of 14 petals, plain rim; air hole indicated but not pierced. Knob handle. Base: inverted branch in almond-shaped groove.

On the basis of the fabric and technique of manufacture this lamp was made in Corinth.
5th to 6th century.

145 (L 4519). Attic lamp   Pl. 35
W. 0.081, L. 0.11. Group 26.
Reddish buff, micaceous clay with some inclusions. Intact. Burnt at nozzle.

Plain disk with framing ring and four holes; herringbone rim. Sides of nozzle double grooved. Solid handle with double groove on upper surface, four on lower; three small circles at junction of handle with disk. Base:
XIO NH C (within double almond-shaped groove)
Cf. *Agora* VII, nos. 2665–2668.
First half of 5th to mid-5th century.

146 (L 4516). Lamp   Pl. 35
W. 0.066, p.L. 0.10. Group 26.
Pinkish white to pink micaceous clay (Munsell 7.5YR 8/2–7/4). Thick reddish brown to red slip (Munsell 2.5YR 4/4–5/8) on upper surface; lamp apparently dipped. Nozzle missing; traces of burning near nozzle.

Circular rayed disk with framing ring; wavy lines on rim, arcs on nozzle. Small solid handle with shallow double groove on top. Base ring.

For shape cf. *Agora* VII, pls. 42–45. The glaze is unusual, and probably the lamp is an import.
Late Roman.

147 (L 4476). Corinthian lamp   Pl. 35
W. 0.065, L. 0.09. Group 26.
Reddish brown clay with white inclusions. Intact.

Square disk with worn cross, framing band; circles at corners; wavy lines on rim. Nozzle: sides double grooved, punched circle. Solid, double-grooved handle with branch on each side. Base: inverted branch within double almond-shaped groove; punched circle at top and bottom.

Derived from a 4th-century Attic lamp type. Cf. *Agora* VII, no. 1430. For the wavy lines on the rim, cf. Garnett, no. 16.
Late 5th to 6th century.

INSCRIPTIONS

ROOM 5

148 (I 2636). Latin inscription   Pl. 36
Max. p.H. 0.082, p.L. 0.285, Th. 0.05. Max. p.H. of letters 0.025, W. of letters 0.02–0.035. Group 19.
Coarse-grained, white marble. Mended from two joining fragments; broken all around. Weathered.

Front surface smoothed, back roughly picked. Front face carved in two planes with inscription on lower vertical plane; the plane above slopes inwards. The upper part of seven letters preserved, well cut with serifs:
OUIVIIV

149 (I 2640). Latin or Greek inscription   Pl. 36
P.H. 0.065, p.L. 0.13, Th. 0.022. P.H. of letters 0.017, W. of letters 0.06. Group 19.
Fine-grained, white marble. Fragment broken all around.

Back and front faces smoothly dressed. Parts of three letters preserved, well cut with serifs:
. IO

150 (I 2667). Latin or Greek inscription   Pl. 36
P.H. 0.275, p.L. 0.198, Th. 0.047. H. of letters 0.065, W. of letters 0.035–0.045. Group 19.
Coarse-grained, white marble. Mended from two joining fragments; broken all around.

Front and back faces smoothly dressed. Part of two lines of letters preserved, well cut with serifs:
C A
A V

151 (I 2643). Greek inscription   Pl. 36
P.H. 0.16, max. p.L. 0.19, Th. 0.045. P.H. of letters 0.03, W. of letters 0.028. Group 19.
Coarse-grained, white marble. Mended from two joining fragments. Lower part of face broken away, but bottom edge partially preserved.

Front and back faces smoothly dressed. Parts of three letters preserved.
O C Π

152 (I 2693). Greek inscription   Pl. 36
P.H. 0.125, p.L. 0.07, Th. 0.05. P.H. of letters 0.04–0.05, W. of letters 0.019. Group 19.
Fine-grained, white marble. Single fragment broken all around.

Front and back faces smoothly dressed. Two letters and abbreviation sign preserved:
. K̄ A

APPENDICES AND CONCORDANCES

APPENDIX I
BRICKWORK SPECIFICATIONS

The brickwork used in the Bath is presented in tabular form, Table 1 for brickwork of walls, benches, parapet walls, etc., Table 2 for hypocaust columns. The type of information given in these tables is based on the study by R. Ginouvès of brickwork at Argos.[1] Munsell soil-color charts were used for the colors of the bricks and of the bonding material of the hypocaust columns when not of mortar.

In attempting to measure and describe the brickwork of the Bath it was not always possible to obtain complete information, either because of partial excavation or because the walls were so well preserved that complete bricks were not visible. Furthermore, in some instances only a small sample could be measured. It seemed desirable, however, to list all available information.

Since the Bath had a life of almost four centuries and throughout that period underwent extensive reconstructions and repairs, there were numerous examples of different brickwork to record. Although some generalizations can be made about the type of brickwork in use, there were enough differences, particularly in the mortar thicknesses and treatment of the mortar, that it seemed necessary to present the information in the tables by location rather than by type of brickwork.

At the present state of the excavation it has not been possible to construct a chronological chart to illustrate by examples from the Bath changes in brickwork in Corinth during the construction phases of the building, from approximately A.D. 200 to A.D. 580. The brickwork of around A.D. 200 (no. 1), however, is dated by the architecture and that of the early 6th century (no. 23) by stratigraphy. A few conclusions can also be drawn about the types of bricks in use.

In the early period, i.e. around A.D. 200, a small, square brick cut diagonally was used, together with bipedales and voussoir bricks (no. 1), and sesquipedales also were apparently used (no. 2). In the 3rd century the same square brick, cut diagonally, continued to be used together with sesquipedales, cut diagonally in eight triangles (no. 8), and slightly thicker sesquipedales cut in two rectangles or possibly four triangles (no. 8). Sesquipedales are also found in reconstruction work in Room 5 (nos. 16b, 19, 20), but these examples are not dated.

In later periods in the building a square brick was used uncut. This type of brick is found in the façade (nos. 4, 6), in Room 2 (no. 7), in Room 3 (nos. 10–12), in Room 5 (nos. 16a, 19a, 20a, 21), and in the façade area (nos. 23, 25). Its size range is 0.28–0.31 by 0.30–0.32 m. The dated examples of these bricks show that in the early 6th century they were used with a mortar thickness about equal to that of the bricks (no. 23). The mortar was smoothed obliquely. The other instances of the use of this brick are not securely dated, although it is possible that it occurs around A.D. 400 (no. 6). The types of bricks used in the Great Bath thus change over the centuries. The bricks also become progressively thinner (from *ca.* 0.04 m. to *ca.* 0.03 m.), and the mortar becomes thicker. Generalizations about dating on the basis of brick and mortar thicknesses can, however, be dangerous. The type of construction seems also to have an effect on mortar thickness. The parapet of the west pool in Room 3 (no. 10), apparently constructed in the same period as the dated brickwork (no. 23),[2] exhibits thicker mortar joints.

It has not been possible to supplement the information gained from the Bath with information from other sites in Greece. The proportions of bricks to mortar in the early brickwork of the Bath (no. 1) compare best with Thermes A at Argos,[3] but these baths are at present dated to the Hadrianic period,[4] a date which does not conform to that proposed for the Great Bath on the Lechaion Road. Thermes B in the Agora at Argos, at present dated only later than Thermes A, also have similar brickwork.[5] The thickness of the

---

[1] Ginouvès, *Théâtron*, pp. 217–245.
[2] See pp. 48–49 above.
[3] Ginouvès, *Théâtron*, p. 233.
[4] P. Aupert, "Thermes A," *BCH* 98, 1974, p. 773, early 2nd century.
[5] Ginouvès, *Théâtron*, p. 238; P. Aupert, "Agora: Les thermes B," *BCH* 107, 1983, p. 853.

APPENDIX I

mortar joints for the early brickwork of the Great Bath (no. 1) is close to that of a construction in Thermes A at Argos, dated to the second quarter of the 3rd century,[6] but the thickness of the bricks is different.

A comparison with brickwork in Rome is equally inconclusive. Hadrianic bricks average 0.038 m. in thickness with a mortar thickness of 0.012–0.015 m.[7] In the Antonine period bricks average 0.033 m. in thickness with a mortar thickness of 0.013–0.018 m.[8] Severan bricks measure 0.025–0.033 m. in thickness with a mortar thickness of 0.005–0.025 m.[9] The thickness of the mortar joints in the early period of the Great Bath (no. 1) compares best with the Severan examples in Rome. The thickness of the bricks, however, is not paralleled in that period.

Until further study of brickwork in Greece has been undertaken, it seems that dating by this method must be based on dated buildings only from the particular site concerned. Corinth does not possess many examples of dated brickwork, although the baths in the South Stoa, dated to around A.D. 300, use bricks similar to late examples in the Great Bath on the Lechaion Road (no. 23).[10]

In conclusion, it seems that on the basis of the brickwork of the Great Bath, bricks in Corinth in the late 2nd or early 3rd century averaged 0.04 m. in thickness and were used with mortar joints with an average thickness of approximately 0.02 m. (nos. 1, 2). These proportions seem to have continued in the 3rd century as attested by the brickwork of the north apse of Room 2 (no. 8). By the early 6th century bricks averaged 0.03 m. in thickness and were used with mortar joints averaging 0.032 m. in thickness (no. 23).

---

[6] Ginouvès, *Théâtron*, p. 234.
[7] G. Lugli, *La tecnica edilizia romana*, Rome 1957, p. 604.
[8] *Ibid.*, p. 608.
[9] *Ibid.*, p. 611.
[10] *Corinth* I, iv, p. 151.

APPENDIX I
TABLE 1: BRICKWORK

LOCATION	BRICKS						
	Color	Original type	Front	Back	Sides	Th.	Th. 10 bricks
1. Main building period: Rooms 1–5, 7, and exterior walls	a. Light reddish brown to light red (2.5YR 6/4–6/6); light gray to pale yellow (5Y 7/2–7/3)	Square bricks cut diagonally in half	0.27–0.30	—	0.21–0.22, 0.19–0.22 (sometimes used as front face)	0.035–0.045 av. 0.04	0.402 0.368 0.395
	b. Pink to reddish yellow (5YR 6/8–7/8)	Bipedales	0.58–0.60	—	0.58–0.60	0.05	—
	c. Reddish yellow (5YR 6/8)	Voussoir	0.59	—	—	Max. 0.05–0.055 Min. 0.024–0.027	—
2. Colonnade: foundations of east stylobate (p. 9)	Pale yellow (2.5Y 8/4); pink (5YR 7/4–8/3)	Sesquipedales cut in eight triangles	0.28–0.29	—	0.21–0.22	0.038–0.04	only 6 courses
3. Tiled court (p. 11)	Reddish yellow (5YR 7/6); yellow (2.5Y 8/4)	Rectangular	0.10	0.10	0.06	0.02–0.03	—
4. Façade: north wall, blocked window (p. 16)	Light reddish brown (2.5YR 6/4)	Square	0.30	0.30	0.30	0.03	only 4 courses
5. Façade: south wall, blocked window (p. 16, fn. 10)	Reddish yellow (5YR 7/6)	Square or rectangular	0.42–0.435	—	—	0.035–0.05	only 3 courses
6. Façade: central wall, reconstruction to south niche and pier (p. 31)	Reddish yellow (5YR 7/6); pale yellow (5Y 8/3–8/4)	Square or rectangular	0.29–0.32	—	—	0.026–0.03	only 6 courses
7. Room 2: north apse pool, parapet wall (p. 38)	Pale yellow (5Y 8/3)	Square or rectangular	0.31	0.31	0.32	0.03, 0.035	only 3 courses
8. Room 2: north apse walls and foundations (a in walls, b and c in upper section of foundations, c in two lower sections) (p. 39)	a. Light reddish brown to light red (2.5YR 6/4–6/6); light gray to pale yellow (5Y 7/2–7/3)	Sesquipedales cut in eight triangles	0.28–0.30	—	0.20–0.21, 0.18–0.20 (sometimes used as front face)	0.035–0.045 av. 0.04	only 8 courses could be measured
	b. Reddish brown (5YR 5/4); light reddish to reddish brown (2.5YR 6/4–4/4)	Square bricks cut diagonally in half	0.27–0.29	—	0.19–0.20	0.035–0.05, av. 0.0425	0.425
	c. Reddish yellow (5YR 7/6–6/6); light reddish brown (5YR 6/4)	Sesquipedales cut in two rectangles (or possibly four triangles)	0.41–0.44	—	—	0.045–0.05, av. 0.045	only 6 courses
9. Room 2: north apse, blocked doorway (p. 39)	Light reddish brown (5YR 6/3)	Square or rectangular	0.49, 0.62	—	—	0.04–0.05, av. 0.045	0.45
10. Room 3: pool against west wall, parapet, and outer step (p. 45)	Pale yellow (5Y 8/3); reddish yellow (5YR 7/6)	Rectangular (or square)	0.28	0.28	0.31	0.03–0.032	only 2 courses
11. Room 3: bench on east side of room (p. 45)	Light reddish brown (5YR 7/3)	Rectangular (or square)	0.28	0.28	0.30–0.31	0.03	only 3 courses

TABLE 1: BRICKWORK

	MORTAR			
Color and composition	Th.	Th. 10 joints	Treatment of joints	Th. 10 bricks and 10 joints
1. White with sand, small pebbles, some finely ground brick	0.015–0.025, av. 0.019–0.022	0.21	An incised line along bottom of horizontal joints	0.60–0.64
same	same	same	same	same
same	—	—	—	—
2. White with sand, small pebbles	0.015, 0.025–0.03 alternately	—	Smooth	—
3. White with a little finely ground brick	—	—	Smooth	
4. White with pebbles, sand, small amount of ground brick	0.025–0.05	—	Smooth	—
5. Pink with coarsely ground brick fragments, small pebbles	0.03–0.04	—	Smooth	—
6. Light gray, coarse with small stones	0.038–0.05	—	Smooth	—
7. Pink, coarse with large quantity of brick fragments	0.047–0.065	—	Smooth	—
8. White with small pebbles, sand, some ground brick	0.015–0.03, av. 0.02	0.20	same as 1	0.60
same	same	—	Careless work. In some areas joints were not dressed	—
same	same	same	same	same
9. White with finely ground brick and sand	0.015–0.03, av. 0.025	0.255	Smooth. Horizontal marks of trowel at top and bottom of joints	0.74
10. Pink with large quantity of coarsely ground brick, some sand and pebbles	0.038–0.04	—	Smooth	—
11. White with beach sand, small quantity of ground brick	0.035–0.04	—	Smooth	—

APPENDIX I

LOCATION	BRICKS						
	Color	Original type	Front	Back	Sides	Th.	Th. 10 bricks
12. Room 3: repair to east wall (p. 45, fn. 26)	Light reddish brown (5YR 6/4)	Square or rectangular	0.30	—	—	0.03–0.04	0.384
13. Room 3: screen wall (p. 46)	Pinkish gray (7.5YR 7/2)	Rectangular	0.56	0.56	0.60	0.035	—
14. Room 5: blocked furnace entrance (p. 51)	Pale yellow (5Y 8/3)	—	—	—	—	0.03–0.04	—
15. Room 5: spur walls at southeast wall of room (p. 51, fn. 45; p. 59, fn. 66)	Pink to light reddish brown (5YR 7/3–7/4 6/3–6/4)	—	0.25–0.30	—	—	0.03 0.05–0.06	only 9 courses
16. Room 5: repair to southeast wall of room (p. 52, fn. 49)	Pink (5YR 7/3–7/4); pale yellow (5Y 7/3)	—	a. 0.27–0.30, majority 0.30 b. 0.40	—	—	0.03–0.035 0.05	0.42
17. Room 5: blocked doorway (p. 53)	Pink (5YR 7/4)	Rectangular or square, cut diagonally in half	0.19–0.35, majority 0.30	—	—	0.035	0.355
18. Room 5: repairs to southwest wall (p. 53)	Reddish brown to reddish yellow (5YR 5/4–6/6)	—	0.34–0.36	—	—	0.035–0.04	0.374
19. Room 5: northwest wall (p. 53)	a. Yellow (5Y 7/4)	—	0.30	—	—	0.03	0.359
	b. Reddish yellow (7.5YR 6/6)	—	0.39–0.40	—	—	0.04	
	c. Yellow (10YR 7/6); reddish yellow (5YR 6/6)	Sesquipedales	0.44	—	—	0.045–0.05	
20. Room 5: northeast wall (p. 53)	a. Red (2.5YR 5/6); pink (5Y 8/3); reddish yellow (5YR 6/6)	Square or rectangular	0.30–0.31	—	—	0.03–0.035	0.353
	b. Yellowish red (5YR 5/6)	Square or rectangular	0.41	—	—	0.03–0.035	
21. Room 5: fallen fragment of vaulting (p. 54)	Pink (5YR 7/4); pale yellow (5Y 8/3)	Square or rectangular	0.30–0.31	—	—	0.03	only 9 courses
22. Room 7: repair to northwest wall and addition to northeast (p. 55)			Same as location no. 5				
23. Service area west of façade (p. 56)	Light red (2.5YR 6/6); pale yellow (2.5Y 8/4)	Square	0.31	0.31	0.31	0.025–0.035, av. 0.03	0.315
24. Service area north of Rooms 2 and 3: northeast and southwest walls of Corridor 1 (p. 57). For apsidal foundations, see above, location no. 8	Reddish yellow (5YR 6/6–5/6)	—	0.17–0.20, 0.26–0.30	—	—	0.04–0.05, av. 0.045	0.455
25. Drain along east edge of tiled court (p. 60)	Reddish yellow (5YR 7/6); pale yellow (5Y 8/3)	—	0.30–0.31	—	—	0.03	only 9 courses

TABLE 1

	MORTAR			
Color and composition	Th.	Th. 10 joints	Treatment of joints	Th. 10 bricks and 10 joints
12. White, coarse with small pebbles, sand	0.02–0.04	0.299	Smooth	0.65
13. —	—	—	—	—
14. Light gray with sand, pebbles	0.03–0.04	—	Smooth	—
15. White with coarse sand, pebbles	0.04–0.045		Smooth	—
16. White with coarse sand, pebbles	0.025–0.035	0.274	Smoothed obliquely	0.715
17. White with coarse sand, some pebbles	0.025–0.03	0.228	Smooth	0.583
18. White with pebbles	0.025–0.04	0.221	Smoothed obliquely	0.595
19. White with sand	0.03	0.286	Smoothed obliquely	0.645
	same		same	
	same		same	
20. Pinkish with large quantity of pebbles, sand, and some ground brick	0.03–0.035	0.306	Smoothed obliquely	0.68
	same		same	
21. Pinkish white with pebbles	0.038–0.04	—	Smoothed obliquely	—
22. Same as location no. 5			same as location no. 5	
23. White with small brick fragments	0.025–0.035, av. 0.032	0.32	Smoothed obliquely	0.635
24. Yellow with a few pebbles	0.02–0.035, av. 0.028	0.28	Smooth	0.76–0.79 (north wall) 0.63–0.64 (south wall)
25. White with finely ground brick, some pebbles, sand	0.025–0.04	—	Smoothed obliquely	—

APPENDIX I
TABLE 2: HYPOCAUST COLUMNS

	BRICKS			
LOCATION	Color	Shape	L. and W.	Th.
26. Room 2 (p. 37)	Reddish yellow 5YR 7/6–6/6; pink (7.5YR 8/4)	Square	0.23 × 0.23	0.03–0.035
27. Room 3: along east and west sides of room in band 2.55 m. wide; a few beneath north apse pool; beneath central pool (p. 43)	Reddish yellow (5YR 6/6); reddish brown (5YR 5/4)	a. Round b. Square c. Square (cap and base)	D. 0.25 0.31 × 0.31 0.32 × 0.32 0.30 × 0.30	0.05–0.062, majority 0.06 0.03–0.035 0.05–0.06
28. Room 3: beneath north apse pool (p. 43)	—	Rectangular	0.28 × 0.31	—
29. Room 3: beneath parapet, north apse pool, from center to east (pp. 43, 44, 48)	Yellowish red (5YR 7/6)	Rectangular	0.30 × 0.32	0.03
30. Room 3: beneath parapet of north apse pool from center to west (pp. 43, 48)	Pink (5YR 7/3)	a. Round b. Rectangular or square broken in half	Same as location no. 27a 0.20 × 0.30	 0.03–0.032
31. Room 3: central area of room at break in floor (p. 43)	Reddish yellow (5YR 7/6) Pale yellow (5Y 8/3)	Square	0.30 × 0.30 0.31 × 0.31	0.03–0.035
32. Room 3: beneath central pool (pp. 43, 48)	a. Same as location no. 27 b. Pink to reddish yellow (5YR 7/4–6/6)	 Rectangular or square, broken	 0.20 × 0.30	 0.03–0.04
33. Room 3: south half of room (pp. 43 and 44, fn. 24)	—	Round	—	—
34. Room 5 (p. 51)	a. Reddish yellow (5YR 7/6) b. same	Round Square	D. 0.28 0.30 × 0.30	0.05 0.03

TABLE 2: HYPOCAUST COLUMNS

BONDING MATERIAL		COLUMNS		
Type	Th.	H.	Spacing	Protective Coating
26. Pale yellow soil (5Y 8/3)	0.01–0.02	0.755	0.36 (east to west); 0.45, 0.26, 0.40 (north to south)	None
27. Very pale brown soil (10YR 7/3)	0.01–0.02	0.935	0.29–0.30	Very pale brown soil (10YR 7/3)
28. Mortar				None
29. Pale yellow mortar with coarse sand	0.025–0.03	0.935	0.40	Very pale brown soil (10YR 7/3)
30. a. Same as location no. 27				
b. Gray mortar with small pebbles	0.03–0.04	0.935	Same as location no. 27	Very pale brown soil (10YR 7/3)
31. White mortar with pebbles	0.025–0.035	Full height not preserved	Irregular; see Pl. 55	Very pale brown soil (10YR 7/3)
32.		0.75		Same as location no. 27
Mortar with many pebbles, coarse sand	0.025–0.04	0.75	0.29–0.30	None
33. Mortar		0.82	—	None
34. Very pale brown soil (10YR 7/3)	0.01–0.018	0.88	0.395	Very pale brown soil (10YR 7/3)
same	same	same	same	same

NOTES TO TABLE 2

27. These columns stand on a base of one thick brick or two square bricks and have a cap of one thick brick.
29. A row of double columns formed the support of the edge of the pool: small ones to the north support the floor of the pool; taller ones behind to the south support the parapet. Only one example was measured for spacing. The protective coating is a very thin layer unlike that on columns of location no. 27.
30. The small rectangular columns are set against the north face of the round columns to support the pool floor.
31. These columns are not in line with the others in the room. There are remains of protective coating on some columns only.
32. The small rectangular columns are set against round columns as supports for the edge of the pool and rest against the clay coating of the round columns.
33. This area has not been cleared. Measurements and color of bricks cannot be obtained.
34. Columns in the northwest side of the room used eleven bricks; four columns preserved on the southeast side used nine. The columns are now destroyed, and the thickness of bonding material for the latter can not now be obtained. The round columns have a base and cap of two square bricks each. Square columns were also used in this room.

APPENDIX II
GROUPS OF FINDS

Thirty-three groups of finds which are important for the history of the building have been catalogued below. The material in them has been treated as evidence for dating rather than as the subject for a study of the various categories (pottery, lamps, etc.) found in the excavation of the Bath. Dates given for the coins are, whenever possible, the dates of issue; otherwise the dates are those of the emperor concerned. Only the coins important for dating a group are identified; others are simply listed as Greek, Byzantine, 4th century, etc., except for Groups 14 and 28 where the dates of all the coins are of interest. All coins in the groups are listed by inventory number, even those that are illegible or have disintegrated. The quantity of material in each group is given in terms of boxes. One box measures 0.36 × 0.15 m. with a height of 0.10 m.

Three groups of particular interest (19, 25, and 26) are discussed in Appendix III.

Group 1

Location: Beneath the tiled court.
Lot no.: 5143
Date: Late 1st or possibly early 2nd century.
Contents: (Lotted, ½ box) Fine and coarse pottery fragments.
Coins: None.
Comments: Group 1 provides a *terminus post quem* for the laying of the paving of the tiled court. At the eastern end of the area cleared, the Byzantine bothros had been cut through the herringbone paving immediately north of the east-to-west drain under the floor. The group consists of pottery found under the floor at this point. No complete profiles were found and only one join. One ridged handle may belong to the early 2nd century; the remainder dates to the 1st.

Group 2

Location: From fallen concrete vaulting in Rooms 1, 2, and 3.
Lot nos.: 3504, 4657, 4658
Date: Late 1st or possibly early 2nd century with two later pieces.
Contents: (Inventoried) **119, 120**; MF 12651, MF 12581 (bronze needle, bronze spike).
(Lotted, 1⅓ boxes) Coarse pottery fragments; fragmentary bronze and iron spikes, fragmentary iron bar, two bronze nails.
Coins: 66-306 (1st century B.C.).
Comments: The pottery and other objects were collected when various fragments of fallen vaulting were broken up so that excavation could continue. One wheel-ridged fragment and one spirally grooved fragment from the fallen apse of Room 3 show no traces of mortar and may have come from the fill beneath the fallen masonry. They are later than the other pottery in the group. The interest of the material lies mainly in the metal objects.

Group 3

Location: Lime-slaking pit in service corridor northeast of Room 3 (Corridor 1).
Lot nos.: 3571, 3572
Date: 3rd century.
Contents: (Inventoried) **130, 131**.
(Lotted, 2 boxes) Coarse pottery fragments.
Coins: None.
Comments: The pottery from the lime pit is mixed in date. The two latest pieces, **130** and **131**, belong to types which begin in the first half of the 3rd century and continue until the 4th (**130**) and 5th (**131**). **131** was found in the lower level of the lime pit, and there is thus no possibility that it was trodden in from the levels above.

The lower dating in the 3rd century, however, is to be preferred for these two pieces since the material in Group 6, which lay directly above the lime pit, dates to the mid- or second half of the 3rd century. The majority of the material in Group 3 dates from the 1st to the early 2nd century. Fragments of white marble revetment and a bipedalis were also found in the fill of the pit. The depth of the pit was *ca.* 0.60 m.

Group 4

Location: Hypocaust of Room 2.
Lot no.: 5147
Date: Mid-3rd century.
Contents: (Inventoried) **132, 133**.
(Lotted, 2 boxes) Fragmentary coarse pottery.
Coins: None.
Comments: The pottery was found on the floor of the hypocaust against the parapet wall of the south pool, in the center. A few 1st-century rim fragments were found with the later material.

Group 5

Location: Drain in Room 4.
Lot no.: 3558
Date: Before A.D. 267.
Contents: (Inventoried) **134, 135**.
(Lotted, ⅓ box) Four fragmentary trefoil-mouth jugs of same type as **134**, three miniature cooking-pot bases of same type as **135**, small bowl base; stone mosaic tesserae.
Coins: None.
Comments: The group dates the period after which the drain was no longer in use.

Group 6

Location: Above the lime-slaking pit in the service area northeast of Room 3 (Corridor 1).
Lot nos.: 3569, 3570, 5173
Date: Mid- or second half of 3rd century.
Contents: (Inventoried) C-66-135, C-66-136, C-66-232 (pottery); MF 12641 (stone mortar).
(Lotted, 2¾ boxes) Fine and coarse pottery fragments; glass-vessel fragments and glass mosaic tesserae; lamp fragments.
Coins: None.
Comments: Group 6 represents the fill above stereo in Corridor 1 and lay directly above the lime pit. The gray ashy fill was *ca.* 0.60–0.80 m. in depth. The bulk of the pottery, including most of a white-slipped amphora (cf. *Agora* V, L 11), was mid-3rd or second half of 3rd century, but there was earlier material of the 1st and 2nd centuries and of the 1st century B.C. The lamp fragments date from the 2nd to early 3rd century.

Group 7

Location: Service area north of Room 2 and northeast of Room 3 (Corridors 1 and 2).
Lot nos.: 3568, 3575, 3577
Date: Late 4th to 5th century.
Contents: (Inventoried) C-66-85, C-66-233, C-66-234 (pottery); MF 12678 (terracotta mask).
(Lotted, 2½ boxes) Fine and coarse pottery fragments; window-glass and glass-vessel fragments, glass mosaic tesserae; bone spatula, bone pins; Attic and Corinthian lamp fragments; terracotta-figurine fragments.
Coins: (Total 2) 66-234 (Elagabalus, A.D. 218–222); 66-227 (illegible).
Comments: Group 7 represents the fill above stereo in Corridor 2 and in the small passageway to the north. The fill, *ca.* 0.20 m. deep, was also found at the east end of Corridor 1, where it had spilled out from Corridor 2 and overlay Group 6. The pottery is mixed in date, the latest being late 4th to 5th century. There is a great deal of 3rd-century and some earlier material. The presence of figurines and a terracotta mask suggests that this fill may have been brought in from outside, because such objects would not be used in a bath. The location of the fill indicated that it was thrown in at the north end and spilled out to the west into Corridor 1.

Group 8

Location: Circular pool in Room 1.
Lot no.: 3503
Date: Last quarter 4th century.
Contents: (Inventoried) L 4521 (lamp fragment); S 2907 (marble hand).
(Lotted, 3 boxes) Coarse pottery fragments; bone pin; window-glass and glass-vessel fragments, glass mosaic tesserae; lamp fragments; iron nail; painted stucco fragments.
Coins: (Total 6) 66-422 (Valentinian II, A.D. 378–383); 68-852 (Valens, ca. A.D. 364–367); 68-850 (Constantius II or Julian, A.D. 346–361); 66-447 (4th century); 68-816, 68-851 (illegible).
Comments: The material provides a *terminus post quem* for the filling in of the pool. The date is based on the coins and reinforced by a 4th-century lamp fragment in the lot (cf. *Agora* VII, no. 974; *Hesperia* 50, 1981, p. 127, no. 6). Six of the pottery fragments appear to be 4th century; the remainder are 3rd with some 2nd-century pieces. The depth of the fill was *ca.* 0.60 m.

Group 9

Location: Foundation trench in the façade area.
Lot nos.: 5186, 5187
Date: Late 4th century.
Contents: (Inventoried) C-68-29, C-68-76, C-68-77 (pottery); S 2896 (marble leg fragment).
(Lotted, 2⅓ boxes) Fine and coarse pottery fragments; window-glass fragment, glass-vessel fragment, two glass mosaic tesserae; lamp fragments; iron fragments, lead disk; two fragments of mosaic flooring, two stone tesserae; three stucco fragments; stamped tile fragment, biconical loomweight.
Coins: (Total 5) 68-184 (Julian, A.D. 355–361); 68-904 (A.D. 355–361); 68-136, 68-185 (Greek); 68-183 (illegible).
Comments: The pottery in the lots belongs to the late 4th century (5186) and to the late 1st to 2nd century (5187). The latter comes from a fill of crumbled mortar and brick fragments found within the trench against the foundations of the façade. It did not appear to have any particular significance, since the nature of the fill of the trench suggests that the trench was used as a dump. The presence of the two fragments of mosaic flooring may be significant, since of the rooms excavated only Room 5 had a mosaic floor with thick bedding. The depth of fill was *ca.* 1.70 m.

Group 10

Location: Over the destroyed floor of the pool in front of the façade.
Lot nos.: 5184, 5185, 5193, 6634
Date: Late 4th to early 5th century.
Contents: (Inventoried) MF 68-119 (terracotta weight); S 2903 (marble drapery fragment).
(Lotted, 2¾ boxes) Fine and coarse pottery fragments; window-glass and glass-vessel fragments; lamp fragments.
Coins: (Total 8) 68-780 (A.D. 395–408); 68-881 (time of Valentinian II, Theodosius I, and Arcadius, A.D. 388–392); 68-779 (Arcadius, A.D. 383–387); 68-965 (Theodosius I, A.D. 383–392); 68-1125 (Theodosius I, A.D. 392–395); 68-122, 68-123 (Constantius II, A.D. 346–361); 68-775 (Greek).
Comments: The group comes from a fill *ca.* 0.20–0.40 m. in depth at the base of the façade and sloping down to *ca.* 0.25 m. to the west. The pottery was mostly late 4th or early 5th century in date, but there were also three later fragments, one of which is late 6th, the second early 6th, the third late 5th. In view of the bulk of the earlier material and the corroboration of the coins, these were considered to be intrusive. All the pottery in the lots was fragmentary with few joins and no complete profiles.

Group 11

Location: Façade area.
Lot no.: 5183
Date: 5th century.
Contents: (Lotted, 2 boxes) Fine and coarse pottery fragments; window-glass and glass-vessel fragments; lamp fragments; bronze wire, iron nail and clamps.

APPENDIX II

Coins: (Total 5) 68-52, 68-121 (Arcadius, A.D. 383–392); 68-53 (Theodosius I, A.D. 388–392); 68-964 (Valentinian II, Theodosius I, or Arcadius, A.D. 383–388); 68-131 (illegible).

Comments: The group represents additional fill that accumulated in the area to a depth of *ca.* 0.30–0.60 m. before the building of the service area. It precedes Group 12 and is later than Group 10. The group is dated by the pottery, all fragmentary, which is later than the coins. Some 4th-century fragments are present in the group. Two sherds appear to be of late 6th-century date but were considered intrusive.

Group 12

Location: Exterior floor level for the service area in front of the façade.
Lot nos.: 4676, 5181
Date: 5th century.
Contents: (Lotted, ⅓ box) Fine and coarse pottery fragments; one glass-vessel fragment, five small window-glass fragments; iron nail and knife blade; fragment of stucco.
Coins: (Total 2) 70-350 (4th century); 68-774 (illegible).
Comments: The group contains material from a hard and uneven level of brick and mortar fragments found to the north, south, and west of the service area. At the base of the façade the fill was deeper (0.30–0.60 m.) than at the west (0.10 m.). At the west it proved to be extremely hard. This level was the uppermost one cut through for the building of the service area. The pottery was fragmentary with no complete profiles. One intrusive fragment of African Red Slip Ware dates to the early 7th century; the remainder of the material appears to belong to the 5th century. The location of the fill suggests that it should be associated with some reconstruction inside the building, the debris from which was tipped out through the windows of Room 3. This would explain why the fill was deeper against the walls.

Group 13

Location: Foundation trenches for the service area against the façade wall.
Lot nos.: 4677, 4678
Date: Early 6th century.
Contents: (Lotted, ½ box) Fine and coarse pottery fragments; window-glass fragments and glass-vessel fragment; two lamp fragments.
Coins: None.
Comments: This group comes from the trenches, *ca.* 0.385 m. deep, cut into the fills represented by Groups 10–12. Only a small amount of material was found, and most of it is not datable. Two of the pottery fragments, however, appear to be early 6th century.

Group 14

Location: Tiled court.
Lot nos.: 4717, 5142
Date: Early 6th century.
Contents: (Inventoried) C-67-58 (pottery); MF 68-69 (lead amulet).
(Lotted, 2⅓ boxes) Fine and coarse pottery fragments; bone pin; window-glass and glass-vessel fragments, two glass mosaic tesserae; lamp fragments; iron wedge and nail; bronze earring(?); two fragments of painted stucco.
Coins: (Total 131) 67-797, 68-284 (Marcian, A.D. 450–457); 68-272, 68-441 (Theodosius II, A.D. 408–423 and 402–408); 67-467, 67-493, 67-559, 67-716, 67-717, 67-721, 67-762, 67-795, 67-813, 67-822, 67-866, 68-283, 68-285, 68-432, 68-435, 68-572, 68-573, 68-1019 (5th-century nummi); 68-277 (Honorius, A.D. 393–395); 67-723, 67-782, 68-268, 68-1015, 68-1016, 68-1018, 68-1022 (Arcadius, A.D. 392–408); 68-433 (Magnus Maximus, A.D. 388); 67-430, 67-466, 67-468, 67-491, 67-497, 67-728, 67-730, 67-731, 67-814, 67-861, 68-267, 68-273, 68-275, 68-276, 68-278, 68-279, 68-281, 68-282, 68-425, 68-426, 68-429, 68-430, 68-434, 68-439, 68-442, 68-563, 68-568, 68-569, 68-626, 68-973, 68-1014 (Theodosius I, or his sons, A.D. 379–423); 68-438, 68-448, 68-1023 (Valentinian II, A.D. 388–392, 379–383, 375–392); 68-1097 (Valentinian II, Theodosius I, Arcadius, and Flacilla, A.D. 383–392); 68-436, 68-1017 (Gratian,

Valentinian II, or Theodosius I, A.D. 378–383); 67-652, 68-627 (Valens, A.D. 375–378); 67-725, 68-562, 68-567 (Constantius II, A.D. 337–361); 67-796 (Maxentius? A.D. 350–353); 67-542 (House of Constantine); 67-469, 67-494, 67-495, 67-720, 67-859, 68-1021 (4th–5th century); 67-541, 67-862, 67-865, 68-271, 68-287, 68-565, 68-566, 68-571 (4th century); 67-674 (Greek); 67-492, 67-496, 67-540, 67-653, 67-718, 67-719, 67-722, 67-724, 67-726, 67-727, 67-729, 67-761, 67-763, 67-798, 67-799, 67-812, 67-860, 67-864, 68-255, 68-269, 68-270, 68-274, 68-280, 68-286, 68-422–68-424, 68-427, 68-428, 68-431, 68-437, 68-440, 68-564, 68-570, 68-624, 68-625, 68-628, 68-1013, 68-1020 (illegible); 67-498, 67-863 (intrusive Byzantine).

Comments: Group 14 comes from the lowest level of fill, 0.20–0.50 m. deep, which lay directly on the floor of the court in the total area cleared. The latest pottery is early 6th century, and there were 3rd-, 4th-, and 5th-century pieces also. The large number of coins is striking.

Group 15

Location: Room 1.
Lot no.: 3501
Date: Late 6th to early 7th century.
Contents: (Inventoried) A 601, A 602 (stone bench supports); **105, 106**, S 2817 (marble hand), S 2827 (marble fragment of togatus), S 2813 (marble relief fragment).
(Lotted, 2 boxes) Fine and coarse pottery fragments; glass-vessel fragments, glass mosaic tesserae; three bronze implements; stucco fragment; terracotta water-pipe fragment.
Coins: (Total 60) 66-454 (Tiberius II or imitation, ca. A.D. 580); 66-418, 66-458 (Justin II? A.D. 565–578); 66-365 (Justinian I, A.D. 527–538); 66-415, 66-423, 66-430–66-434, 66-436–66-439, 66-442, 66-443, 66-448, 66-457, 66-459 (barbarous minimi, 6th century); 66-446 (barbarous minimus, 5th century); 66-389, 66-393, 66-396, 66-407, 66-411, 66-413, 66-444 (minimi, 5th–6th century); 66-391, 66-392, 66-394, 66-404, 66-406, 66-410, 66-414 (4th and 5th centuries); 66-305 (3rd century); 66-405, 66-408, 66-409, 66-412, 66-416, 66-417, 66-420, 66-424–66-429, 66-435, 66-440, 66-441, 66-445, 66-449–66-453, 66-455 (illegible or dissolved).
Comments: The group represents the material from the destruction fill of the room, which covered the entire floor in a layer *ca.* 0.35–0.80 m. thick. The latest fine wares date from the late 6th to early 7th century. The four Byzantine sherds are either contamination from the stratum above or from a drain. The pottery is fragmentary with no complete shapes or profiles, and most of the sherds are coarse wares which, with the exception of the spirally grooved fragments, are nondescript. A relatively small quantity of glass was found.

Group 16

Location: Room 2.
Lot nos.: 4683, 5145
Date: 6th century.
Contents: (Inventoried) **94**.
(Lotted, ¾ box) Fine and coarse pottery fragments; three glass-vessel fragments, small fragment of window glass, glass mosaic tesserae; iron fragments; terracotta-tube fragment, water-pipe fragment, and pipe fragment from a vent.
Coins: None.
Comments: Group 16 represents the only fill found over the floor of Room 2 that was not contaminated by Byzantine sherds (see Lots 2273–2275 for material within the two pools and over the floor at the south end of the room). The fill lay directly beneath (Lot 5145) and, at the same level, to the north of (Lot 4683) a large mass of fallen vaulting. The depth of fill was *ca.* 0.50 m. Most of the pottery was coarse ware and not closely datable, but one fragment appears to be late 6th-century fabric from Palestine.

Group 17

Location: Room 3.
Lot nos.: 4662–4665
Date: Late 6th to early 7th century.
Contents: (Inventoried) **109**, S 2857 (marble arm), S 2898 (marble leg?), **96, 97**, A 741 b (revetment with dipinti), **113**.

(Lotted, 3 boxes) Fine and coarse pottery fragments; window-glass and glass-vessel fragments, glass mosaic tesserae; bronze patch, iron clamps; stucco fragment; terracotta-tube fragments, *tegulae mammatae* fragments.

Coins: None.

Comments: The material in Group 17 was found in a layer of earth and ash, *ca.* 0.70–1.25 m. thick, over the floor of the room, over the floor of the hypocaust beneath the breaks in the floor of the room, and also in a small area up to the west wall of the room beneath the preserved floor. The material in the ash level which lay directly on the floor of the room produced pottery which did not seem different in date from that in the earth fill above, and both are consequently discussed together as evidence for the destruction period of the room, although they are still stored in separate lots. The ash layer on the floor of the hypocaust produced little pottery. The chief interest of this fill was the great number of terracotta tubes, evidence for the construction of the screen walls of the room. Twenty-two *tegulae mammatae* fragments were also found, and two were saved. The quantity of window glass was noticeable when compared with Groups 15 and 16. Some of it was found in the north apse pool, but most came from the center of the room and the west side.

Group 18

Location: Room 4.
Lot no.: 3557
Date: Late 6th to early 7th century.
Contents: (Lotted, ½ box) Fine and coarse pottery fragments; window-glass fragment, glass mosaic tesserae, glass-vessel fragments; stone mosaic tesserae; terracotta water-pipe fragment.
Coins: (Total 7) 68-1012 (Maurice Tiberius, A.D. 582–583); 66-174 (possibly 6th century); 66-178 (5th century); 66-179 (4th century); 66-177 (3rd century); 66-180, 66-181 (dissolved).
Comments: Group 18 contains material from the fill, 0.10–0.34 m. deep, which lay over the destroyed floor of the room. The pottery is very fragmentary, but one fine-ware rim dates to the late 6th or early 7th century. Only a few glass-vessel fragments were found, but there was a large quantity of mosaic tesserae.

Group 19

See APPENDIX III

Group 20

Location: Room 7.
Lot no.: 5170
Date: 6th century.
Contents: (Inventoried) A 746 (revetment with dipinto).
(Lotted, ½ box) Four coarse pottery fragments; iron pins; three fragments of marble revetment with dipinti; terracotta-tube fragments.
Coins: None.
Comments: Group 20 contains the material from the earth fill, *ca.* 0.35 m. thick, which lay over the destroyed floor of the pool in Room 7. Only one datable fragment of pottery was found, which places the abandonment of the pool in the early 6th century, but in view of the evidence from the other rooms it was probably abandoned later. The interest of the group lies in the fragments of marble revetment with dipinti, which were found in this room as well as in Room 3 and in the area in front of the façade.

Group 21

Location: Façade area.
Lot nos.: 4673–4675, 4682, 5175–5180, 5189–5192, 5203
Date: Late 6th to early 7th century.
Contents: (Inventoried) C-67-96, C-67-97, C-68-31 (pottery); **110**.
(Lotted, 7 boxes) Fine and coarse pottery fragments; glass-vessel fragments, window-glass fragments, three glass mosaic tesserae; lamp fragments; bronze nail, hinge fragment, fragment with relief design; iron nails and clamp, two very small iron clamps; lead strip; terracotta-tube fragment, water-pipe fragments.

Coins: (Total 9) 68-464, 68-846 (5th century); 68-954, 68-776, 68-777, 68-847, 68-953 (4th century); 67-886, 67-952 (illegible).

Comments: Accumulation of material in the façade area after the construction of the service area and before the laying of marble slabs in the northwest corner is represented by Group 21. The fill was *ca.* 1.20–1.75 m. thick and lay above the fill represented by Group 12 and below Group 23. A great quantity of pottery was recovered from the fill. The latest dates from the late 6th to early 7th century, but the coins were all earlier. Particularly striking in these lots was the great quantity of window glass.

Group 22

Location: Foundation trench for the north drain from the service area in front of the façade.
Lot no.: 5194
Date: Early 6th century.
Contents: (Lotted, ½ box) Coarse-ware pottery fragments; glass-vessel fragments, window-glass fragment; lamp fragment.
Coins: None.
Comments: Only a small amount of material was found in the trench, which was *ca.* 0.60 m. deep. Several large fragments of storage vessels joined with fragments in Groups 21 and 23.

Group 23

Location: Façade area.
Lot nos.: 4672, 5171, 5188
Date: Late 6th to early 7th century.
Contents: (Inventoried) MF 12837 (window glass).
(Lotted, 1 box) Fine and coarse pottery fragments; glass-vessel fragments, window-glass fragments; iron nail, lead fragments; curved terracotta-brick fragments from furnace flue.
Coins: 67-810 (5th century).
Comments: The group represents the latest accumulation in the façade area before the final earthquake brought down the marble blocks. The fill, 0.25–0.57 m. deep, lay directly above the marble slabs in the northwest corner and above the lots discussed in Group 21. It is, therefore, later, but the pottery, which was all fragmentary, does not appear to be different from that in the levels below. The chief interest of the group is the great quantity of window glass that was found, some of it in large fragments (max. p.L. 0.18 m.) and some preserving one edge.

Group 24

Location: Latrine.
Lot nos.: 5132, 5133
Date: Late 6th to early 7th century.
Contents: (Lotted, 1⅓ boxes) Fine and coarse pottery fragments; five glass-vessel fragments; three lamp fragments; iron nails; terracotta-tube fragment, water-pipe fragments.
Coins: (Total 4) 68-460, 68-661 (5th century); 68-524 (illegible); 68-682 (intrusive Byzantine).
Comments: Group 24 dates to the period when the latrine had gone out of use, since it was found in an uneven layer *ca.* 0.50–0.75 m. deep, over the destroyed floor of the latrine. The date is based on the fine wares.

Groups 25 and 26

See APPENDIX III

Group 27

Location: Lime pit west of the colonnade.
Lot nos.: 4740, 5136, 5137
Date: Early 6th century.

APPENDIX II

Contents: (Lotted, 1¼ boxes) Fine and coarse pottery fragments; glass-vessel fragments, glass mosaic tesserae, window-glass fragments; two fragments of mosaic, one with glass tesserae, the other with stone; iron nails.

Coins: (Total 2) 67-229, 67-262 (illegible, dissolved).

Comments: From the lowest level of the fill, *ca.* 1.10 m. deep, came a fragment of an early 6th-century storage jar. The remainder of the material is 5th century.

Group 28

Location: House in the colonnade.
Lot no.: 4736
Date: Third quarter of the 6th century.
Contents: (Lotted, ⅓ box) Coarse-ware pottery fragments.
Coins: (Total 81) 67-400 (Justin II, A.D. 565–578); 67-336, 67-343, 67-351, 67-352, 67-354, 67-355, 67-357, 67-363, 67-364, 67-366, 67-379, 67-381, 67-382, 67-407, 67-409 (Justinian I, A.D. 527–565); 67-393 ("Vandalic", A.D. 530–533); 67-405 (Justin I, A.D. 518–527); 67-345, 67-346, 67-348, 67-378, 67-380, 67-384, 67-385, 67-388, 67-392, 67-395, 67-397, 67-401 (Anastasius I, A.D. 491–518); 67-350, 67-372, 67-377 (Leo I, A.D. 457–474); 67-373 (Marcian, A.D. 450–457); 67-328 (Theodosius II, A.D. 402); 67-332 (5th century); 67-370 (late 4th–5th century); 67-330 (4th century); 67-329, 67-331, 67-333–67-335, 67-337–67-342, 67-344, 67-347, 67-349, 67-353, 67-356, 67-358–67-362, 67-365, 67-367–67-369, 67-371, 67-374–67-376, 67-383, 67-386, 67-387, 67-389–67-391, 67-394, 67-396, 67-398, 67-399, 67-402, 67-403, 67-406, 67-408 (illegible or disintegrated).

Comments: Group 28 represents the material from below the floor of the house. It was isolated in a level 0.22–0.38 m. deep against the south face of the north wall in the area where the hearth was found. In the remainder of the room the same fill was dug (Lots 4722, 4725–4728, 4730, 4733, 4734, 4737), but it was disturbed by a large bothros, and therefore only Lot 4736 is included in the group; it was sealed by the floor, and there was no disturbance. The pottery, all fragmentary, appears to date to the early 6th century, and except for the one coin of Justin II, the coins date to the first half of the 6th, to the 5th, and to the late 4th centuries.

The large number of coins scattered through this small extent of fill is surprising. A. R. Bellinger, who studied them, suggested that the great numbers of coins of small denomination could be explained as admission fees to the Bath, dropped on the way in. It does not seem, however, that this can be the case, since the accumulation of fill over the court, the construction of a service area against the façade, the destruction of the mosaic floor in the colonnade, and the digging of a lime pit in the entranceway suggest that this area was no longer being used as an entrance to the Bath.

Group 29

Location: House in the colonnade.
Lot no.: 4735
Date: Late 6th to early 7th century.
Contents: (Inventoried) **128, 129**.
(Lotted, 1 box) Coarse pottery fragments; iron nails.
Coins: None.
Comments: Fill, 0.30–0.46 m. deep, was found above the floor of the house in an undisturbed level along the north wall. Two complete storage amphoras, **128, 129**, presumably belong to the last occupancy of the house. The remainder of the group comprises coarse household wares, including fragments from vessels similar to the two complete examples.

Group 30

Location: Pit in the floor of the colonnade.
Lot no.: 4731
Date: Early 6th century.
Contents: (Inventoried) C-67-36, C-67-64, C-67-65 (pottery).
(Lotted, ½ box) Coarse pottery fragments.
Coins: None.

Comments: The group is important as evidence for the destruction of the colonnade in the early 6th century. The depth of fill was *ca.* 0.39–0.49 m.

Group 31

Location: Service area north of Room 2 and northeast of Room 3 (Corridors 1 and 2).
Lot nos.: 3561, 3567, 3574
Date: First half of 6th century.
Contents: (Inventoried) C-66-66 (pottery).
(Lotted, 2 boxes) Fine wares (2 fragments); coarse-ware pottery sherds; glass-vessel fragments, glass mosaic tesserae; lamps.
Coins: (Total 4) 66-214 (Justin I, A.D. 518–527, or Justinian I, A.D. 543–565); 66-207 (late 4th–5th century); 66-213 (Theodosius I? A.D. 388–392); 66-225 (dissolved).
Comments: The material in this group comes from the ash levels below those represented by Group 32. Different layers of ash were dumped in the service corridor forming an ashy level *ca.* 0.15–0.50 m. thick. The latest coin indicates a date for the group in the first half of the 6th century. The pottery is fragmentary, and there is little fine ware, but neither the lamps nor the coarse ware appear to be as late as the lots in the ash layers at a higher level. Some 3rd- and 5th-century fragments were present in the fill.

Group 32

Location: Service area north of Room 2 and northeast of Room 3 (Corridors 1 and 2).
Lot nos.: 3560, 3565, 3566, 3573
Date: Late 6th to early 7th century.
Contents: (Lotted, 3 boxes) Fine and coarse pottery fragments; one green-glazed Byzantine sherd (intrusive); three window-glass fragments, glass-vessel fragments; one complete lamp and lamp fragments; stone mosaic tesserae.
Coins: (Total 9) 66-212 (Justin II and Sophia, *ca.* A.D. 565–577); 66-223 (Justin II, A.D. 567/8); 66-211 (Justinian I? A.D. 527–538); 66-192 a (Valentinian I, A.D. 364–375); 66-192 b, 66-221 (Greek); 66-190, 66-191, 66-222 (illegible).
Comments: Group 32 represents the latest period of use of the service area. Ashy fill appears to have been dumped here from the hypocausts of the rooms. An uneven level of different types of ash, ranging in depth from 0.10 to 0.35 m., was found. The date of this group is based on the fine wares and the coins. The pottery was all fragmentary with no complete profiles.

Group 33

Location: Façade area, Rooms 3, 4, 5, and 7.
Lot nos.: 2377, 2378, 3549–3551, 4661, 4666, 4671, 5174
Date: 12th–13th century.
Contents: (Inventoried) C-65-178, C-67-95 (pottery); A 515, A 516 a–d (stone moldings); S 2750, S 2867, S 2902 (marble drapery fragment, marble arm, marble hand); MF 12107 (terracotta tube); I 2644 (inscription).
(Lotted, 6 boxes) Byzantine glazed wares; Roman coarse ware; Turkish sgraffito, one fragment; glass mosaic tesserae; iron clamps, spike; lead fragments from clamping of blocks; bronze stylus; two fragments of mosaic floor, stone mosaic tesserae; terracotta tubuli fragments, tube fragments, brick fragment with dotted stamp in shape of foot, stamped tile fragment.
Coins: (Total 4) 65-71 (Nicephorus III, A.D. 1078–1081); 65-59, 65-64 (4th century); 68-670 (dissolved).
Comments: Group 33 comes from a layer 1 meter thick of destruction fill of crumbled bricks and mortar, which lay over the late 6th- to early 7th-century levels. The group is mainly interesting for the non-ceramic material which provides evidence for the decoration and construction of the rooms.

APPENDIX III

GROUPS 19, 25, AND 26

Lack of space has prevented the detailed publication of all groups of material from the Great Bath which are important for its history. Some individual pieces appear in the Catalogue, but for most of the material a listing of the contents of the groups is all that has been possible (Appendix II). It has seemed worthwhile, however, to present three of the groups in more detail, since they are not only important for the chronology of the Bath but also represent material typical of the late 6th to early 7th century in Corinth.

Group 19 belongs to the interior of the Bath, to Room 5, and dates to the period when the building had been abandoned but before its final destruction by earthquake. The material from Room 5 is typical of that found over the floors of all the rooms and may thus be taken to represent the destruction period of the building as a whole. The other two groups, 25 and 26, come from the drain within the latrine in the colonnade along the west side of the tiled court and from the drain which ran along the colonnade. Both date to the period when these drains had been abandoned. They were dug separately but have been considered together, since the latrine drain emptied into the colonnade drain and although the colonnade drain could have continued in use after the latrine had been abandoned, the reverse is not possible. If, therefore, the silting up did not occur at the same time, the latrine drain must have gone out of use first, and its fill thus provides a *terminus post quem* for the colonnade drain.

Group 19

Location: Over the floor of Room 5, within collapsed flooring, within the ash fill of the hypocaust.
Lot nos.: 2379-2383, 3552, 3554-3556, 4667, 4668, 4670
Date: Late 6th to early 7th century.
Contents: (Inventoried) **99**, **109** (sculpture); **116–118** (terracotta); **136**, **137** (pottery); **139–141** (lamps); **148–152** (inscriptions).
(Lotted, 319 sherds, total amount 7 boxes)
Pottery: bowl and dish fragments of African Red Slip Ware (Hayes, forms 99, nos. 7, 18 or 22; 104, B; 105); imitation of African Red Slip Ware (cf. Hayes, form 104); bowl or dish fragments, Late Roman C (Hayes, forms 3; 10, A2); red-ware body fragments; micaceous water-jar toe and body fragments; amphora fragments with white-painted decoration (cf. *Agora* V, M 329); wheel-ridged body fragments (cf. *Agora* V, M 333); spirally grooved and combed sherds; ampulla toe (early Christian) and possible imitation of one; cooking-pot fragments; flat-based pot with concave walls, black fabric; jug base.
Bone: counter or stopper (cf. *Corinth* XII, nos. 1688, 1689).
Glass: many fragments of light-olive and pale green bottles (necks, conical bases, body fragments); dark green bottle fragments; green bottle base and handle; neck fragments with coils and threads; dark green goblet bases; cup fragments with rims folded inward. A few mosaic tesserae, green and blue. Fragments of window glass (Lots 2379, 2382, 3552).
Lamps: fragments of seven lamps of same type as **140**. One glazed lamp fragment.
Metal: bronze buckle with pierced plate (for type, cf. *Corinth* XII, no. 2187); flat bronze circlet; three bronze fragments with one smooth surface (Th. 0.018, 0.017, 0.01), four smaller fragments; iron nails (L. 0.035, 0.05); iron T-clamp; iron arrowhead with leaf-shaped blade; iron knife blade; iron instrument perforated at one end (cf. *Corinth* XII, no. 1463); lead button(?); lead fragment.
Stone: marble relief fragment; revetment fragment with scratched lunate sigma.
Terracotta: tube fragments; water-pipe fragment; Corinthian pan- and cover-tile fragments; projection from *tegula mammata*; small terracotta ring weight, two larger weights.
Coins: (Total 16) 67-487 (Maurice Tiberius, A.D. 586/7); 66-155 (Maurice Tiberius, A.D. 582–602); 66-143 (Tiberius II and Anastasia, A.D. 578–582); 67-429 (Justin II, A.D. 565–578); 66-145, 66-154 (6th century); 65-65, 67-476, 67-488 (5th century); 67-489 (4th century); 65-66, 66-141, 66-142, 66-157, 67-428, 67-490 (illegible).

Comments: Group 19 contains material from various fills in Room 5. A layer of earth (1.20 m. thick) was found over the preserved and collapsed floor of the room (Lots 2379, 3552, 4667). Beneath this in one area and above collapsed floor debris was a burnt layer (Lot 2381); collapsed floor debris was found in the central area of the room and against the southwest wall at the west (Lots 2380, 3554, 3555, 4668). Over the floor of the hypocaust were found two types of ash fill, one dark (Lots 2382, 4670), the other gray (Lots 2383, 3556). It was expected that these two fills would represent the last period of use of the hypocaust, rather than reflecting the period after the abandonment. The material from these fills, however, was disappointingly similar in date to that from the levels above, and joins were found between fragments in the earth fill (Lots 3552, 4667) and in the ash (Lots 2382, 4670), and between those in collapsed floor debris (Lot 4668) and in the ash (Lot 4670). Non-joining fragments of the same pot were found in the earth and ash fills (Lots 2379, 4670) and between the two kinds of ash fill (Lots 3556, 4670). It seems, therefore, that the soft nature of the ash allowed material from the destruction period to sink into it. Consequently, although individually the fills probably represent the periods of last use of the room and its subsequent destruction, the material has been discussed together as total evidence for the destruction period of Room 5.

A great many fragments of glass vessels were found in this room as compared to the number found in the other rooms of the building. The largest quantity was found in the ash fills (Lots 2383, 3556), but fragments were also found in good quantity in fallen floor debris (Lot 4668). Other lots had a handful each. Although no complete vessels were found, there were several examples of rims and bases from the same vessel, without body fragments. There were few joins. The main shapes represented are toilet bottles with long necks, especially in Lot 2383.

Within the ash fill, olive pits and egg shells were found. Their presence is presumably an indication of the type of fuel used. Olive pits, chaff, sawdust, straw, and charcoal are cited as fuel used in the Thermes de Banasa (R. Thouvenot and A. Luquet, *Les Thermes de Banasa* [Publication du Service des Antiquités du Maroc 9], 1951, p. 55). For calculations of the amount of fuel needed to operate the heated rooms of even a small bathing establishment, see T. Rook, "Development and Operation of Roman Hypocausted Baths," *Journal of Archaeological Science* 5, 1978, pp. 269–282.

Group 25

Location: Latrine drain.
Lot no.: 5134
Date: Early 7th century.
Contents: (Lotted, 14 sherds, ⅓ box)
Pottery: rim fragment from bowl, African Red Slip Ware (Hayes, form 104, A); 1 body sherd, African Red Slip Ware; rouletted rim from bowl, Late Roman C (Hayes, form 3, B); rim fragment from bowl, possible imitation of Late Roman C (Hayes, form 3, D); spirally grooved sherd; ridged sherd (cf. *Agora* V, M 333); micaceous cooking-pot rim; neck fragment from small amphora or pitcher; two coarse-ware jar fragments; rim-and-wall fragment from a bucket; two early Roman body sherds.
Terracotta: water-pipe fragment.
Coins: 68-688 (Phocas, A.D. 602-610).
Comments: See Group 26.

Group 26

Location: Drain along colonnade.
Lot nos.: 4718, 5140
Date: Late 6th to early 7th century.
Contents: (Inventoried) **112** (sculpture); **121–127** (pottery); **138** (glass); **142–147** (lamps).
(Lotted, 72 sherds, total amount: 2 boxes)
Pottery. *African Red Slip Ware:* base from large plate (Hayes, form 105); sherd from plate with knobbed rim (Hayes, form 104, B); rim and base sherds from flanged bowl (Hayes, form 91, C); rim fragment from bowl (Hayes, form 99, C); rim fragment from large bowl (Hayes, form 68); two fragments from rims of bowls (Hayes, form 57/58); rim fragment (close to Hayes, forms 69–77); rim fragment from bowl (Hayes, form 50). *Late Roman C:* fragment from dish with knobbed rim (Hayes, form 10, A); two dishes, one quarter of one preserved (Hayes, form 2); two fragments, rims of bowls (Hayes, form 3, E) and two base fragments (Hayes, form 3); dish, one quarter of rim preserved (Hayes, form 1, D); three stamped

fragments (Hayes, motifs 1, 6, and 71); rim sherd from bowl (cf. **121**). *Attic*: five sherds from plates (cf. *Agora* V, M 289); body sherd from jug with gouged decoration (cf. *Agora* V, M 320). White-painted amphora sherd, black fabric (possibly 7th-century Palestinian); four micaceous water-jar toes of late shape but solid, one of same shape and open (cf. *Agora* V, M 373 for shape); micaceous water-jar body fragments; sherds from five white-painted amphoras (cf. *Agora* V, M 329–331); ridged body sherd (cf. *Agora* V, M 333); spirally grooved sherds; upper part of amphora (cf. *Agora* V, M 324); sherd from amphora with red paint; three coarse-ware lids.

Glass (½ box): window-glass fragments, light-green to dark-green; base of dark green rectangular bottle; cylindrical necks from jugs, light blue and pale green; rim fragments from cups or bowls, blue and green; colorless and pale green goblet bases; colorless and pale green toilet-bottle necks and bases; colorless fragment from wall of vessel with optic blowing.

Lamps (all fragmentary): six Corinthian imitations of North African lamps; five imitation Attic lamps (*Corinth* IV, ii, type 28); imitation Attic glazed lamp; two round lamps (*Corinth* IV, ii, type 32; cf. O. Broneer, *Isthmia*, III, *Terracotta Lamps*, Princeton 1977, no. 3171); nozzle, Corinthian imitation of an Attic lamp (cf. *Agora* VII, no. 2844); lamp of local design; Attic base with signature XIO N[HC]; handle (*Corinth* IV, ii, type 27).

Terracotta: tube fragment; figurine fragment.

Coins: (Total 43) 68-555 (Justinian, A.D. 539–540); 67-577, 68-543, 68-548 (4th century); 67-578–67-597, 67-604, 67-832, 68-261, 68-542, 68-544–68-547, 68-549–68-554, 68-556–68-560 (illegible or disintegrated).

Comments: Group 25 is dated by the coin of Phocas which was found on the floor of the latrine drain below a fill 0.50–0.80 m. in depth. The pottery in this group was very fragmentary, and the datable pieces do not appear to be as late as the early 7th century. The latest is a rim sherd of African Red Slip Ware dating to *ca.* A.D. 530–580. A great quantity of datable material was found in Group 26, however, from the drain along the colonnade, in a fill whose depth ranged from 0.55 to 2.00 m. The latest of the African Red Slip and Late Roman C wares in this group belong to types which continue into the 7th century. Some of the coarse wares, i.e. the micaceous water-jar toes, belong to the late 6th century. Although none of the coins found in this drain are as late as the 7th century, the coin of Phocas found in the latrine drain provides a *terminus post quem* for Group 26.

Three catalogued pieces from Group 26 are of special interest. The glass jug, **138**, is unusual in that it combines the late technique of optic blowing with an earlier jug shape. The Late Roman C bowl, **121**, is a transitional shape not hitherto recognized in this fabric, and the bowl in Asia Minor "Light-Coloured" Ware, **124**, is one of the few examples of this fabric so far recognized at Corinth. (For another, see Corinth inv. no. C-68-348 a, b.)

CONCORDANCES

I. LOT NUMBERS AND GROUP NUMBERS

Lot No.	Group No.	Lot No.	Group No.	Lot No.	Group No.
2377, 2378	33	4661	33	5142	14
2379–2383	19	4662–4665	17	5143	1
3501	15	4666	33	5145	16
3503	8	4667, 4668, 4670	19	5147	4
3504	2	4671	33	5170	20
3549–3551	33	4672	23	5171	23
3552	19	4673–4675	21	5173	6
3554–3556	19	4676	12	5174	33
3557	18	4677, 4678	13	5175–5180	21
3558	5	4682	21	5181	12
3560	32	4683	16	5183	11
3561	31	4717	14	5184, 5185	10
3565, 3566	32	4718	26	5186, 5187	9
3567	31	4731	30	5188	23
3568	7	4735	29	5189–5192	21
3569, 3570	6	4736	8	5193	10
3571, 3572	3	4740	7	5194	22
3573	32	5132, 5133	24	5203	21
3574	31	5134	25	6634	10
3575, 3577	7	5136, 5137	27		
4657, 4658	2	5140	26		

II. FIELD INVENTORY NUMBERS (Notebook 357) AND CATALOGUE NUMBERS

Inv. No.	Cat. No.	Inv. No.	Cat. No.	Inv. No.	Cat. No.	Inv. No.	Cat. No.
7	87	53	23	81+56	15	116	95
8	56	54+35	12	85	57	118	51
11	80	55	79	86	36	119	78
17	24	56+81	15	87	14	120	77
24	100	57	6	88	58	121	93
32	7	58	71	89	1	122	91
33	9	59+62+79	17	90	2	123	40
34	10	60	19	91 a, b	92	124	32
35+54	12	61	18	94	74	138	73
36	43	62+59+79	17	95	31	142	102
37	70	63	34	96	75	146	88
38	29	64	21	97	33	148	44
39	8	65	46	98	25	149	90
40	30	66	60	99	52	150	98
41	81	67	13	101	53	151	65
42	45	68	11	103	72	152	41
43	61	69	16	104	26	153	50
45	63	71	35	105	68	154	28
46	3	72	20	106	64	155	4
47+48	5	74	47	107	37	156	55
48+47	5	76	67	110	62	157	54
49+52	42	77	22	111	66	158	86
50	69	78	59	112	76	159	89
51	27	79+59+62	17	113	49	160	38
52+49	42	80	48	114	39		

III. INVENTORY NUMBERS AND CATALOGUE NUMBERS

Inv. No.	Cat. No.	Inv. No.	Cat. No.	Inv. No.	Cat. No.
A 593	99	C-69-99	122	MF 12658 a, b	120
A 594	101	C-68-104	124	MF-68-33	138
A 686	94	C-68-105	123	MF-68-47	119
A 741 a	96	C-68-337	132		
A 741 c	97	C-68-338	133	S 2749	107
A 743	84	C-68-347	127	S 2767	111
A 744 a	82			S 2815	106
A 744 b	83	FM 79	116	S 2824	108
A 745	85	FM 88	113	S 2828	105
A 987	68	FM 91	115	S 2853	109
A 987	68	FM 92	114	S 2899	112
		FP 203 a	117	S 2900	110
C-65-152	136	FP 203 b	118	S 2905	103
C-65-153	137			S 2906	104
C-66-243	130	L 4361	141		
C-66-244	131	L 4375	139	I 2636	148
C-66-245	134	L 4455	140	I 2640	149
C-66-246	135	L 4476	147	I 2643	151
C-67-62	128	L 4513	143	I 2667	150
C-67-63	129	L 4514	144	I 2693	152
C-68-47	126	L 4515	142		
C-68-33	125	L 4516	146		
C-68-79	121	L 4519	145		

INDEX

References are to pages or (**bold face**) catalogue numbers

Abacus, cutting down of 22, 26, **59–62**
Acanthus: 24, 28, **21–26, 59–62, 80, 81, 94**; scroll **100, 101**
Achaia, province of 64
Alaric 31[77], 37, 62
American School of Classical Studies at Athens 1
Anathyrosis 9, **47, 50, 77**
Antonine period 28, 61, 87
Apse, addition of: to Room 2, 38–39, 40, 42–43; to Room 3, 30–31
Arches: brick 43, 46, 47, 49–50, 56; in vault construction 47; over niche 35; relieving 35, 36, 37–38, 40, 41, 42, 47, 53; shallow, as lintel 35, 36, 41
Argos, brickwork at 86–87. *See also* Baths
Asia Minor, influences from 21, 24, 28
Athens: two-fascia epistyle in 28; monopteros, in Greek Agora at 28
Attis(?), head 16, **110**

Banasa, Thermes de, fuel used in 104
Base moldings: 15, 40, 48, 53; for pilasters 40, 42
Bases, column: in Rome 27; from colonnade 9, 10, 12, 61, 63[10], **90, 91**; from marble façade 18, 26, 27, **1–6**; from Room 4 50, **98**; from service area 56[61] 61, 63[10], **102**; from Temple of Tyche at Corinth 27; restoration of, in marble façade 22; re-used 9, 26; unfinished at back **1–6, 90, 102**
Basins 12, 37
Baths, at Argos: in Agora 86; Thermes A 64, 86–87
———, at Corinth: Greek 1[2]; in South Stoa 1[2]; in the Gymnasium area 1[2], 30; near the fountain of Hadji Mustapha 1[2]; north of the Peribolos of Apollo 1[2], 30, 63; north of the Theater (?) 1, 63[10]; of Eurykles 1, 1[2], 63; of Hadrian 1, 63–64; west of the Odeion 1[2]
——— *See also* Banasa, Miletus, Trier
Bench supports 98
Benches 34, 38, 39, 44, 45, 48
Blocks, unfinished 24, 25, **77, 78**
Boilers 59
Bone **95, 96, 97, 103**
Bothroi: Byzantine 4, 11; Turkish 49[38]
Boundary wall 1
Bricks: bipedales 41, 86; from furnace flue 58, 100; sesquipedales 86; voussoir 34, 35, 36, 41, 86; with V-shaped notch 15. *See also* Appendix I, *passim*; Herringbone
Building materials 3–4
Byzantine: construction 4–5, 7, 8, 13; walls 5, 8, 13. *See also* Bothroi; Drains; Houses; Pottery

Caldarium 2, 43
Capitals: Corinthian 19, 22, 26, 27, 28, **21–26, 59–62, 80, 81**; Ionic 10, 48, 53; pilaster 40, 41, 61[2], **94**; re-used 26; unfinished 25, 29, **80, 81**; unfinished at back 22, 26, **21, 22, 62**
Captives' Façade: 11, 24, 28; redating of 11
Centering, cuttings for 19, **7, 22, 26, 80**
Channels, water. *See* Conduit; Drains; Gutter; Water channel
Chemtou, marble from 3. *See also Giallo antico*
Chisel, claw 7, **11, 26, 81**
Cipollino 3. *See also* Karystos
Cisterns(?) 56[61]
Clamps and pins: bronze 35, 36, 47, **119**; cuttings for 8, 15, 19, 20, 21, 26, 35, 39, 45, 46, 53, **16, 25, 27–31, 34, 36, 37, 41, 43, 47, 50, 59–61, 63–65, 67, 69, 70, 72, 74, 80, 81, 89, 92, 95, 104**; iron 18, 46, 49, 53, 55, **27, 28, 31, 34**
Coffers, irregularly shaped **69, 71**
Coins, cache of 4, 43. *See also* Appendices II–III *passim*
Colonnade: 2, 7, 8–11; later history of 9, 10, 12–13
Columns: fluted 19, 22, 26, 27, 64[10], **13–20, 53–58**; spirally fluted 13, 25, **79**; unfinished 26, **10, 11**; unfluted 8, 10, 18–19, 22, 26, 37, 48, 50, 53, **7–12, 51, 52**
Commodus, temples to, at Corinth 28
Concrete 3, 14, 37
Conduit, water: modern 2–3, 14. *See also* Drains; Gutter; Water channel
Console blocks 24–25, 26–27, 28, **75, 76**
Consoles: 23–24; diagonal 23–24, 29, **69, 70, 71**; ovolo as crowning molding of 24
Cornice: 21, 23–24, 26, 28, 53, **34–41, 69–74**; coffered 53, **100, 101**. *See also* Geison blocks
Cyma recta 18, 27, **1–6, 82–85**
Cyma reversa 15, 18, 21, 23, 24, **27–50, 63–70, 72–74, 86, 87, 92, 95, 100, 101, 103**

Destructions. *See* Alaric, Earthquakes, Herulians, Sacks and conquests
Dinsmoor, W. B., restored plan of building by 2, 42
Dipinti: on pottery **125, 126**; on walls of building 47, 55, **96, 97**, 98, 99
Doorsill 35. *See also* Threshold
Doorways: 2, 35, 36, 37, 38, 39, 40, 41, 42, 49, 53, 54, 61. *See also* Doorsill; Threshold
Dowel holes 18, 19, 26, **13, 23, 24, 27, 30, 31, 59–61, 70, 98**
Drains: Byzantine 5; Roman 9, 11, 13, 34, 37, 38, 43, 44, 48, 54, 60, 61, 62. *See also* Conduit; Gutter; Water channel

Earlier building on site. *See* Site, earlier building on
Early travelers, building seen by 1³, 5
Earthquakes 4, 5, 17, 31, 32, 37, 48, 49, 55, 62
Eleusis, two-fascia epistyle at 28
Empolion cuttings 9, 18, 19, 22, 26, **1, 2, 12, 16, 42, 44-46, 53**
Entablature. *See* Epistyle-frieze blocks
Entranceway: 7-8, 11-12, 14, 29, 63; later history of 12, 32, 62
Epistyle: three-fascia 23, **63-68, 95**; two-fascia 20-21, 23, 28, **27-33, 68**
Epistyle-frieze blocks: 8, 10, 11, 14², 19-21, 22-23, 26, 27, 28, 41, 60⁷², 61, **27-33, 63-68, 92, 95**; proportions of 23, 26. *See also* Masons' marks
Euboia, marble from 3. *See* Cipollino; *Fior di pesco*; Karystos
Eurykles: C. Julius Eurykles Herculanus 63⁹; of Sparta 1. *See also* Baths, at Corinth, of Eurykles
Eusambatis 10
Excavations: of 1896 1; of 1965-1968 2-3; difficulties encountered 2-3; significance of 64

Façade, marble: 2, 8, 11¹⁵, 14-32 (Chapter II); area at base of (Room 6) 29-31; later history of 31-32, 62; chronology of 25-29, 62; re-used material in 26-28; unassigned blocks from 24-25, 26-27, **75, 76**
Façade, marble, restoration of, on paper: 14, 15, 17, 30; in angles 20, 21, 23, 24; problems with 17, 27
Figurines 95, 105
Fior di pesco 3, 15, 16, 22, 33, 39, 41, 50, **52, 82-85**
Floors: 12; cement (concrete) 8, 11, 37; construction of, within building 33, 34, 37, 43-44, 49, 52; of hypocaust 37, 43, 51⁴³, 54; marble 29, 33, 38, 43; mosaic 8, 12, 49, 50, 52, 59, 96
Flues: furnace 56⁶¹, 58; vents 98, in walls 40, 41, 42, 46, 49-50, in vaults 47, 47³²
Formwork: for foundations 14, 30; for vaults 3, 47; for walls of service corridor 57
Foundations: of colonnade 9, 11; of entranceway 7, 11; of façade 14, 30; of Room 2 39, 56; of Room 3 57; of Room 5 52, 63; trench for, in façade area 30, 31
Fountain group 37, **105**
Frankish constructions 4-5
Frieze. *See* Epistyle-frieze blocks
Frigidarium 2, 33, 34
Fuel. *See* Banasa
Furnaces 37, 42, 43, 51, 54, 58-59, 61. *See also* Flues; Heating systems

Ganymede(?), head 16, **110**
Geison blocks 10, **93**. *See also* Cornice
Giallo antico 3, 19, 22, 28, 36, 50, **13-20, 58**
Giuliani, C. 47
Ginouvès, R. 86

Glass: vessels of **138**, 95-102 *passim*, 103, 104, 105; window 17, 95-102 *passim*, 103, 105. *See also* Tesserae
Goths, sack by. *See* Alaric
Graffito **137**, 103
Granite 3, 48
Graves 5, 37
Groups: *1* 11, 61; *2* 37, 47, 61; *3* 42, 48, 57; *4* 43, 48; *5* 50, 54, 58, 61; *6* 42, 58, 61; *7* 58; *8* 37; *9* 31, 60; *10-12* 17, 31, 56; *13* 17, 56, 59; *14* 12, 31; *15* 36, 37, 62; *16* 43, 62; *17* 46, 48, 49, 62; *18* 50, 62; *19* 55, 59, 62; *20* 55, 56, 62; *21* 17, 32, 62; *22* 60; *23* 17, 32; *24-26* 13; *27-30* 12-13; *31, 32* 58, 62; *33* 16, 32, 49, 52, 54, 55
Guilloche 18, **1-4, 31**
Gutter: along colonnade 10; in latrine 13. *See also* Water channel

Hadrian: Library of, at Athens 24; time of 12, 27, 61, 63¹⁰, 86, 87; Villa of 47; Baths of 1, 63
Hearth, in 6th-century house 12
Heating systems 58-60. *See also* Flues; Furnaces; *Testudo alvei*; Tubes; Tubuli; Vaults, heating of; Walls, heated
Herakles 37, **105**
Hermes 41¹⁹, 48, **109**
Herringbone pattern, brick paving in 11
Herulians 54⁵⁹, 61
Houses: Byzantine 4-5; in colonnade 4, 7, 8, 9, 12-13, 62; modern 35; Turkish 5
Hypocaust: 37, 43, 48, 51, 55; columns of. *See* Appendix I, Table 2

Identification of building 63
Interaxial spacing: of entranceway 7-8; of colonnade 9-10
Inscriptions 10, 12, 60⁷², **148-152**, 102, 103. *See also* Dipinti; Graffito; Isthmian Games
Irrigation channel. *See* Conduit
Isthmian Games, victors' list from 13
Ittar, Sebastian, 1802 plan of building by 1-2, 33, 33¹, 35, 36, 40¹⁵, 42, 45
Ivy pattern, in mosaic 49

Karystos, marble from 3, 8, 18, 26, 39, 50, **7-11**

Lamps: 95-97 *passim*, 99, 100, 102, 103, 105; Attic **141, 143, 145**; Corinthian **139, 140, 142, 144**; imported **146**
Lapis lacedaemonius 3, 4, 33, 35, 36, 37, 40, 41, 48, 50, 53
Latrine, in colonnade: 4, 7, 8, 9, 13, 62; footing slabs from 17¹⁴, 53
Lead: 96, 99, 100, 103; used with dowels 19, 26, 102
Leaf frieze 18, 28, **1, 2, 63, 64, 75, 92**

Leaf, on abacus 27[47], **26**, **59**
Leaves, water **27**, **38**, **75**
Lechaion Road: 1, 2, 4, 7, 8, 10, 11, 12, 64. *See also* Entranceway; Shops
Lepcis Magna, Severan Basilica at 28
Lesbian leaf 18, **1**, **27**, **34**, **69**, **92**, **95**
Lime pit, in entranceway 7, 12, 62; in service area 42, 57
Lion's head spout 52, **99**
Loomweight **96**
Lotus and palmettes 29, **63–66**, **68**, **92**, **95**

Marble: bluish gray 15; gray 38, **96**; gray veined **79**; grayish white 40, **99**; greenish gray **97**; pinkish **95**; red 19, **12**; white 3, 9, 12, 22, 33, 34–35, 36, 38, 39, 40, 41, 43, 44, 45, 48, 50, 53, 55, **1–6**, **21–51**, **59–78**, **80**, **81**, **86–94**, **98–112**. *See also* Cipollino; *Fior di pesco*; *Giallo antico*; Karystos; Proconnesos; *Rosso antico*
Marble blocks, storage of, on site 11[15]
Marble façade. *See* Façade, marble
Marmara 3. *See also* Proconnesos
Masons' marks, on epistyle-frieze blocks 8, 26, **31**, **92**
Metalwork 47, **119**, **120**, 94, 96–103 *passim*
Miletus, Baths of Capito 30
Moldings: stone 54, 102; stucco 50. *See also* Base moldings
Mortar. *See* Appendix I *passim*
Mosaic 8, 12, 16, 34, 35, 36, 52, 59, 101. *See also* Floors; Tesserae

Niches: apsidal 15, 16, 35; barrel vaulted 16; bricking up of 30; decoration of 16, 34–35; platforms in front of 15, 16, 18; rectangular 15–16, 34, 35, 36; restoration of 16, 35
Numidia, marble from 3, 28. *See also Giallo antico*

Olympia, two-fascia epistyle at 28
Opus incertum 52, 53, 63
Oven 5

Palmettes 23, **34**, **37**, **38**, **100**, **101**. *See also* Lotus and palmettes
Pan, head of 37, **106**
Parapets: of marble façade 24; of pools 30, 34, 38, 39, 40, 44, 45, 55; openwork 30, **86**
Pausanias 1[1], 63
Pediment 24
Peloponnesos, marble from. *See Lapis lacedaemonius*
Philippi, theater at 28
Pier cap 15, 18
Piers 14–15
Pilaster 40. *See also* Capital, pilaster
Pins. *See* Clamps and pins
Pits: in colonnade 8, 12; Turkish, clay-lined 5. *See also* Bothroi; Lime pit

Plague of A.D. 542 62
Plan: early phase of Room 2 41–42; of building 1–2, 3, 14; restored, of Sebastian Ittar 1–2, 33, 33[1], 35, 36, 41, of W. B. Dinsmoor 2, 33, 42
Plaster, painted. *See* Stucco, painted
Plinths 9, 10
Podium 14, 15, 17
Podium cap 18
Polykleitos, Roman copy of head by 41
Pools 2, 14, 29–30, 31, 33–34, 37–40, 42, 43, 44–46, 48–49, 52, 55, 60, 61, 62
Poros 7, 9, 12, 40, 53
Porphyry. *See Lapis lacedaemonius*
Portrait heads 37, 48, **107**, **108**
Pottery: Asia Minor "Light-Coloured" Ware **124**; Athenian Ware **131**, **133**; Byzantine 4[15], 102; Frankish 4[15]; Roman, African Red Slip Ware **123**, **136**, Late Roman C **121**; Turkish 4[14], 102. *See also* **122**, **125–130**, **132**, **134**, **135**, Appendices II–III *passim*
Pour channels 9, 10, 18, 22, 26, **1–3**, **42**, **44–46**, **90**
Proconnesos, marble from 3, 15, 22, 33, 34, 35, 38, 39, 40, 45, **53–57**

Ram, sculpture of 48, **109**
Rebate 9
Relief 13, 41, 54, **68**, **103**, **104**, 98, 103
Repairs: to blocks **34**, **63**, **70**; to colonnade 9, 10; to furnace 58; to hypocausts 43, 44[22], 51, 54, 58; to marble façade 15–16, 20, 23, 25, 26, 27, 29, 31, 55; to walls of building 15, 31, 34, 37, 40, 41, 45, 48, 50, 53, 54, 55
Roads 5, 64. *See also* Lechaion Road
Re-use: of blocks 9, 11, 12, 13, 22, 26–27; of wall plaques 33, 38, 41
Revetment 16, 30, 34, 35, 36, 37, 38, 39, 40, 41, 42, 45, 49, 50, 53, 55, 61, **82–85**, **94**, **96**, **97**, **99**, 99, 103
Ribbon, twisted 28, **27**, **92**
Room 1: 2, 33–37; axis of, different from Rooms 2 and 3 3, 36, 63; chronology of 37, 62; plan of, in 1802 33, 35, 36
Room 2: 2, 37–43; axis of 37; chronology of 41–43, 48, 61; early plan of 38, 39, 40, 41–42
Room 3: 2, 14, 30–31, 43–49; axis of 43; chronology of 48–49, 62
Room 4: 2, 49–50, 61; chronology of 50, 61
Room 5: 2, 14, 30, 50–55; chronology of 54–55, 61, 62, 63; converted into service area 55, 59; earlier walls of 52
Room 6: 55. *See also* Façade; Chapter II
Room 7: 14, 16, 55–56; chronology of 55–56
Rosettes 29, **26**, **59**, **69**, **70**, **73**, **94**, **100**
Rosso antico 3, 4, 36, 53
Roumania 46, 49

S-scrolls 23, 29[62], **63**, **75**
Sacks and conquests 62[5]. *See also* Alaric, Herulians

Scaffolding holes 34, 36, 46
Sculpture 16, 37, 41, 48, 50, 53, **103–112**, 96, 98, 99, 102. *See also* Attis(?); Fountain group; Ganymede(?); Herakles; Hermes; Pan; Polykleitos; Portrait heads; Ram; Relief; Seated figure; Statue support (?)
Seated figure 54, **111**
Severan period 12, 27, 29, 61, 87
Service areas 2, 12, 23, 31, 52, 55, 56–58, 61, 62, 63
Setting lines 15, 16, 18, **25, 42, 77, 80, 88**
Shops, on Lechaion Road 2, 4, 7, 8, 11
Sima 28
Simitthu, marble from 3. *See also Giallo antico*
Site: location of 1; earlier building on 3, 52, 63–64; history of 1–2, 4–5, 63–64
Sluice 60
South Basilica, at Corinth 28
Sparta, marble from 4. *See also Lapis lacedaemonius*
Stairway, of 6th-century house 12
Statue support (?) 60, **112**
Steps: marble 8, 10; blocks for 10, 23, 54, 56. *See also* Benches
Stucco: 48, 96–99 *passim*; painted 50, 96, 97. *See also* moldings
Stylobate: of colonnade 9, 12; of entranceway 7, 12; of marble façade 21–22, 26, **42–50**

Tegulae mammatae 46, 53, 99, 103
Tenaro, Cape, marble from 4. *See also Rosso antico*
Tepidarium 2
Terracotta **113–118**, 95, 98–100 *passim*, 102, 103, 104, 105
Tesserae: glass 16, 36, 47, 95–99 *passim*, 101, 102; stone 8, 12, 16, 35, 49, 95, 96, 99, 101, 102
Testudo alvei 59
Thunderbolt **71**
Threshold block, of 6th-century house 12

Tile: 103; stamped **117, 118**, 96, 102
Tiled court: 2, 7, 8, 10–11, 31, 62; later history of 12, 13, 62
Topography of Corinth, Byzantine to present 4–5
Trier, Barbarathermen 30
Tubes, from heating system 46, 49, 53, 55, **113–115**, 98, 99 *passim*, 100, 102, 103, 105
Tubuli 53, **116**, 102
Tunisia, marble from 3. *See also Giallo antico*
Turkish levels 5. *See also* Bothroi; Houses; Pits; Pottery

Vaults: 36, 41, 47, 50, 54, 55, 56, 56[61], 57, 62; heating of 43, 47; metalwork in 47. *See also* Flues; Formwork
Veneer. *See* Revetment
Vents. *See* Flues
Voussoir. *See* Bricks, voussoir

Walls: base, brick and mortar 53, *opus incertum* 52, 53; channels in 15, 30; heated 43, 46, 52, 53, 55. *See also* Flues; *Tegulae mammatae*, Tubuli
———, of colonnade 8–9, 11; of entranceway 7, 11; of façade 14–17, 31; rebuilding of 31, 53; of rooms of building 34–35, 39, 40–41, 45–47, 49–50, 52–53, 54–55. *See also* Byzantine
Water channel 49, 58. *See also* Conduit; Drains; Gutter; Water systems
Waterpipes 49, 52, 98–99 *passim*, 100, 103, 104
Waterspouts 34, 37, 52, **99**
Water systems 60. *See also* Conduit; Drains; Sluice; Water spouts; Waterpipes
Wave pattern, in mosaic 8, 12
Weights 103. *See also* Loomweight
Windows: 14, 16–17, 36, 45–46, 50–51; glass for. *See* Glass, window; moldings for 17, **87–89**; mullion for 17[14]

PLATES

PLATE 1

a. Colonnade and tiled court, from the west

b. Colonnade and tiled court, from the east

PLATE 2

a. Façade area, from the south

b. Façade area, from the north

PLATE 3

a. Foundation trench in the façade area, from the northwest

b. Service area against the central wall of the façade, from the west

PLATE 4

a. Foundations of the north wall of the Lechaion Road entranceway, from the south

b. Inscription on the lower step of the colonnade

c. Central wall of the façade, foundations at the northern end, from the west

d. Inscription built into the 6th-century house

e. Latrine, from the east

PLATE 5

a. Room 2, north end, from the north

b. Service area north of Room 3 (Corridor 1), from the northwest

PLATE 6

a. South pool in Room 2, from the north

b. Room 3 before excavation of the central pool, from the south

a. Central pool in Room 3 after removal of most of the fill, from the east

b. Southeast wall of Room 5, south end, from the northwest

PLATE 8

a. Southeast wall of Room 5, north end, and northeast wall, from the southwest

b. Southwest wall of Room 5, from the northeast

PLATE 9

b. Room 7, north corner, from the southwest

a. Room 4, west side, from the northeast

PLATE 10

c. Service corridor wall beneath the north apse of Room 3, from the north

a. East wall of Room 2, south end, from the north

b. Northwest wall of Room 5, from the southeast

1

3

PLATE 12

4

17, 15

7, 8

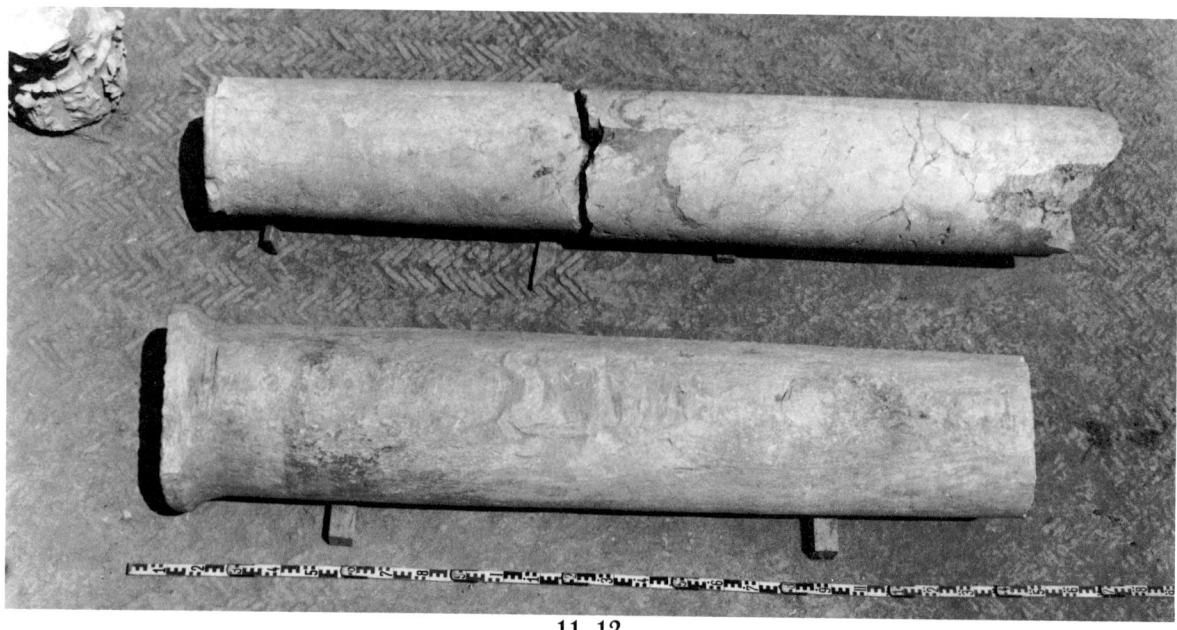
11, 12

PLATE 13

21

22

23

24

25 26

PLATE 14

27

29

30

PLATE 15

31

The Captives' Façade, Corinth

PLATE 16

35

37

34

36

PLATE 17

42

38

43

PLATE 18

53

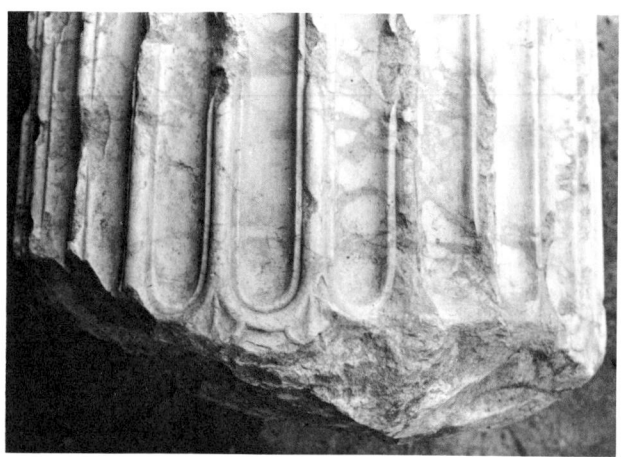

53, detail

55

PLATE 19

59

61 and 60

61

62

PLATE 20

63

64

66

PLATE 21

68, front (above) and back (below)

PLATE 22

69

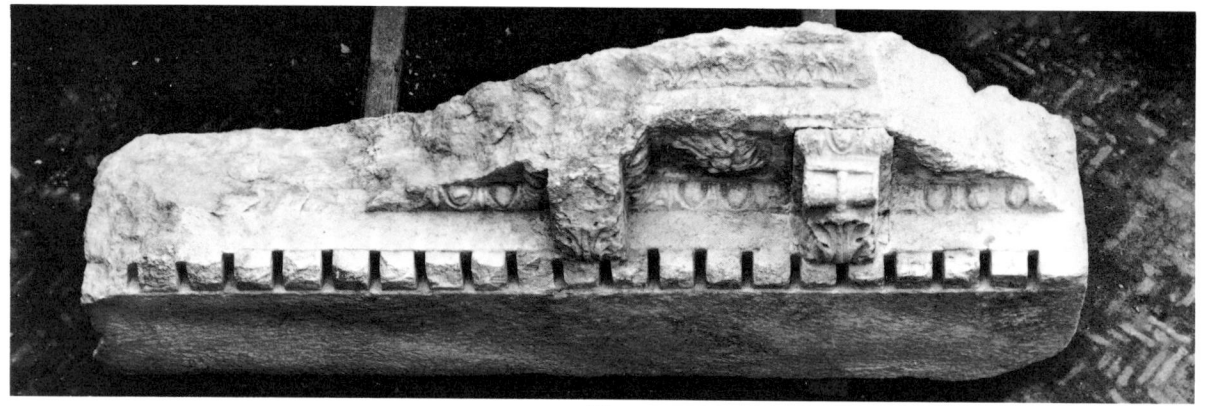

70

71

PLATE 23

75

75 and 76

79

80

81

PLATE 24

82

86

84

85

87

PLATE 25

93

92, back

92, front

91

PLATE 26

94

95

96

97

PLATE 27

99

100

101

103

104

a. Fountain group of Herakles and the Nemean Lion **105**

b. Head of Pan **106**

c. Male portrait **107**

d. Head **108**

PLATE 29

PLATE 30

a. Head **110**

b. Seated figure **111**

c. Statue support **112**, front

d. **112**, back

PLATE 31

a. Head and chest of a ram 109

b. Tube from heating system 113

c. Stamped tile 117

d. Tubulus 116

e. Stamped tile 118

PLATE 32

a. Spike and clamp 119

b. Plate, African Red Slip Ware 123

c. Shaft and crosspiece 120

d. Stamped base 122

e. Bowl, Asia Minor fabric 124

PLATE 33

a. Storage jar, dipinto **125**

b. Storage amphora **127**

c. Storage jar, dipinto **126**

e. Glass jug **138**

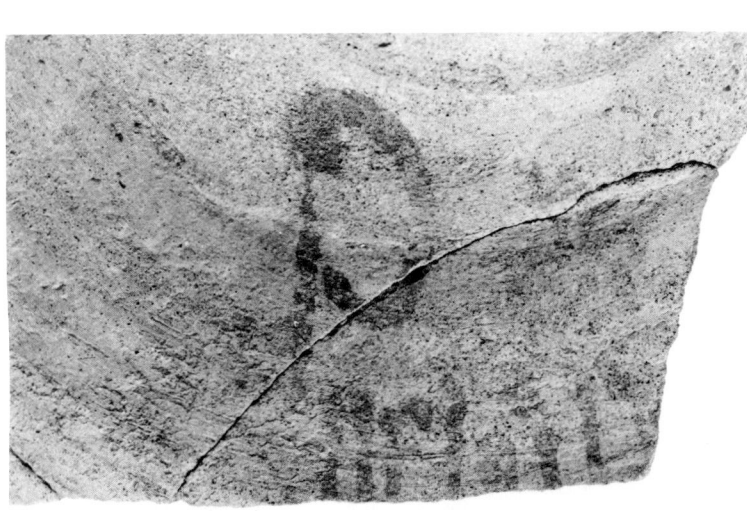

d. **126**, detail

PLATE 34

a. Storage amphora **128**

b. Storage amphora **129**

c. Bowl or dish, African Red Slip Ware **136**

d. Amphora, graffito **137**

PLATE 35

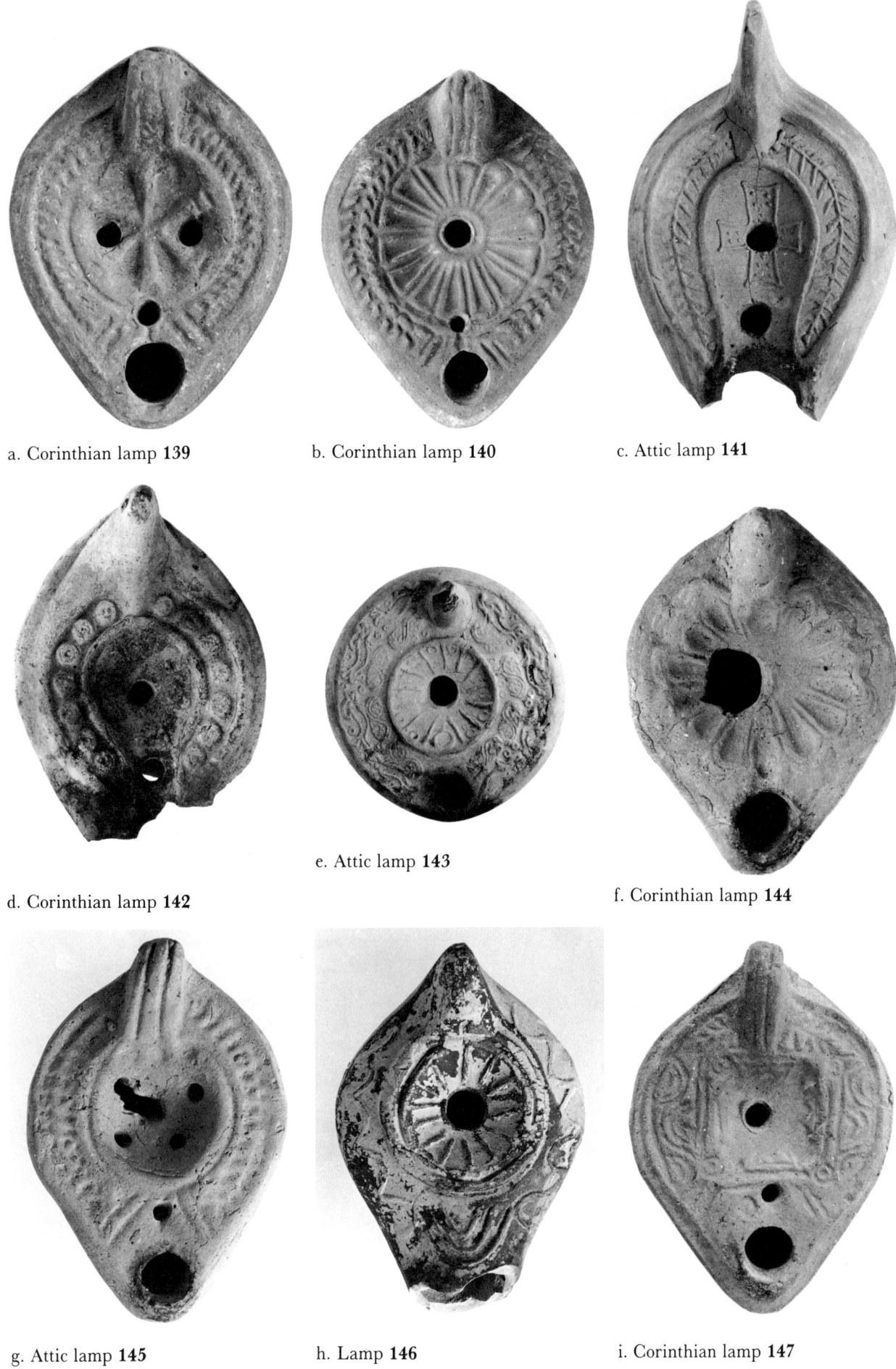

a. Corinthian lamp **139**

b. Corinthian lamp **140**

c. Attic lamp **141**

d. Corinthian lamp **142**

e. Attic lamp **143**

f. Corinthian lamp **144**

g. Attic lamp **145**

h. Lamp **146**

i. Corinthian lamp **147**

PLATE 36

a. Latin inscription **148**

b. Latin or Greek inscription **149**

c. Greek inscription **152**

d. Latin or Greek inscription **150**

e. Greek inscription **151**

PLATE 37

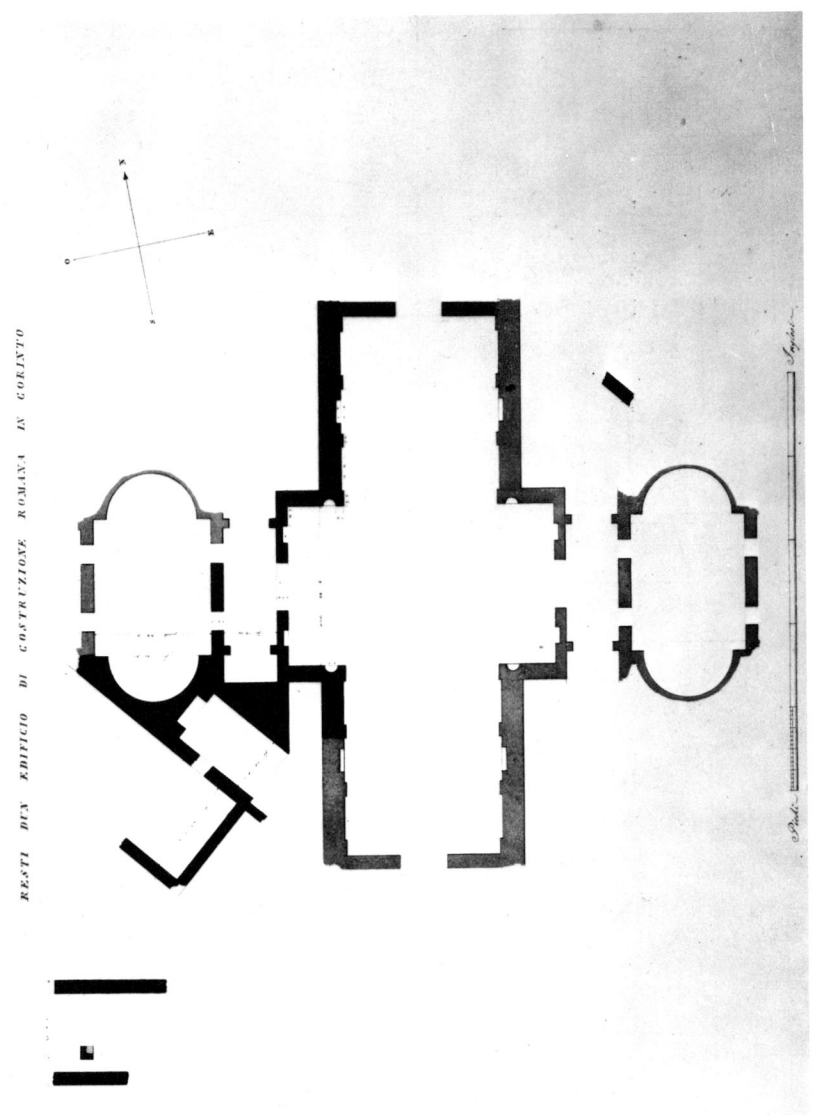

a. 1802 plan (Sebastian Ittar. By courtesy of the Trustees of the British Museum)

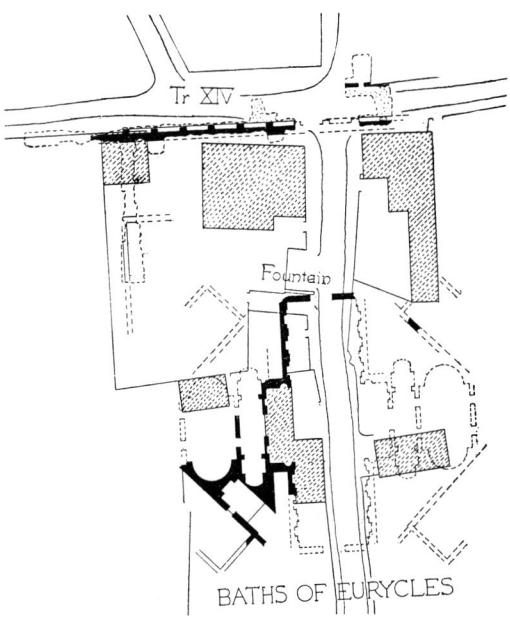

b. 1910–1911 plan (William B. Dinsmoor)

PLATE 38

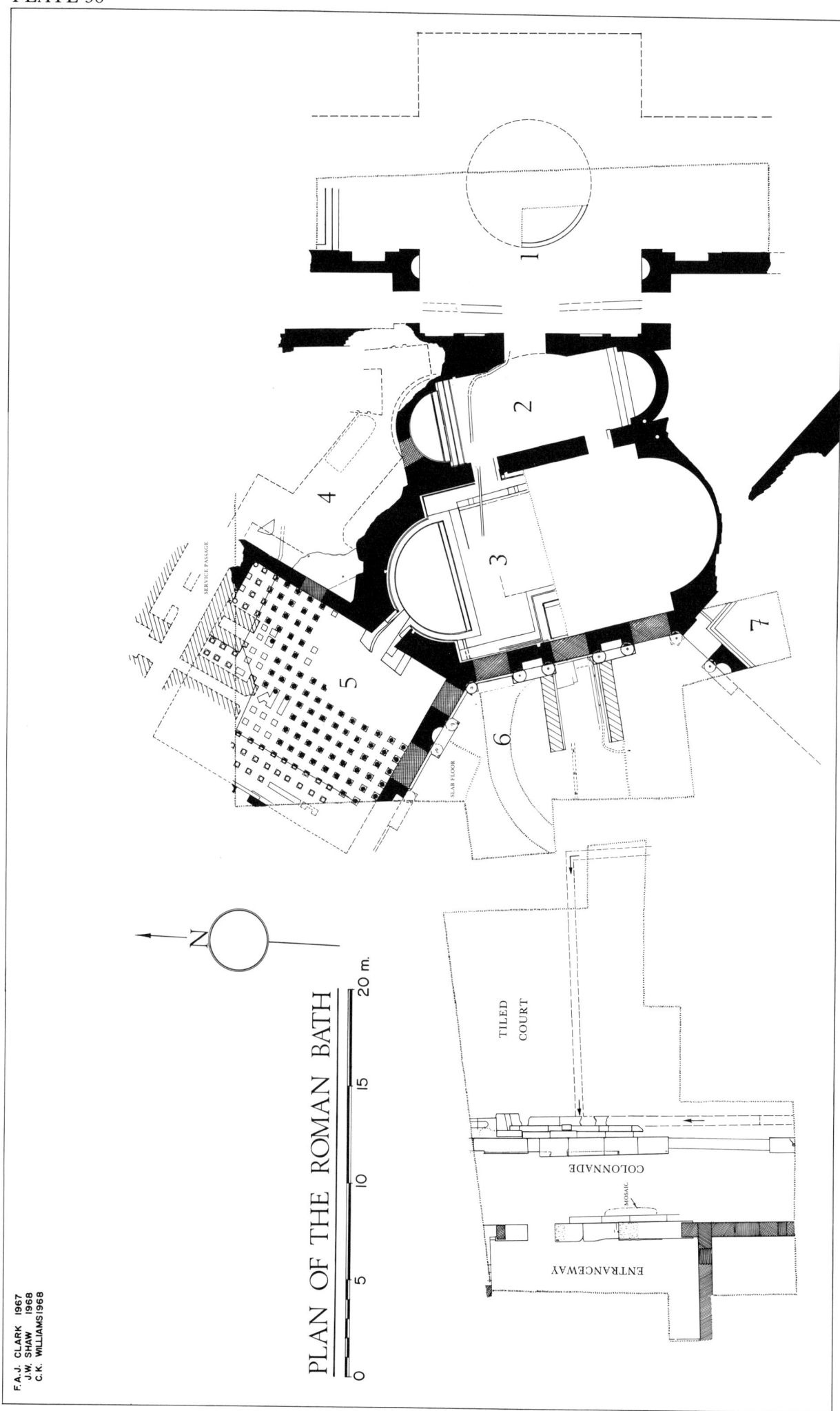

Plan of the Great Bath on the Lechaion Road

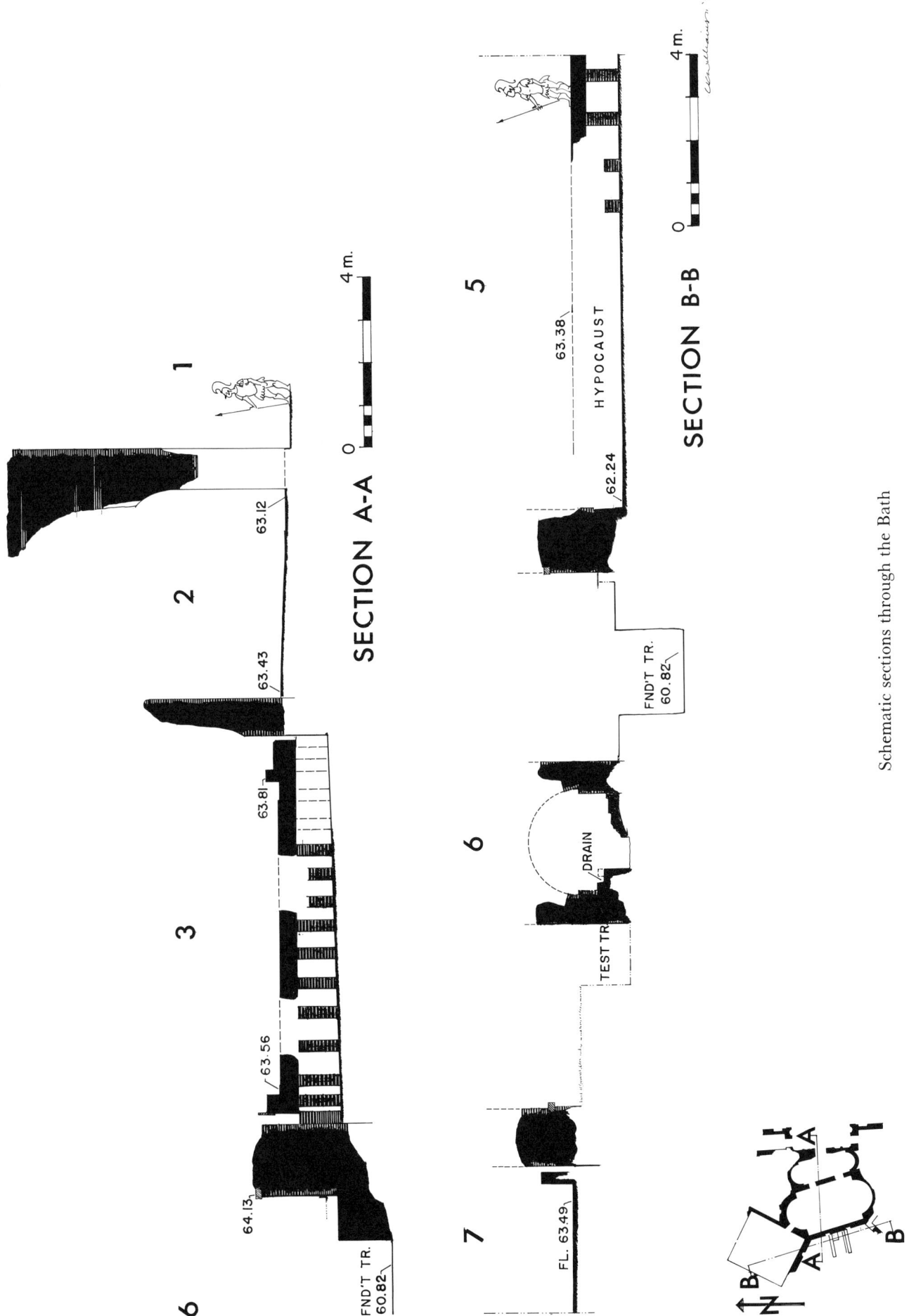

PLATE 39

Schematic sections through the Bath

PLATE 40

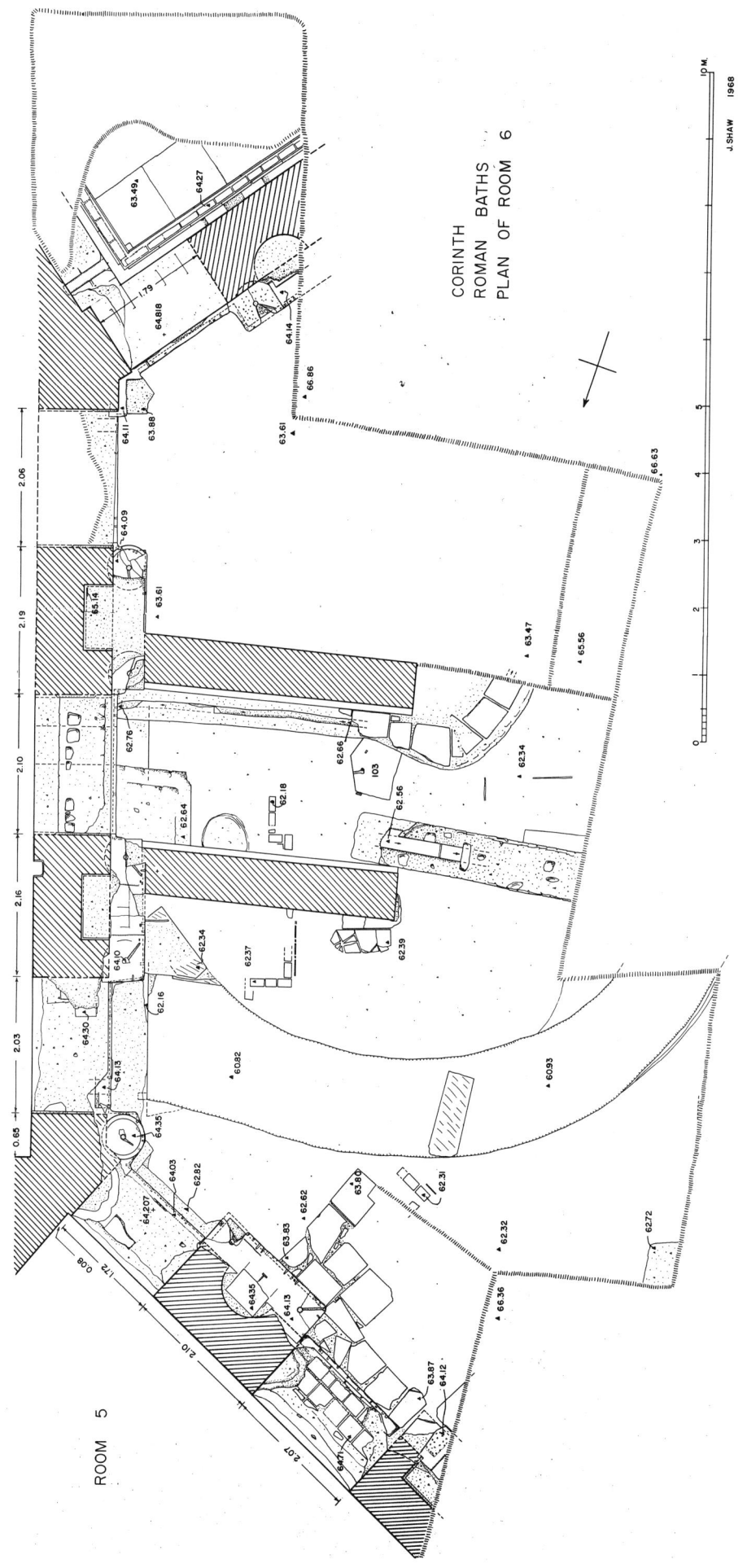

Plan of the Façade Area, actual state (Room 6)

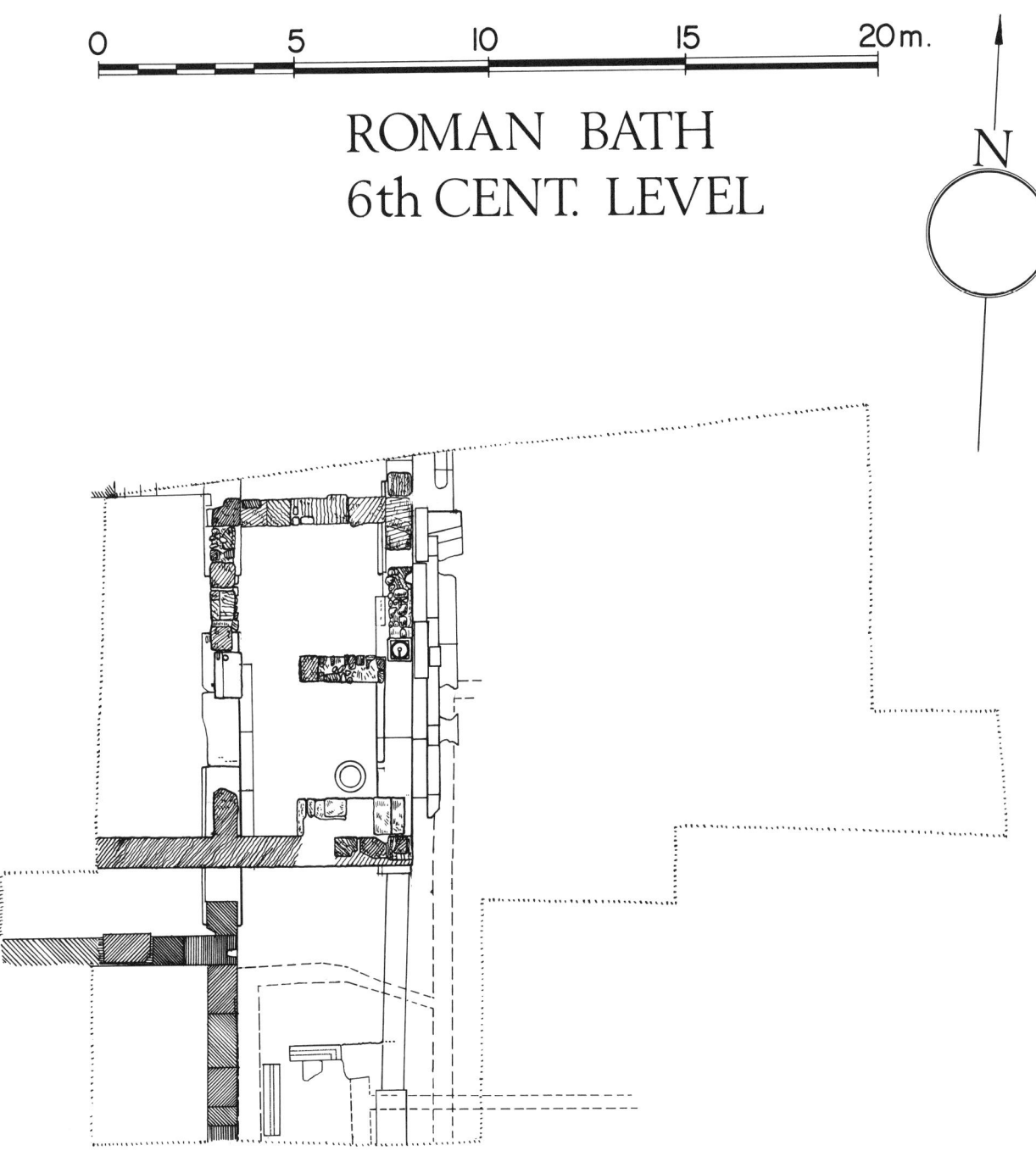

Plan of the 6th-century house and latrine

PLATE 42

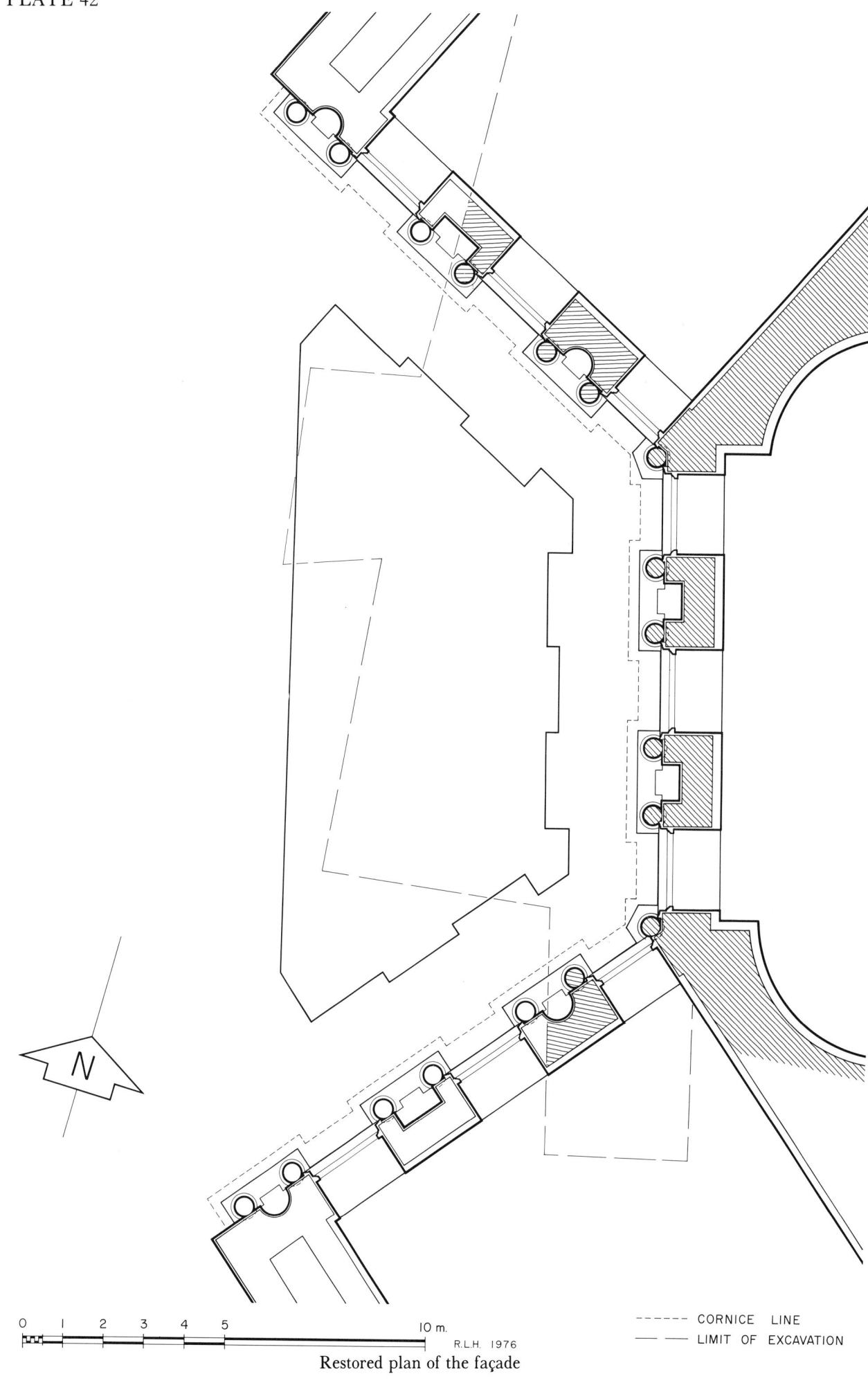

Restored plan of the façade

--- CORNICE LINE
— LIMIT OF EXCAVATION

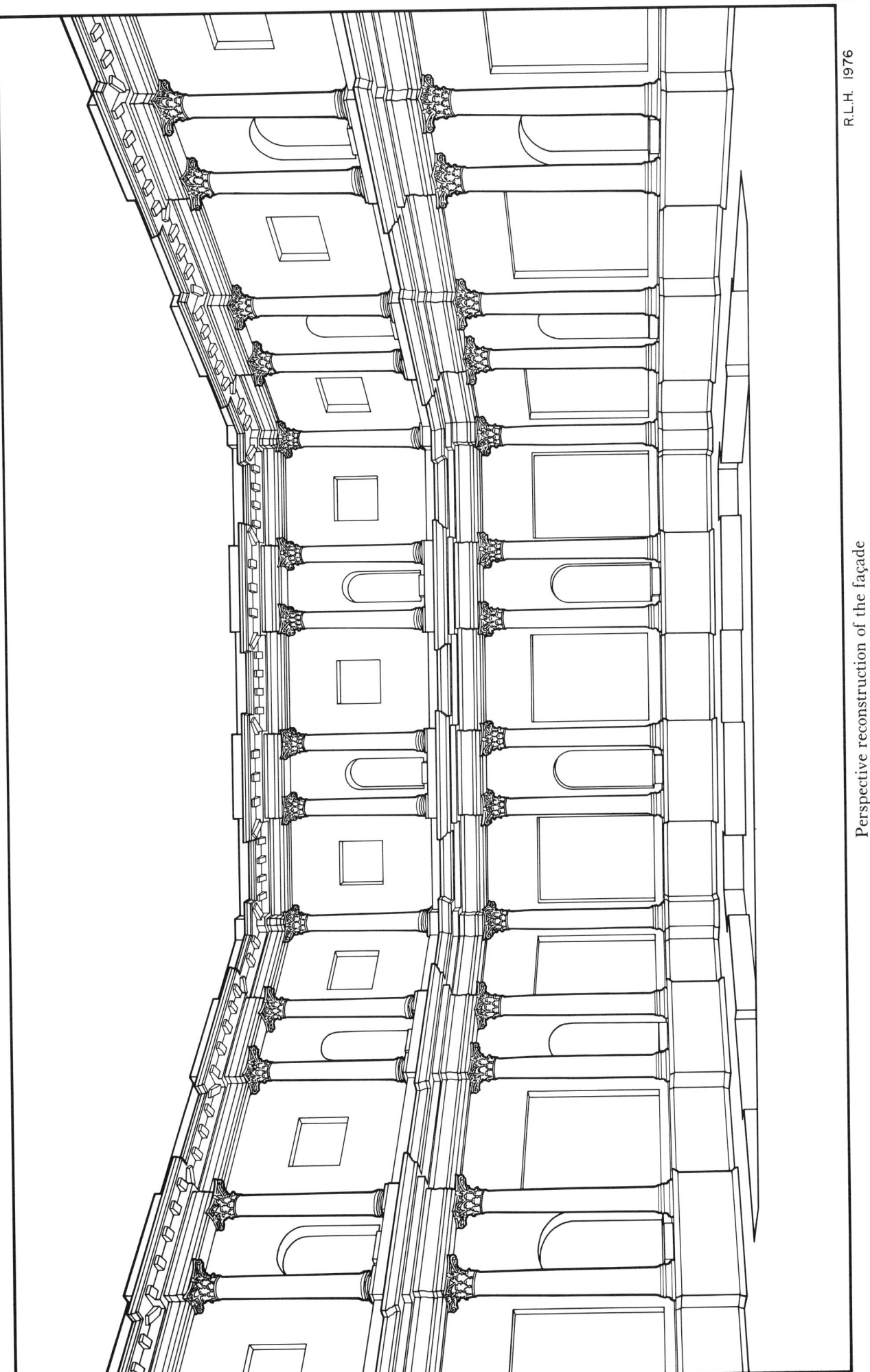

Perspective reconstruction of the façade

PLATE 43

R.L.H. 1976

PLATE 44

Restored north wing, elevation

PLATE 45

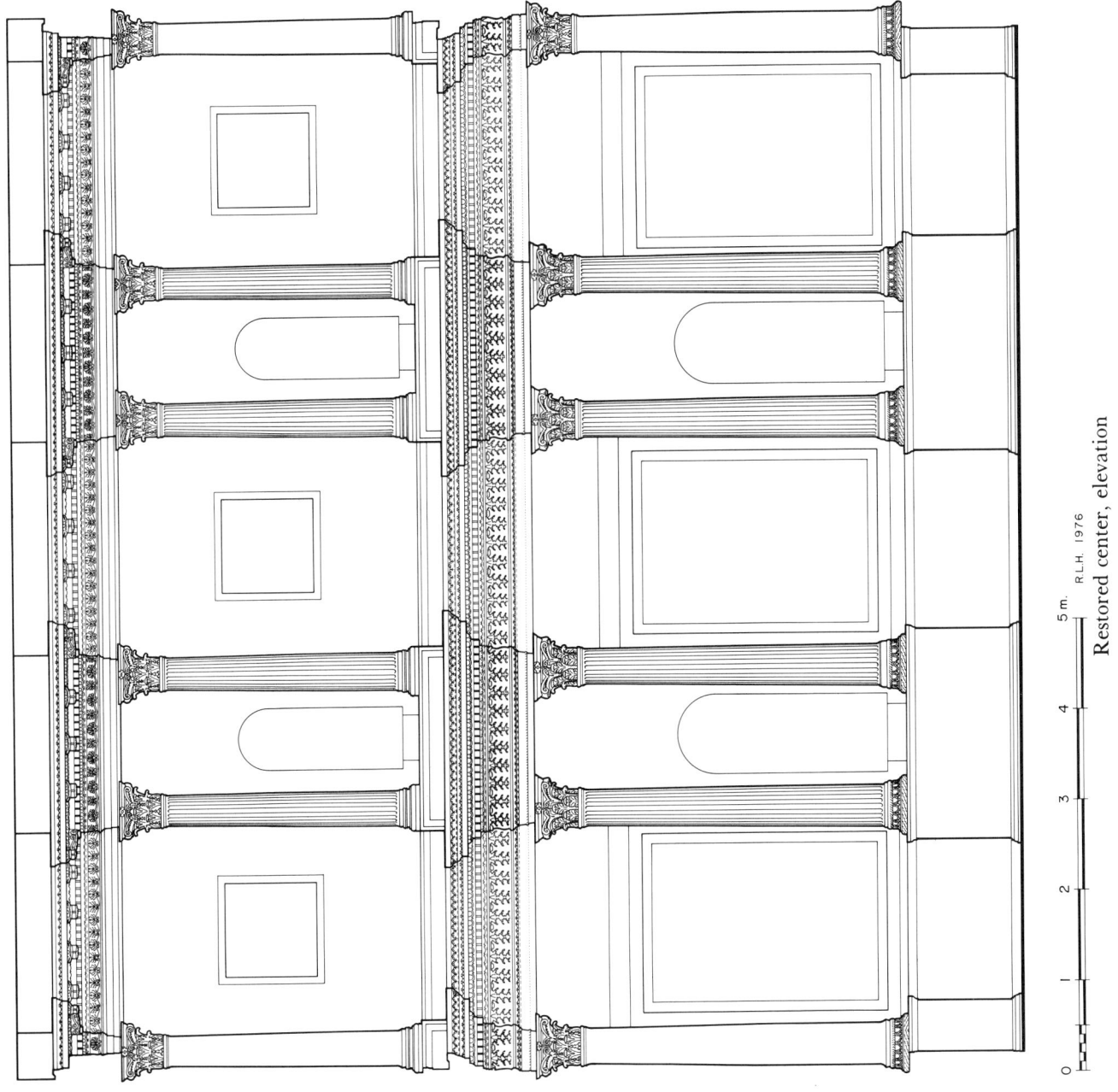

Restored center, elevation

PLATE 46

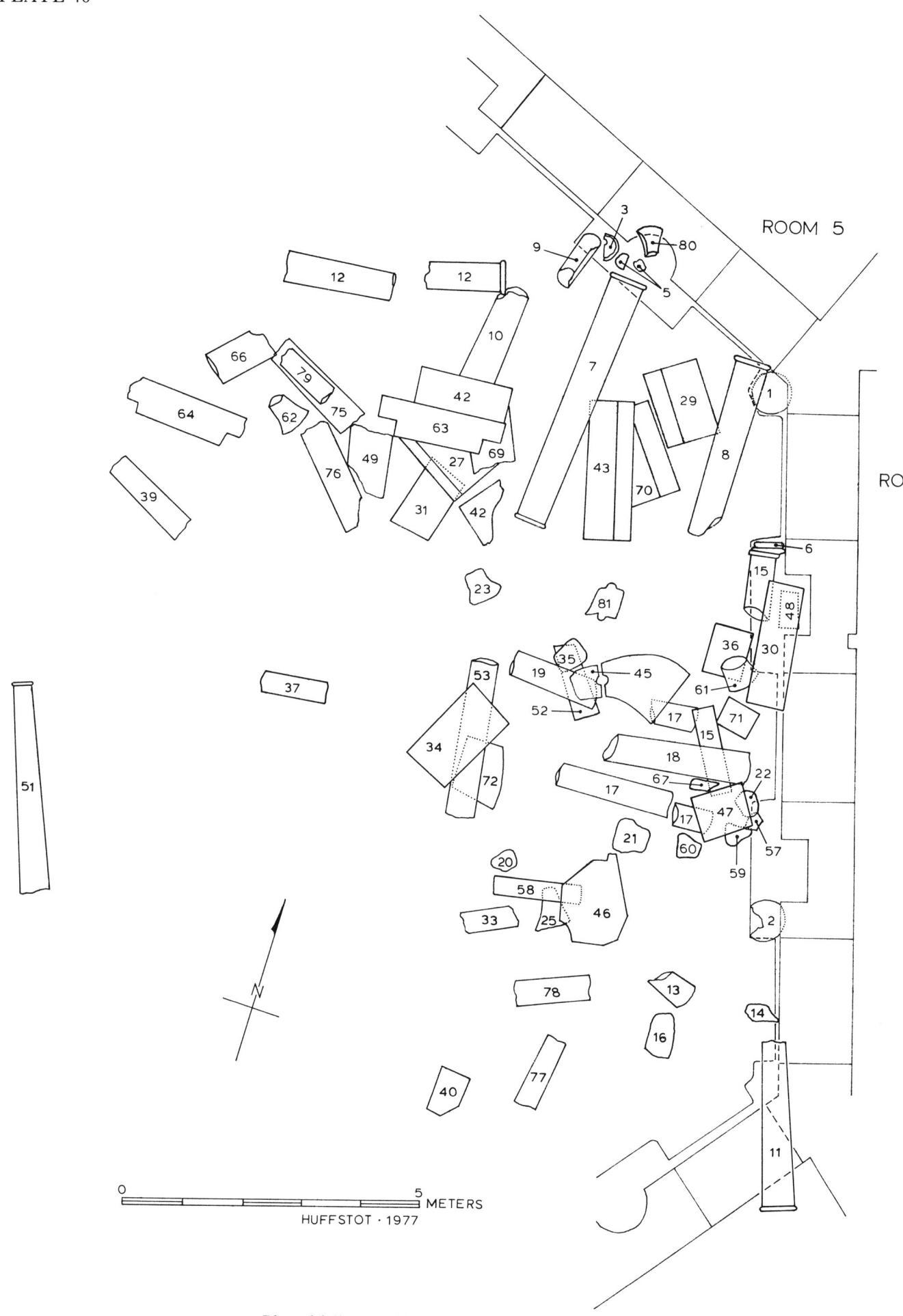

Plan of fallen marble blocks in the façade area

PLATE 47

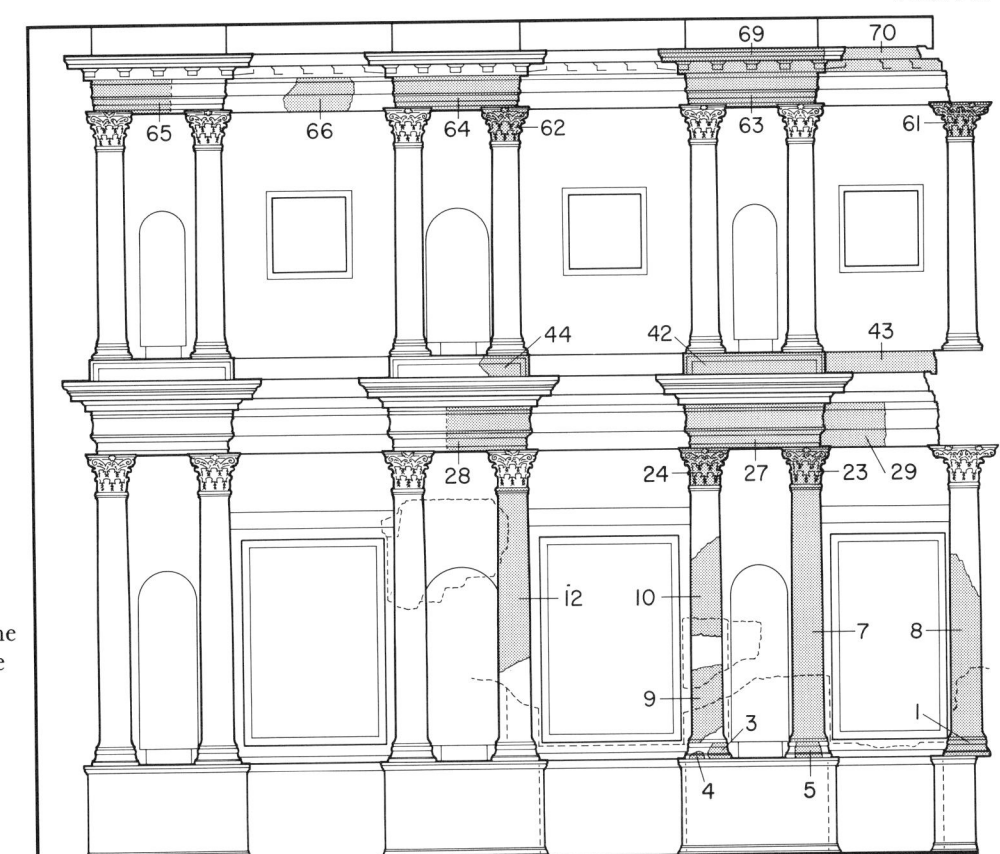

a. Preserved blocks in the north wing of the façade

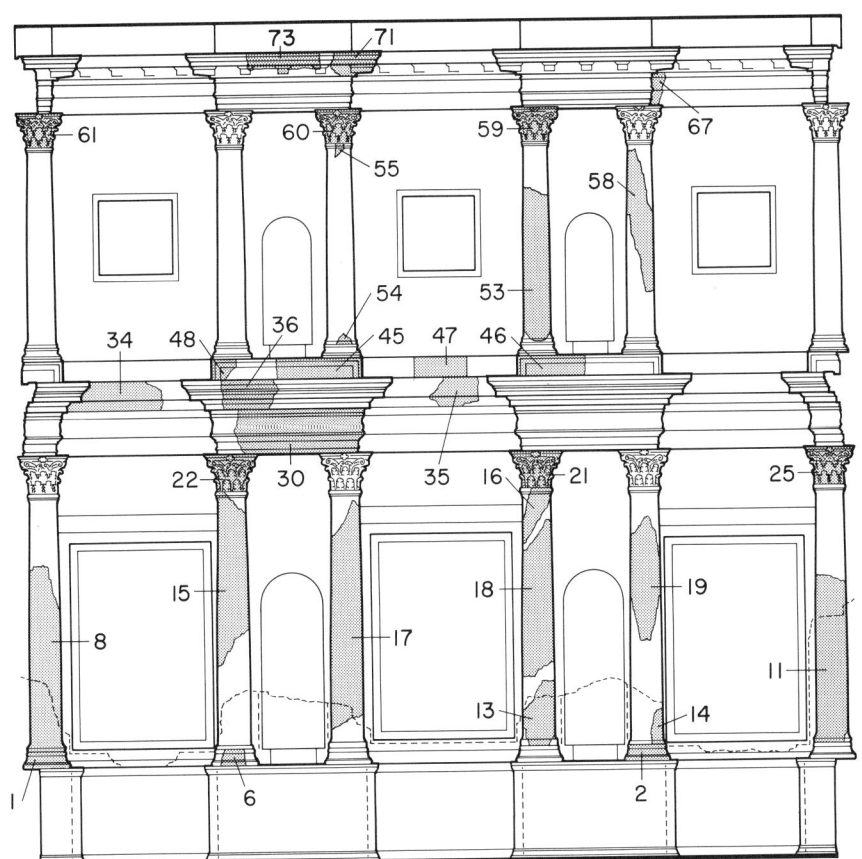

b. Preserved blocks in the center of the façade

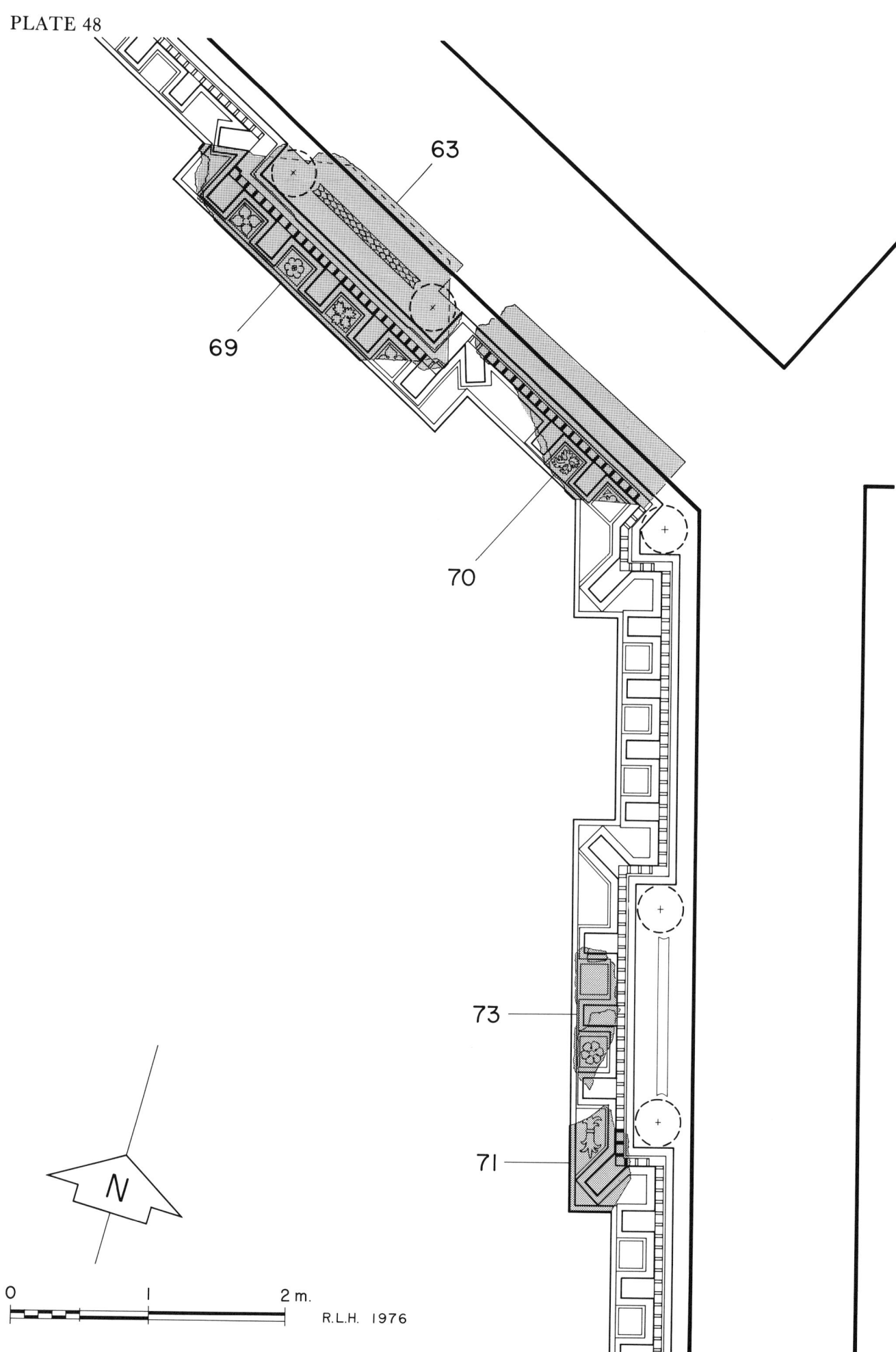

Reflected plan of the soffit of the façade cornice, upper order

PLATE 49

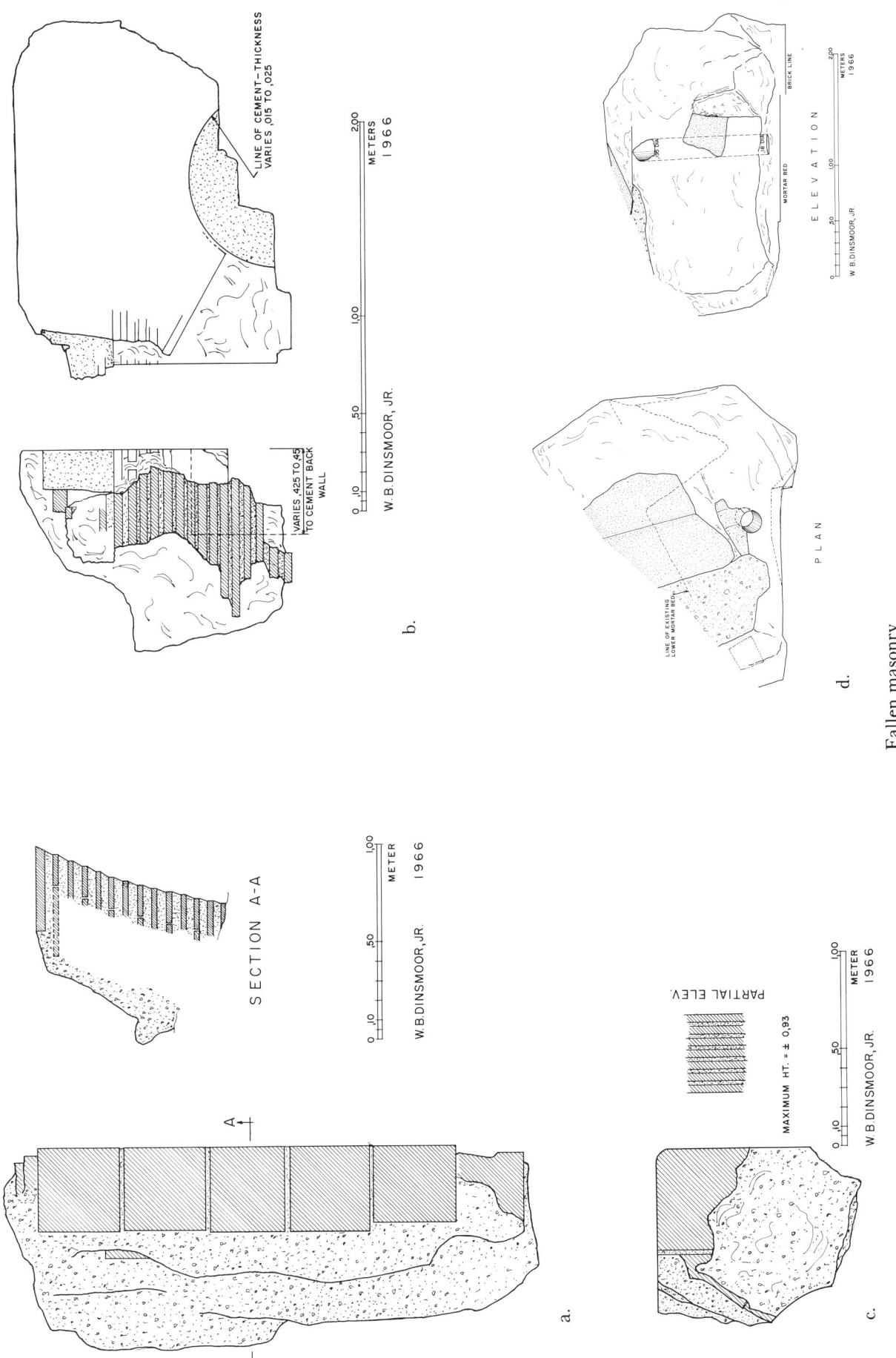

Fallen masonry

PLATE 50

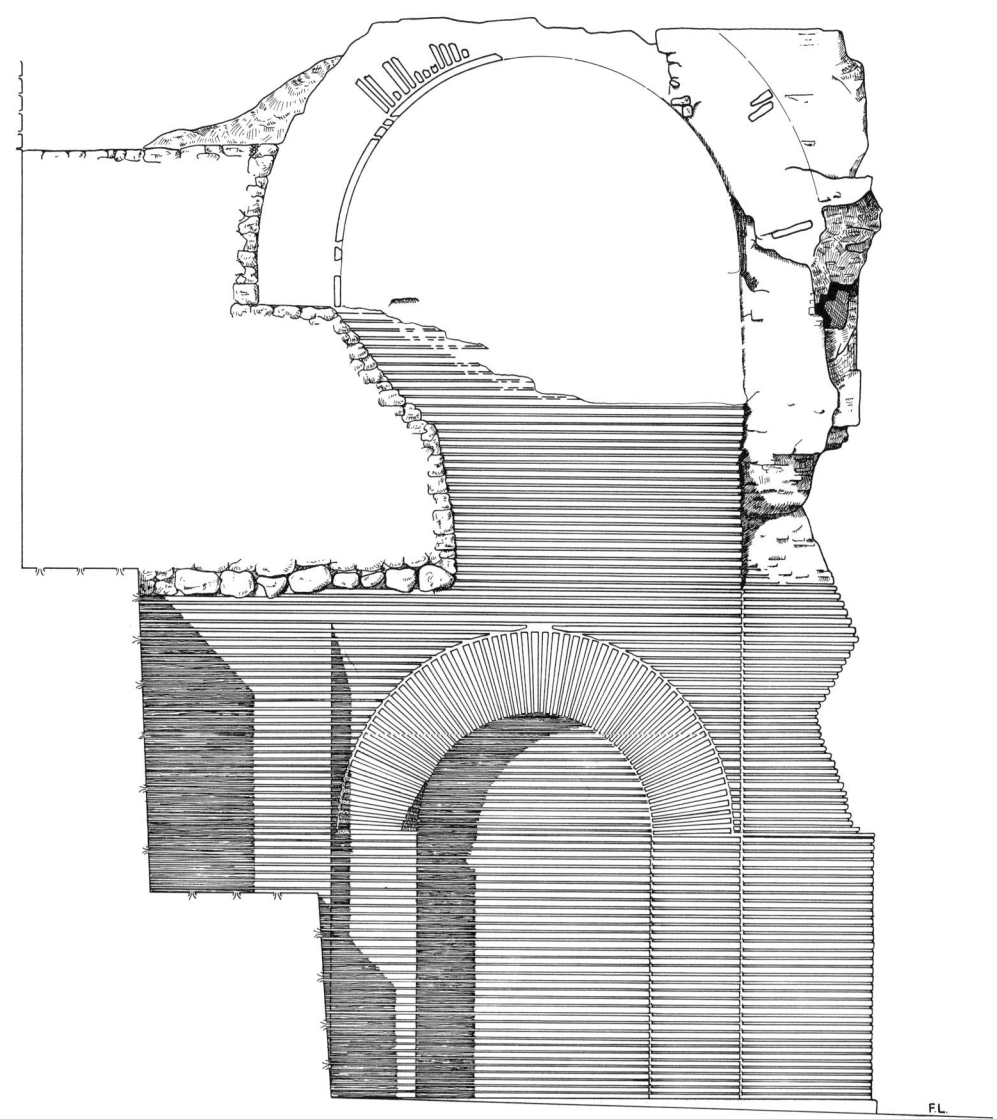

ELEVATION

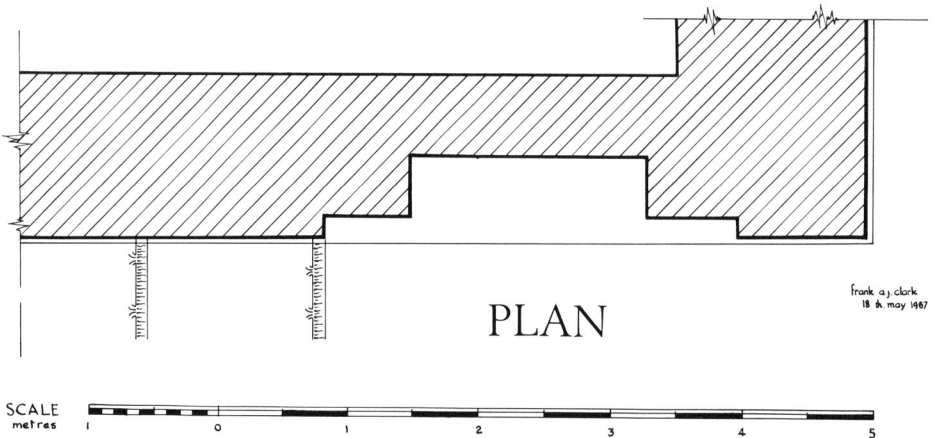

PLAN

ELEVATION E
Plan and elevation, west wall of Room 1, south end

PLATE 51

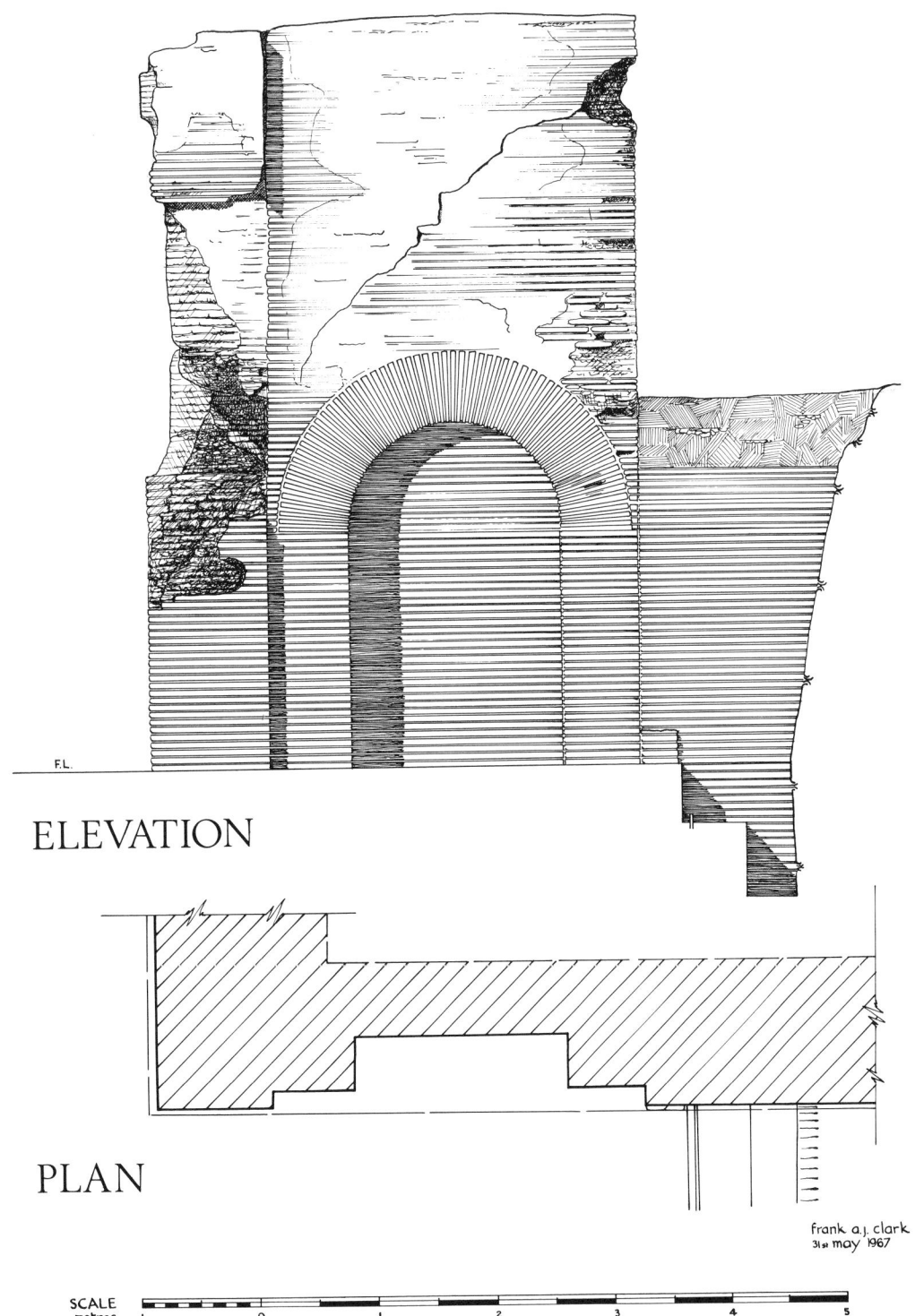

ELEVATION A
Plan and elevation, west wall of Room 1, north end

PLATE 52

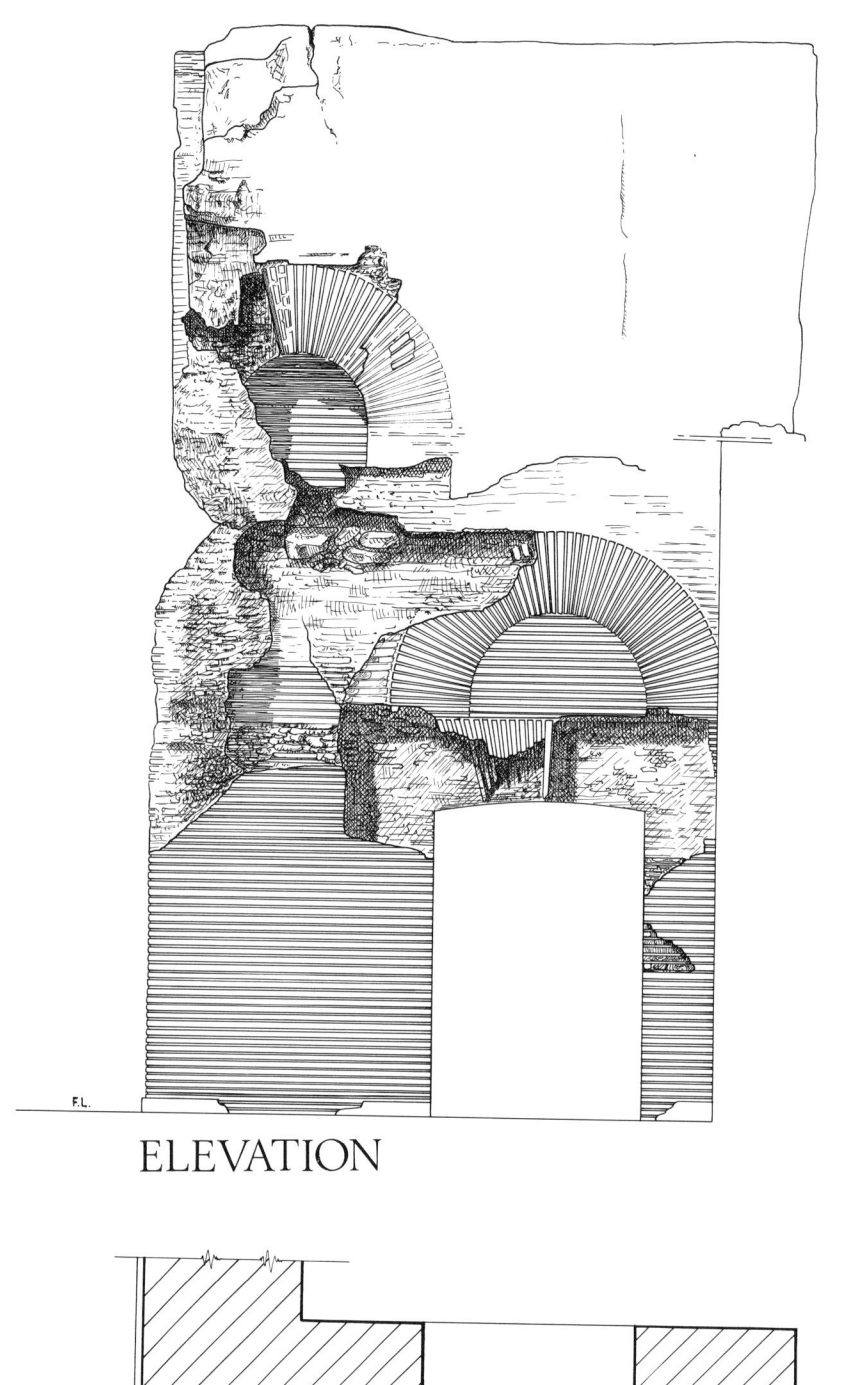

ELEVATION

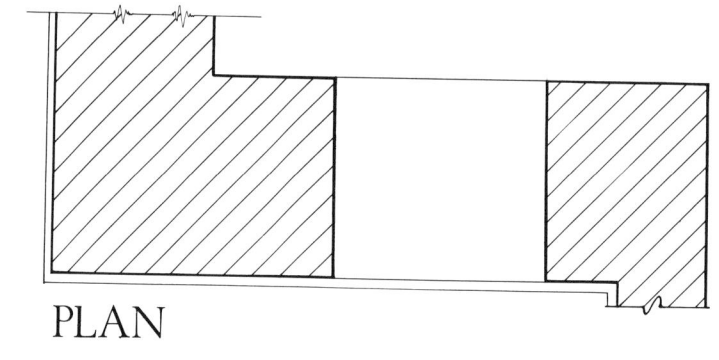

PLAN

ELEVATION D
Plan and elevation, south wall, west section of Room 1

PLATE 53

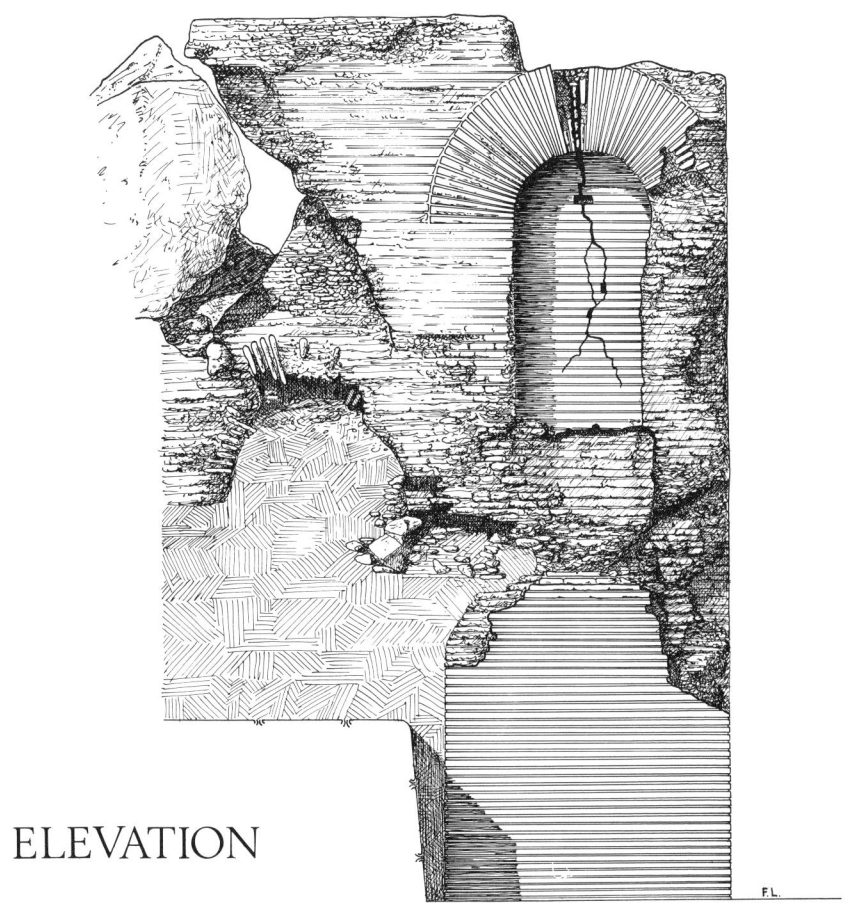

ELEVATION

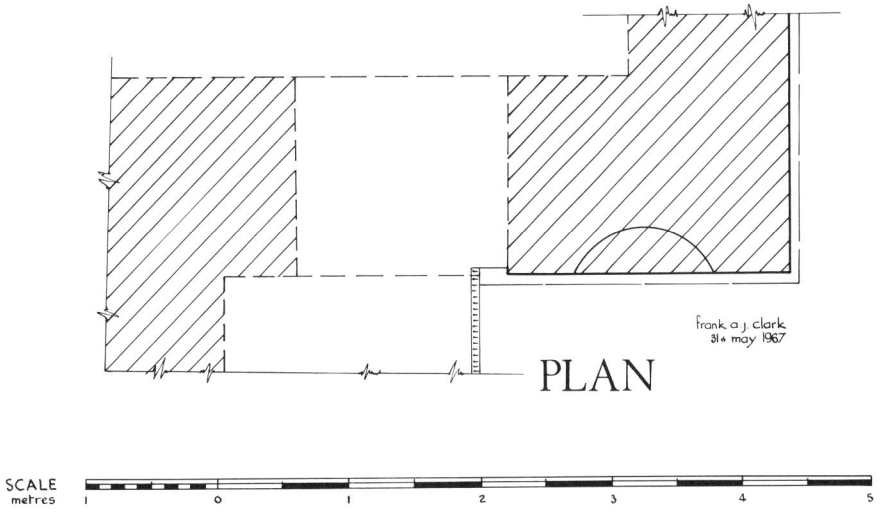

PLAN

ELEVATION B
Plan and elevation, north wall, west section of Room 1

PLATE 54

b. Section of wall between Rooms 1 and 2

a. Plan and elevation, west wall, west section of Room 1

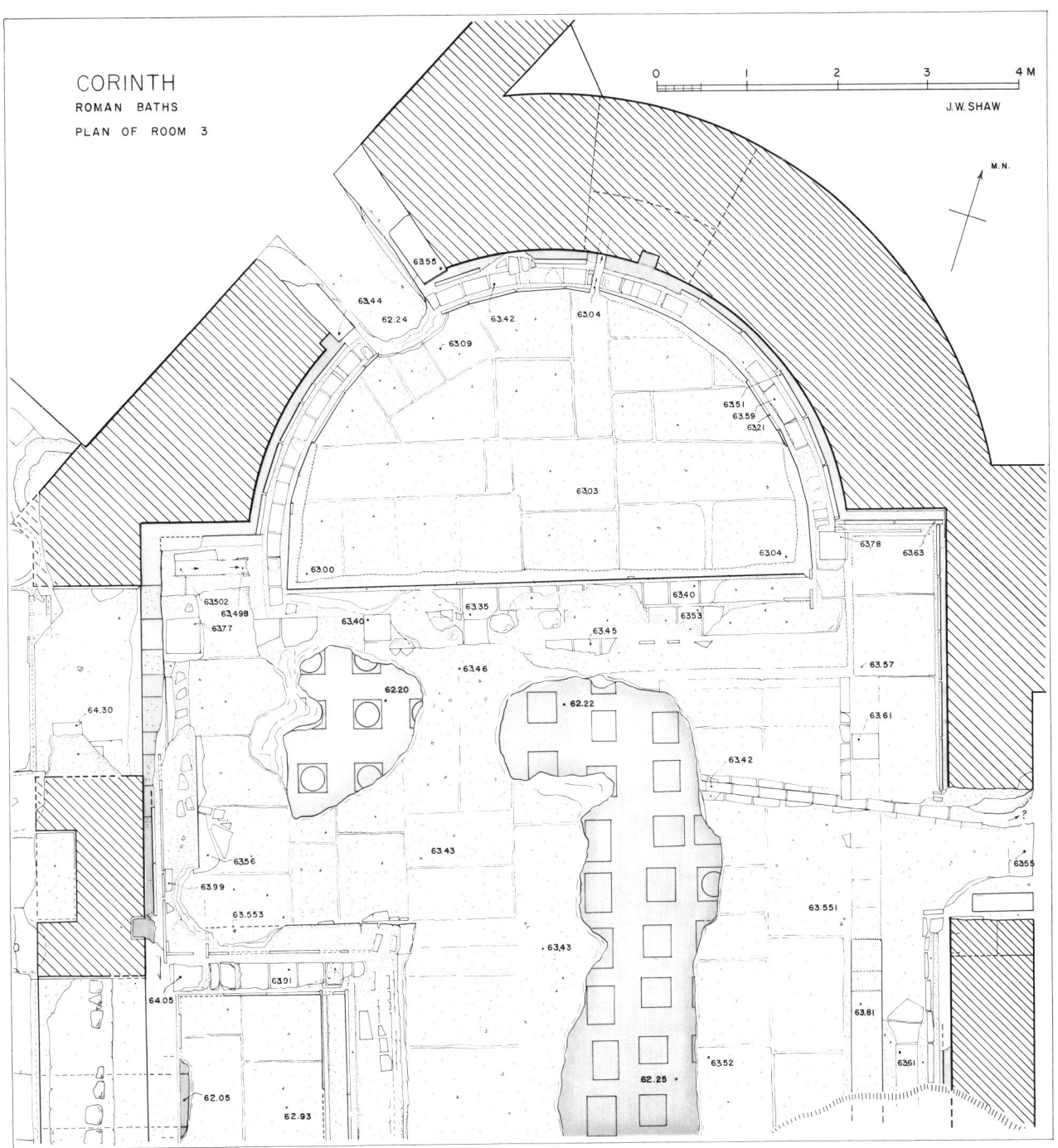

Plan of Room 3

PLATE 56

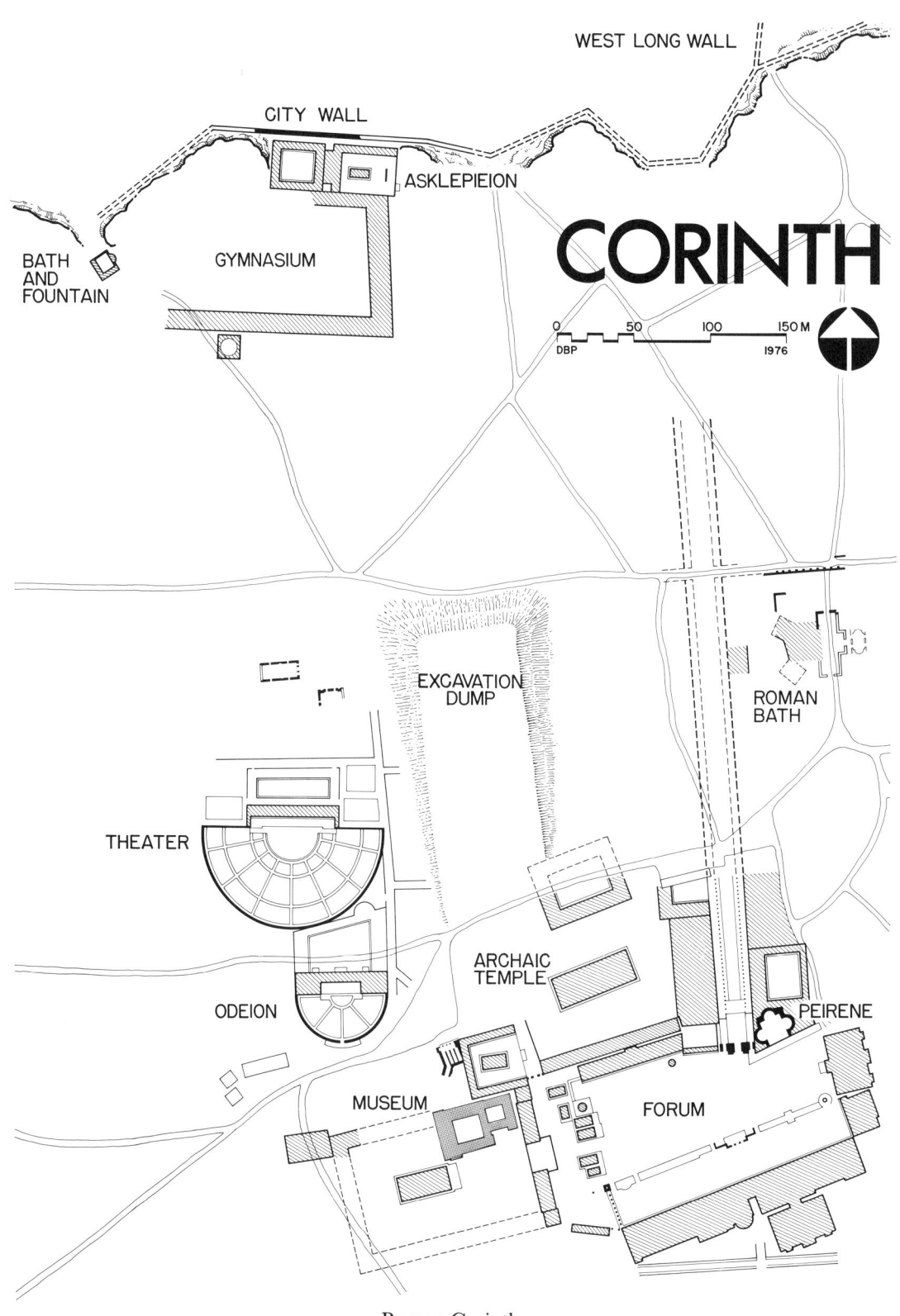

Roman Corinth